A CULTURAL HISTORY OF THE EMOTIONS
IN THE MODERN AND POST-MODERN AGE

Edited by Jane W. Davidson and Joy Damousi

BLOOMSBURY ACADEMIC
LONDON • NEW YORK • OXFORD • NEW DELHI • SYDNEY

BLOOMSBURY ACADEMIC
Bloomsbury Publishing Plc
50 Bedford Square, Loncon, WC1B 3DP, UK
1385 Broadway, New York, NY 10018, USA
29 Earlsfort Terrace, Dublin 2, Ireland

BLOOMSBURY and the Diana logo are trademarks of Bloomsbury Publishing Plc

First published in Great Britain 2019
This edition published in Great Britain, 2022

Copyright © Bloomsbury Publishing, 2019

Jane W. Davidson and Joy Damousi have asserted their right under the Copyright, Designs and Patents Act, 1988, to be identified as Editor of this work.

Cover image: 1945: An audience, mostly servicemen, enjoying a comedy show at the BBC. (© Erich Auerbach / Getty Images)

All rights reserved. No part of this publication may be reproduced or transmitted in any form or by any means, electronic or mechanical, including photocopying, recording, or any information storage or retrieval system, without prior permission in writing from the publishers.

A catalogue record for this book is available from the British Library.

A catalog record for this book is available from the Library of Congress.

ISBN:　HB:　978-1-4725-3579-5
　　　　PB:　978-1-3503-4527-0
　　　　Set: 978-1-3503-4769-4

Series: The Cultural Histories Series

Typeset by RefineCatch Limited, Bungay, Suffolk
Printed and bound in Great Britain

To find out more about our authors and books visit www.bloomsbury.com and sign up for our newsletters..

CONTENTS

LIST OF ILLUSTRATIONS		vi
GENERAL EDITORS' PREFACE		ix
	Introduction *Joy Damousi and Jane W. Davidson*	1
1	Medical and Scientific Understandings *Mark Jackson*	19
2	Religion and Spirituality *Anastasia Scrutton*	37
3	Music and Dance *Wiebke Thormählen*	53
4	Drama *Mary Luckhurst and Peta Tait*	73
5	The Visual Arts *Charles Altieri*	91
6	Literature *Gillian Whitlock and Grace Moore*	111
7	In Private: The Individual and the Domestic Community *Peter N. Stearns*	129
8	In Public: Collectivities and Polities *Emma Hutchison and Roland Bleiker*	145
NOTES ON CONTRIBUTORS		161
NOTES		165
REFERENCES		173
INDEX		195

LIST OF ILLUSTRATIONS

INTRODUCTION

0.1 Fritz Lang directing a scene for *Metropolis*, 1927. Granger/Bridgeman Images. — 6

0.2 Ginger Rogers and Fred Astaire in *Swing Time*, 1936. Photo by RKO Radio Pictures/Getty Images. — 7

0.3 Martin Luther King Jr. in Washington, 1963. Photo by CNP/Getty Images. — 11

0.4 Beatlemania: police control crowds of fans as the Beatles arrive at the ABC Theatre, July 1964. Photo by Trinity Mirror/Mirrorpix/Alamy Stock Photo. — 14

CHAPTER 1

1.1 Walter Bradford Cannon (1871–1945). Wellcome Library, London. Wellcome Images, V0026158. Photograph by Bachrach, 1934. *Copyrighted work available under Creative Commons Attribution Only license CC BY 4.0 http://creativecommons.org/licenses/by/4.0/.* — 23

1.2 Patient suffering from war neuroses: shell shock. Wellcome Library, London. Wellcome Images, L0023554. Photograph taken from Arthur Frederick Hurst, Medical Diseases of the War (1918). *Copyrighted work available under Creative Commons Attribution Only license CC BY 4.0 http://creativecommons.org/licenses/by/4.0/.* — 24

1.3 James–Lange and Cannon–Bard theories. — 26

1.4 Virginia Johnson and William Masters. Photo by Bettmann via Getty Images. — 32

1.5 Marie Stopes (1880–1958), Wikimedia Commons. — 33

CHAPTER 2

2.1 Carl Jung (1875–1961). Photo by Hulton Archive/Stringer Getty Images. — 43

2.2 "Priest of the Devil, Nicholaes Witsen (1641–1717). Amsterdam, 1705. The earliest known depiction of a Siberian shaman." © The British Library Board. — 43

2.3 Yoga. Photo by Felix Hug via Getty Images. — 46

ILLUSTRATIONS vii

CHAPTER 3

3.1 Members of the Ballets Russes, *The Rite of Spring*, Paris, 1913. Photo by Bettmann via Getty Images. 54

3.2 Rudolf von Laban teaching dance, 1931. Photo by Ullstein Bild/Ullstein Bild via Getty Images. 57

CHAPTER 4

4.1 *Waiting for Godot*, from left: Carl Raddatz, playwright/director Samuel Beckett, Stefan Wigger in rehearsal at the Schiller. Photo by Everett Collection Inc/Alamy Stock Photo. 80

4.2 Amiri Baraka (1934–2014) speaking at the Congress of African People held in Atlanta, 1970. Photo by Robert Abbott Sengstacke/Getty Images. 82

4.3 South African playwright Athol Fugard (center) with actors John Kani (left) and Winston Ntshona (right). Photo by *Evening Standard*/Getty Images. 83

4.4 Rokia Traore (left) and Tina Benko in Toni Morrison's *Desdemona*, 2013. Photo by Lieberenz/Ullstein Bild via Getty Images. 84

4.5 Playwright Sarah Kane (1971–99). Photo by Marianne Thiele/Ullstein Bild via Getty Images. 87

4.6 Playwright Caryl Churchill (b.1938). Photo by United News/Popperfoto/Getty Images. 87

CHAPTER 5

5.1 Henri Matisse, *The Open Window*, 1905. Photo by FineArt/Alamy Stock Photo. 94

5.2 Egon Schiele, *Self-Portrait with Lowered Head*, 1912, Wikimedia Commons. 95

5.3 Kasimir Malevich, *Suprematism: Eight Red Rectangles*, 1915. Photo by Fine Art Images/Heritage Images/Getty Images. 96

5.4 Barbara Hepworth, *Figure for Landscape*, 1960. Photo by Peter Barritt/Alamy Stock Photo. 98

5.5 Jackson Pollock, *Autumn Rhythm Number 30*, 1950. Photo by Peter Horree/Alamy Stock Photo. 99

5.6 Jackson Pollock, *Number I (Lavender Mist)*, 1950. Photo by B Christopher/Alamy Stock Photo. 99

5.7 Robert Rauschenberg, *Monogram*, 1955–59. Photo by SuperStock/Alamy Stock Photo. 101

5.8 Sophie Calle, detail of *Prenez Soin de Vous*, 2007. Photo by Eric Vandeville/Gamma-Rapho via Getty Images. 104

5.9	Sophie Calle, detail of *Prenez Soin de Vous*, 2007. Photo by Eric Vandeville/Gamma-Rapho via Getty Images.	105
5.10	Gerhard Richter, *Ema (Nude on a Staircase)*, 1966. Photo by Peter Horree/Alamy Stock Photo.	106
5.11	Gerhard Richter, *Ice (2)*, 1989 (oil on canvas). © Gerhard Richter 2018 (0084).	108

CHAPTER 6

6.1	Charles Dickens with two of his daughters, c.1865. © National Portrait Gallery, London.	121
6.2	Author Azar Nafisi (b.1948). Photo by Steve Pyke/Contour by Getty Images.	122
6.3	Author Peter Carey (b.1943). Photo by David Levenson/Getty Images.	124

CHAPTER 7

7.1	Classroom with boy wearing dunce cap (1906). Stereo photograph by Underwood & Underwood, 1906/Everett Collection/Bridgeman Images.	134
7.2	Kensington Palace after Diana's death. Photo by Sally and Richard Greenhill/Alamy Stock Photo.	137
7.3	Celebrity Kim Kardashian. Photo by London Red Carpet/Alamy Stock Photo.	140

CHAPTER 8

8.1	Reason and emotion in diplomacy and decision making: Churchill, Roosevelt, and Stalin at the Yalta Conference in February 1945, The National Archives photo no. 111-B-4246 (Brady Collection).	148
8.2	Anger, culture, and protest: Occupy Wall Street, October 25, 2011, Wikimedia Commons. *This file is licensed under the Creative Commons Attribution 3.0 Unported license.*	151
8.3	Affective predispositions and diplomatic hostilities: British aircraft carriers during the Suez Crisis, 1956, Wikimedia Commons.	154
8.4	Representations of terrorism and the circulation of affect: visual depiction of the terrorist attacks of September 11, 2001. Photo by Michael Foran via Wikimedia Commons. *This file is licensed under the Creative Commons Attribution 2.0 Generic license.*	158

GENERAL EDITORS' PREFACE

The general editors, volume editors and individual authors of this series have many organizations to thank for helping to bring it into existence. They gratefully acknowledge assistance from the Arts and Humanities Research Council (UK); the European Research Council Project, The Social and Cultural Construction of Emotions, University of Oxford, and its Director, Professor Angelos Chaniotis; the Leverhulme Trust; and the Wellcome Trust. Above all, the series has depended on support from the Australian Research Council Centre of Excellence for the History of Emotions (CE110001011). The project was conceived as a key part of the Centre's collaborative research work and has benefited greatly from the generous help of its academic and administrative staff.

The general editors also express their deep gratitude to the volume editors and authors for their time, expertise and gracious willingness to revise essays in the light of readers' comments. Many other people helped in reading, tracing images and advising in various ways. Our thanks go to Merridee Bailey; Jacquie Bennett; Sophie Boyd-Hurrell; Frederic Kiernan; Mark Neuendorf; Fiona Sim; and Stephanie Thomson; and to the patient staff at Bloomsbury: Dan Hutchins; Claire Lipscomb; Beatriz Lopez; and Rhodri Mogford. We especially acknowledge Ciara Rawnsley, who as Editorial Assistant for the entire series has tirelessly helped authors and done indispensable and meticulous work on all aspects of the volumes' preparation.

This series is dedicated to the memory of Philippa Maddern (1952–2014) who was an original general editor, and an inspiring friend, mentor and colleague to many of the contributors.

Introduction

From the Modern to the Digital World: New Order, New Emotions

JOY DAMOUSI AND JANE W. DAVIDSON

As this volume attests, the twentieth century ushered in distinctive understandings of emotions that transformed how inner life was subsequently understood, especially through the rapidity of change brought about by the massive technological advancements of the period. The automobile transformed itself into a high-speed sports car and a symbol of danger, sex, and money. The airplane made travel over great distances possible and desirable, the allure of holiday destinations creating new ways to experience leisure and pleasure that permitted people of limited financial means to travel at low cost to escape to a new horizon, albeit only for a week or two. In fact, by 1969, it was even possible to visit the Moon—the horizon for excitement and expectation seemed limitless.

In addition to actual transport, the exponential growth in film and TV made journeys to far-flung places or even the deepest recesses of the mind possible through creative imagery. The advent of the computer, then the personal computer and the Internet, coupled with advances in telecommunications, recordings, and radio, meant that the immediacy of experience was shaping how, why, and where emotions were to be expressed: everyday life could be accompanied, monitored, or controlled through these digital and highly accessible means.

During the course of the century, theories of emotion responded to the new technologies and practices, and revolutionized ideas of the place of emotions in all spheres covering medicine and science, philosophy, politics and economics, religion, education, and artistic endeavors. This change is captured particularly in the rise of the history of emotions as a field of academic inquiry, which has provided new scholarly bases for exploring the role and impact of emotions in our lives. Key texts expressing these theoretical developments include Stearns and Stearns (1985), Reddy (2001), Rosenwein (2006), Scheer (2012), and Plamper (2015), although new theoretical developments continue to emerge.

For a series on the cultural history of emotions spanning antiquity to the modern day, volume and chapter divisions are necessary. In this volume, we have followed a remit to examine the period 1920 to the present, beginning with medical and scientific discovery and ending with collectivities and polities, but since the past century has been a time of incredible change in relation to technology and speed of communication, we have decided to focus some of this introductory chapter on the aspects of twentieth-century life and emotions that the main body of the book could not include. Even so, in the few words we have available, we are not comprehensive. Using the world wars and the Cold War period as time-markers, we explore matters ranging from health and well-being to arts and entertainments to reveal the new language for how emotion was framed and experienced.

THE GREAT WAR: EMOTIONS, MOURNING, AND SCIENCE

The First World War created a devastated landscape; the scale of loss and mourning and the cultural practice of it was transformed, leaving desolation in its wake. The public and private expression of grief took place at all levels of society and across class, gender, and ethnicity. Men and women mourned their dead; the living returned from the battlefield broken and wounded. Some never recovered from their injuries; others remained haunted by psychological trauma.

The short- and long-term impacts of the war continue to be assessed a century hence. Much of this evaluation is in terms of the theories that emerged from the cataclysmic event that shaped a generation. Emotions operated at various levels during and immediately after the war. The emotions of the soldiers became a focus of debate and discussion, and those of families and the broader community were writ large across the nations which endured the war. There is no sharper example of the strength of emotion than in the mourning practices and grief that engulfed that generation. Rituals of mourning became central to cultural life. Mourning for the dead became more than a private issue, and the expression of grief took many forms. The scale of death where twice as many men died in the First World War as were killed in all the major wars between 1790 and 1914. Across Europe and beyond, death and grief were palpable (Damousi, 2014). The commemorative movement that emerged aimed to channel the devastation of the war through public events to ritualize emotional expression through public meetings including remembrance services, processions, and concerts.

Concurrently, the war gave rise to a method of analyzing emotions that would define the relationship to emotional life and interiority in the twentieth century. Sigmund Freud's name had gained currency throughout the prewar period, especially in relation to his work on dream analysis.[1] His theories on the unconscious had gained currency, but it was his theories on dream analysis and trauma that spoke to doctors on the battlefront who were attempting to manage the new condition of shell shock. Doctors were baffled by a condition where the nerves were literally shattered without any physical impact. Freud convinced them it was a condition of the mind, not the body. His was a scientific method, and thus the analysis of emotions became a science.

The centrality of the war and the treatment of shell shock has been described as being the key to understanding the shift towards emphasizing emotions and psychology experienced in the 1920s (see Mark Jackson, Chapter 1). Shell-shock became increasingly seen as an emotional rather than a physical condition. The tensions which Jackson discerns in the medical treatment of shell-shocked soldiers encapsulate some of the ongoing themes which emerge in the scientific interpretations of the role of emotions throughout the twentieth century. The ambiguous tensions between body and mind, and the separation of science from psychology and psychiatry led to continued stresses in the relationship between science and emotions. Shell-shock, and the arguments it generated surrounding its treatments, captured and anticipated the ambivalence of science and medicine to the role of emotions and the repression or expression of them in health. Beyond this example, other telling examples such as the relationship between emotions and metabolic dysfunction point to the ongoing tension between disease and emotions at this time.

The war did see a shift to scientific, rational, and medicalized approaches to assessing emotional life. Freudian ideas of the unconscious, of language and slips of the tongue, and notions of repression and the interpretation of dreams continued into the interwar years (Schwartz, 1999). The connection to medicine of these theories through the rise of psychosomatic medicine further connects emotions and medical practices. In the 1930s, such theories began to flourish with the rise of views that linked the mind and body in medicine in the work of psychoanalysts Franz Alexander and psychiatrist Helen Flanders Dunbar. Both Alexander and Dunbar were influenced by Freudian ideas about childhood trauma and argued that the mind and body were inseparable.

Freud's theories too, appealed beyond the medical field to other aspects of modern life in the postwar world. The postwar age was highly industrialized, technologically advanced and frenetic. It was seen as a period of alienation and isolation for the individual who was engulfed by the machine. Industrialization, urbanization, and population growth defined the period, and according to Walter Benjamin "the physical and perceptual shocks of the modern urban environment" affected individuals and communities (Singer, 1995). In this modern period, new artistic forms emerged to understand modern life, bringing distinct ways to redefine the self and emotional life and dispense with previous representations of it.

FROM 1920S TO 1940S: MODERNITY, THE ARTS, AND EMOTIONS

The modernity of the twentieth century created new emotional landscapes in the literature of such writers as Virginia Woolf, James Joyce, and the poet T. S. Eliot. Emotions were not simply embedded in the story. The very structure of the work, its language and form, was revolutionary in how emotions were articulated. For Woolf, emotions and emotional life were central to her conceptualization of relationships. These were at the core of her understanding of the very form of fiction. It is the "relations of emotions" that are of deep interest to her. As Emily Blair notes, the arrangement of her emotions shapes the novel itself. "The connexion is not of events but of emotion", Woolf writes (Blair, 2007). By the middle of the twentieth century, the essence of the modernist project placed emotions at the core of how language was to be manipulated. Joyce's works such as *A Portrait of the Artist as a Young Man* (1916) and *Ulysses* (1922) can only be understood, some argue, as emotional and not simply intellectual works. This applies to the structure of *Ulysses* in particular—with its free-flowing stream of consciousness and inner monologues—aimed at representing emotional states, moods, and feelings (Blamires, 1984). The modernist poet of the century, T. S. Eliot, transformed how emotion was represented in literary form. In the classic poem *The Waste Land*, and similar to Joyce, Eliot adopts a highly fragmented, disjointed structure, to create an emotional landscape of dislocation and desolation not previously captured in this form.

New forms of theater were developed and explored a centuries-old medium in new directions (see Luckhurst and Tait, Chapter 4). Framed around performance and audience, theater continued to shape emotions, but with the modern project injecting a new meaning. Through the work of Stanislavsky and realist acting, a focus on realist representation and coherent characterization emerged. Realist drama was also framed around gendered notions of female as emotional and male as unemotional—an enduring stereotype which has infused other mediums across the century. Brecht's contribution challenged many of the conventional practices of how emotions had been performed upto that point. For Brecht, the aim was to create a critical distance of narrative and emotions. To that end, Brecht (1987) sought to make the audience believe that what it sees on the stage is merely an account of past events that should be watched with critical detachment.

Brecht possessed violently anti-bourgeois attitudes; his collaborations with composers Kurt Weill (*Die Dreigroschenoper,* 1928 [*The Threepenny Opera*], and the opera *Aufstieg und Fall der Stadt Mahagonny,* 1930 [*Rise and Fall of the City of Mahagonny*]), and Paul Hindemith and Hanns Eisler in *Lehr-stücke* ("exemplary plays") generated didactic works for critical reflection.

Brecht's notable plays include *Mutter Courage und ihre Kinder* (1941, *Mother Courage and Her Children*). Though written about the Thirty Years War, its parallels to modern life were obvious. The same is true of others: *Der gute Mensch von Sezuan* (1943, *The Good Woman of Stzuan*), set in prewar China; *Der Aufhaltsame Aufstieg des Arturo Ui* (1957, *The Resistible Rise of Arturo Ui*), a parable of Hitler's rise to power set in prewar Chicago; and *The Caucasian Chalk Circle* (first produced in English, 1948; *Der kaukasische Kreidekreis,* 1949), the story of a child caught between its highborn mother, who deserts it, and the servant girl who looks after it (Parker, 2015).

In the realm of classical music composition, new debates challenged a long-standing familiar relationship between music and the representation of emotion (Wiebke Thormählen, Chapter 3). With modernism in music, tonality was abandoned, removing the culturally learned associations of tension and resolution, thus forcing audiences to reflect on their own expectations. Arnold Schoenberg's twelve-tone techniques challenged what it was possible to recognize, memorize, and "feel" while engaging with music. In a similar vein, the musical fabric of timbres, rhythms, and pulses was unpicked by composers like Edgar Varèse, who forced listeners to search for meaning: was the sound painful or pleasurable; was it an industrial soundscape or a piece of music?

The modernist endeavor in dance departed from the long tradition of narrativity in ballet. Isadora Duncan conceived of dance as a means of revealing the human condition. Emotion and motion were bound together through physical enactments of emotional states and their transformation. Rudolf von Laban investigated the body as a route to accessing a natural self, and more than this, he perceived dance as a route to binding communities in physicalized rituals of emotion.

In the visual arts, the modernist trend was to break from realist representation and to consider the human condition in a much rawer emotional state. The emotions sought were those that could not be put into words, but rather presented in raw energy, color, and abstraction. In the works of the Cubists, Abstract Expressionists, and Surrealists, the eye and the capacity to perceive were set awry as the mind's interior content was scrutinized (see Charles Altieri, Chapter 5).

All these artistic efforts grappled with the ways in which our affective states are central to how we experience the world. The effect of their endeavors was not of the magnitude of the popular arts, where mass engagement and communal emotion were often both a motivator and a response. While popular song has been a form used within communities for millennia, the new developments in radio, film, TV, and sound recording meant that song became an integral and important part of everyday life, with sentiments and messages that could be shared across geographic divides.

Popular protest song, which can be traced back for centuries, provided powerful evidence of the role of artistic affect not only to move the masses, but to make art accountable in the face of the social and political inequities of the twentieth and twenty-first centuries (Rosenberg, 2013). The topics of songs of protest have included civil liberties, civil rights, women's rights, economic injustice, politics, and anti-war subjects. For example, in the 1920s and 1930s, the widespread poverty due to the Great Depression following the First World War inspired singers to comment on the hardships they experienced. American singer Aunt Molly Jackson sang with hungry coal miners in Kentucky in 1931, sharing songs like the "Hungry Ragged Blues" and "Poor Miner's Farewell". Racial discrimination was protested against in popular songs by Fats Waller: "(What Did I Do to Be So) Black and Blue" (1929) and "Strange Fruit" (1939), which was an anti-lynching song performed and recorded by Billie Holiday. The opera/musical *The Cradle Will Rock*, directed by Orson Welles and staged in New York in 1937, was pro-union and its content was so emotive that it was shut down for fear of social unrest.

Technological advancements and the emergence of film—the distinctive medium of the twentieth century—used a range of emotions to press its message. Through genres including historical epic, horror, thriller, fantasy, even the western, film shaped emotions of love, anger, pain, and fear. In the 1920s and the silent era, Charlie Chaplin moved from the vaudeville theater to the movie screen and in a dazzling display of slapstick comedy, social satire, and moments of great sincerity and tenderness, his Little Tramp character grappled with life's challenges in the most emotional of displays. In *The Gold Rush* (America, 1925) the Little Tramp functions as a symbol of romantic idealism, the sole gold prospector in the great American wilderness. The tragi-comedy of the starving prospector eating a stewed shoe is heart-wrenching, as is the scene of a New Year party he imagines, including a famous dancing dinner rolls sequence, where he waits for a girl who never arrives (Wheeler and Forster, 2013).

Other key films of the 1920s were based around real historical events: for example, *Potemkin* (Russia, 1925), directed by Sergei Eisenstein, about the 1905 Russian Revolution; and *The Big Parade* (America, 1925), by director/producer King Vidor, perhaps the most famous, precedent-setting war film from the silent era. It was the first realistic war drama and big box-office success of MGM Studios. The script was based on a story by Laurence Stallings, who had endured terrible wartime experiences as a marine in Northern France. The emotional power of this film lay in the capacity to capture the impact of the war on an ordinary man caught up in its horrors.

It would be impossible to speak of the impact of film in the twentieth century without mentioning *Metropolis* (Germany, 1927), directed by Fritz Lang. It was heralded as a German Expressionist masterpiece and helped to generate the science-fiction genre. Its setting is the futuristic twenty-first century city of Metropolis, offering an allegory of man versus machine and of the class struggle. The film is, without doubt, a response to economic misery and the rise of fascism in a pre-Hitler Weimar Republic Germany (von Harbou, 1972).

Across the 1930s and 1940s, films based on history flourished, such as *Stagecoach* (America, 1939), directed by John Ford, a western that propelled John Wayne to stardom. But war themes continued, including the compelling film based on Erich Maria Remarque's pacifist novel about German boys' experiences as soldiers during the First World War, *All Quiet on the Western Front* (America, 1930), directed by Lewis Milestone. In addition, love stories, especially those depicted in song and dance, were created for their "feel-good" and escapist content to counter the aptly labeled Depression Era. American stars of this genre included Fred Astaire and Ginger Rogers, with the movies *Top Hat* (1935, directed by Mark Sandrich) and *Swing Time* (1936, directed by George Stevens) bringing

FIGURE 0.1: Fritz Lang directing a scene for *Metropolis*, 1927. Granger/Bridgeman Images.

escapism and impeccable performance skills in lavish productions to dazzle and enchant audiences (Hyam, 2007).

Other escapist genres of films that developed with emergent technology were animations. *Snow White and the Seven Dwarfs* (America, 1937) by Walt Disney was the first full-length animated feature in color to have an official soundtrack and a motion picture soundtrack album. The impact of the film was so great that when it was finally released on home video in 1994, it sold fifty million copies worldwide. The film is replete with sing-along songs including "Heigh Ho", "Whistle While You Work", and "Someday My Prince Will Come".

From the 1940s, many well-known movies with amazingly complex emotion plots were produced with casts of star actors, amazing music, and special effects. Significant examples are: *The Maltese Falcon* (America, 1941, directed by John Huston); *Casablanca* (America, 1942, directed by Michael Curtiz); *It's a Wonderful Life* (America, 1946, directed by Frank Capra); *The Best Years of our Lives* (America, 1946, directed by William Wyler); *Bicycle Thieves* (Italy, 1948, directed by Vittorio Di Sica); *All About Eve* (America, 1950, directed by Joseph L. Mankiewicz); *Rashomon* (Japan, 1950, directed by Akira Kurosawa); and *On the Waterfront* (America, 1954, directed by Elia Kazan). *Vertigo* (1958), *North by Northwest* (1959), and *Psycho* (1960), directed by British director Alfred Hitchcock, also enlarged the emotional repertoire of cinema. As the century progressed, film coupled with the explosion of mass digital media changed the accessibility of art information, resulting in forms of entertainment in the realm of immediate and self-selecting experience, often for explicit emotional outcomes.

FIGURE 0.2: Ginger Rogers and Fred Astaire in *Swing Time*, 1936. Photo by RKO Radio Pictures/Getty Images.

IN PRIVATE AND IN PUBLIC

While the representation of emotions was being rewritten in twentieth-century arts, the expression of emotions in the private realm was also undergoing radical transformation. Victorian and Edwardian models of emotional expression and of the discussion of feelings rapidly changed in the years after the Great War. One area where this was most apparent was in advice literature written after the 1920s. There was a sharp increase in literature about how to rear children, the role of emotions in family life, and how to deal with nerves and the anxiety of modern-day living. Popular magazines, especially women's magazines, were filled with advice columns about how to manage the stresses and emotions of the modern world. Women's advice columns increasingly became the repository of intimate and personal details, and so began to blur the distinction between public and private emotions.

Issues surrounding "nervousness" and "worry" dominated newspaper and magazine advertisements during this period, but it was in the area of childrearing advice where emotions were most commonly discussed. "Over-anxiety" on the part of the mother fosters fear in the child, readers of *Women's Weekly* were told. "To deliberately awaken fear in a child", noted the *Everylady's Journal*, "should be treated as a criminal offence". By the 1930s, psychological and scientific terminology had entered into popular speech on how to manage the emotions. In these magazines, the mind and body were seen as inseparable. During the 1930s, the importance of emotional life was identified as central to the modern self. A popular text that enunciated this view was a book called *How to be Happy Though Human*, by the psychiatrist Dr. W. Beran Wolfe. The central theme in the book was that the self could be fashioned and that individuals could have control over their behavior, including their emotions. "Most of us are complete strangers to our deeper selves", he wrote. Knowledge of one's self was to be encouraged. He cites everyday examples of how self-knowledge about emotions can enhance daily existence.

The shift from Victorian modes of dealing with emotions to the modern form included more scientific guides to dealing with private life (see Peter Stearns, Chapter 7). The notion of "happiness"—a major theme in Wolfe's writings—is a major thread from the nineteenth to twentieth centuries. Stearns argues that this connects to cheerfulness that also found its way into childhood advice manuals. In contrast to this is the emotion of grief and the shifting attitudes towards grief, especially in relation to the death of a child. Other emotional states such as envy, love, and friendship can be seen to shift in terms of expectations and the increasing influence of psychology. Stearns concludes that private life in the twentieth century could be seen as captured by themes of deformalization, and de-intensification, to which we can also add a more scientific approach to reading emotions in private life.

The shadow cast over these developments during the first decades of the twentieth century throughout Europe is the rise of Nazism and the Third Reich. International relations, political movements, and the role of emotions in both have only recently captured the attention of scholars (see Hutchinson and Bleiker, Chapter 8). The use of propaganda by the National Socialists effectively mobilized intense emotions. Nicholas O'Shaughnessy argues that the core aspect of Nazism was "the dethronement of reason and the celebration of emotion":

> Nazism felt rather than thought, and therefore the nature of its propaganda appeal was also to feeling rather than thinking. The mobilization of emotion lay at the heart of everything the Nazis did; propaganda's operational formula. For Goebbels, the role of the propagandist was to express in words what his audience felt in their hearts.
>
> —O'Shaughnessy 2003

Eric Fromm, the German psychoanalyst and sociologist, identified the need to examine Nazism through an analysis of emotions in his 1941 publication *Escape from Freedom*. In his work, Fromm emphasized what Neil McLaughlin has referred to as "the centrality of the emotional dynamics of mass political violence". His work also points to the sociology of nationalism and emotions (McLaughlin, 1996). Wilhelm Reich's work on the mass psychology of fascism drew out the psychological, psychoanalytical, and emotional appeal of fascism. Published in 1933, Reich argues that the rise of fascism can be traced to sexual repression. He argued that Nazism managed to manipulate the unconscious and mobilize mass support. The social and cultural conditions in Germany of a repressive family structure, a destructive religion, and a sadistic system of education connected with unconscious emotions, trauma, and fantasies that were exploited by Nazi politics and violent practices (Reich, 1933).

The Second World War ushered in a new focus on psychology and emotions. By 1939, the "expert" was entrenched in everyday life and emotions central to it. With the onset of war, the military employed psychological experts. The lessons of the First World War were not too distant; seeking to avoid the disaster of shell shock, in America and Britain in particular, psychologists and psychoanalysts were employed to deal with psychotic personnel. A fundamental difference between the two world wars was that psychology was used more explicitly to assess fear, shame, anxiety, and malingering without the moral judgments expressed in the First World War (Damousi, 2005). One further area where the nexus of emotions and politics has developed is in relation to the Cold War, and it is the postwar world to which we now turn.

POSTWAR PERIOD: 1950S TO THE PRESENT

The Cold War has been seen not only as a matter of public life but as an era in which private life was infused with emotions. During the Cold War period, politics demanded personal commitment and shaped one's entire social existence, in a deeply emotional process. Memoirs of those who lived during this era clearly reveal an intense dimension to living. Families could be divided, friendships torn apart, and lives shattered through political differences. In America, the devastating impact of the Cold War on the careers of artists, writers, filmmakers, and left-wing activists is well-known. Others have written how the Cold War had a destructive impact on their families. Mark Aarons, from a communist family, wrote how:

> The Cold War did not knock on our front door and politely ask to enter. It insidiously seeped in, infesting every nook and cranny of our home, as formless and menacing as the impenetrable mid-winter inversion smogs that, once lifted, left behind sooty fingerprints and the acrid odour of thousands of coke-fired *Cosi* stoves.
>
> —Curthoys and Damousi 2014: x

Not all commentaries on the Cold War evoked emotions of fear, anxiety, and relationships torn asunder. It also provided material for humor. In *Dr. Strangelove* (America, 1964, directed by Stanley Kubrick), black satire mimics the extremes of Cold War politics and mobilizes humor to send a deadly message about the insanity of war. Starting with the French New Wave of the 1960s and German directors of the early 1970s, filmmakers across the latter half of the century make emotions visible through different film genres. After the war, politics on film begin to influence the postwar generation and help to reshape and reinterpret the Second World War and its devastation. In particular, films such as *Ivan's Childhood* (Soviet Union 1962, directed by Andrei Tarkovsky,), *The Conformist* (Italy, 1970, directed by Bernardo Bertolucci), *The Tin Drum* (Germany, 1979, directed and cowritten by Volker Schlöndorff), and later *Au Revoir Les Enfants* (France, 1987, directed by Louis Malle) evoke a new interpretation of the horror and impact of war, through deeply emotional rendering of its legacies (Wheeler and Foster, 2013).

In the theater, influences of the political movements of the 1960s and 1970s, where identity politics began to challenge the very notion of the coherent self and unified emotional responses, pursued traces left by Brecht. But their theatrical experimentation developed new approaches to acting and the role of psychology in how actors work. Samuel Beckett introduced another framework in which characters were asked to draw on emotional states to explore the alienation of characters. More than that, he challenged the idea of the unitary individual, and so ushered in post-modernist theater. This fragmentation of the individual brought with it new aspects of emotional life—a focus on the trivial as well as a complete removal of realism. For Beckett, the aim of his theater was to strip back the idea of an essential human self and to challenge the concept of the unified self and character.

The postwar period also heralded social movements during the 1960s and 1970s, as the baby boomer generation began to protest in ways which were passionate, angry, and overtly designed to confront and destabilize the norms their parents had worked so hard to achieve. The most enduring and dramatic of these movements was the women's movement, which insisted that women needed to express their anger and vocally articulate their oppression. Its language was often revolutionary and exhorted women to protest and mobilize. "The personal is political" was the catchcry and slogan. This meant that the movement supported consciousness-raising groups which aimed to express themselves, articulate their emotions, and counter alienation and isolation. In 1973, one consciousness-raising group wrote of the importance of women discussing their feelings that they had a

> [g]ood feeling of trust, closeness and sisterhood. Everyone has an opportunity to say whatever she feels; there is no attempt on anyone's part to 'run' the group or tell women what they should think, or to talk anyone down.
>
> —Damousi 2005: 293

Political protests continue to be deeply framed by emotional responses. Protests by gay and lesbian activists post-1970s, most notably Stonewall, have been fierce and driven by a passionate political agenda. The campaign for civil rights for African Americans, protests by First Nations, and the assertion of Indigenous rights have defined the politics of the later twentieth and early twenty-first centuries. One of the greatest speeches of the century, Martin Luther King's "I Have a Dream" from August 1963, was delivered with poise but also with the deepest emotion. It reads in part:

> I have a dream that one day this nation will rise up and live out the true meaning of its creed: "We hold these truths to be self-evident; that all men are created equal."
>
> I have a dream that one day on the red hills of Georgia the sons of former slaves and the sons of former slave owners will be able to sit down together at the table of brotherhood . . .
>
> I have a dream that my four little children will one day live in a nation where they will not be judged by the color of their skin but by the content of their character.
>
> I have a dream today.
>
> I have a dream that one day down in Alabama, with its vicious racists, with its governor having his lips dripping with the words of interposition and nullification, that one day right down in Alabama little black boys and black girls will be able to join hands with little white boys and white girls as sisters and brothers.
>
> I have a dream today . . .
>
> This is our hope. This is the faith that I will go back to the South with. With this faith we will be able to hew out of the mountain of despair a stone of hope. With this faith, we will be able to transform the jangling discords of our nation into a beautiful symphony of brotherhood.
>
> http://www.let.rug.nl/usa/documents/1951-/martin-luther-kings-i-have-a-dream-speech-august-28-1963.php

FIGURE 0.3: Martin Luther King Jr. in Washington, 1963. Photo by CNP/Getty Images.

In the more than fifty years since this speech much has changed, but protest continues to remind us of the freedom of speech and civil liberty and equality King died for.

In 2017, the 45th President of the United States was keen to make his own views public, and employed digital media as his preferred way to connect with his electorate and global partners. Yet, his outspokenness resulted in a backlash when the Women's March, which took place in Washington D.C. in January 2017, was organized by thousands of women wearing "pussy hats" and marching in protest against allegations that Donald Trump boasted he grabbed women by their genitals. The wider aim of the protest was to garner the energy to protest gender inequality and attacks on women's rights and dignity that persist in the modern world. The statement of principles demanded at the rally was:

- Accountability and justice for police brutality and "[dismantling] the gender and racial inequities within the criminal justice system"
- Freedom from sexual violence
- Ratification of the Equal Rights Amendment to the Constitution that would guarantee equal protection based on gender
- Affirmation that all domestic and caretaking work is work, even if unpaid, and that women—especially women of color—bear the brunt of that burden
- "The right to organize and fight for a living minimum wage" for all workers, labor protections for undocumented and migrant workers, and "solidarity with sex workers' rights movements"

- Comprehensive reproductive rights, LGBTQ rights, and immigrant and refugee rights.
  https://www.vox.com/2017/1/21/14342942/womens-march-inauguration-trump-protest-goals-feminism-demands

As mentioned above, popular music, specifically song, has played a central part in mobilizing social and political protest, and this has especially been the case as industrial development has facilitated mass distribution of songs through ever-changing media technologies: Edison cylinders, the radio, the gramophone, hi-fi stereo, CDs, iPods, and most latterly, Internet downloads.

The most notable protest singers of the postwar period in the USA were Woody Guthrie ("This Land is Your Land") and Pete Seeger ("Where Have All the Flowers Gone", "We Shall Overcome"), both members of the labor-movement band *The Almanac Singers*. Intriguingly, the band's first album urged non-intervention in the Second World War, but only weeks after it was issued, Hitler invaded the Soviet Union and *The Almanacs* switched to a pro-war position. Widely criticized in the press for switching positions, *The Almanacs* show the power of the pop music band as its capacity to reach a large public. Indeed, after the Second World War, Seeger and colleagues formed a new band, *The Weavers*, and their songs continued to support racial justice and world peace. During McCarthyism, they were placed under surveillance and blacklisted, lost airplay, and DECCA records canceled their contract (Rosenberg, 2013).

Another artist who suffered as a consequence of the "witch hunts" of the 1950s was classical singer, actor, athlete, and civil rights activist Paul Robeson. In defiance of the bans and investigations of Robeson, labor unions in the USA and Canada organized a concert in 1952 at the International Peace Arch between Washington State and British Columbia. Robeson stood on the American side of the border and sang for a crowd estimated at 20,000 to 40,000 people (Swindall, 2015).

By the 1960s and 1970s, the protest songs of Bob Dylan, Joan Baez, and many others captured the very emotional core of the young protest generation, raising awareness and sharing collective emotions about social injustices. Soul singers of the period, such as Nina Simone ("Mississippi Goddam", 1964), Otis Redding and Aretha Franklin ("Respect", 1967), and James Brown ("Say it Loud, I'm Black and I'm Proud", 1968) all demanded equal rights for African Americans. In 1969, Jimi Hendrix made a startling musical assault on "The Star-Spangled Banner" at the Woodstock Festival which was famously interpreted as a political statement against the Vietnam War. The music was undeniably raw and shocking. Woodstock was the most dramatic mass event, attracting half a million rock fans (Lang, 2009).

Another highly significant figure across the period was Jamaican musician Bob Marley, who challenged, among many topics, nuclear proliferation and poverty. In the UK, in 1965, *The Who* performed "My Generation" with Pete Townshend, dressed in Union Jack suits, smashing guitars, and catching the tide of teen rebellion. It was a key moment in British pop, and a strong evocation of the amphetamine-fueled aggression present in the country at the time (Barnes, 1982). In stark contrast, British singer David Bowie created *Ziggy Stardust* in 1972. Bowie told an interviewer: "I'm gay, and always have been". Whether this was ever true is irrelevant; Bowie's androgynous alter ego was the first of his exotic personae, and revealed how a pop star could influence mass behavior. As glam rock took hold, men began growing their hair and wearing exotic make-up. Moods, emotions, and lifestyle choices were in a state of flux (Duncan, 2017).

Perhaps the most significant outbreak of pop-based pandemonium was punk's crowning glory in *The Sex Pistols* and their 1977 hit "God Save the Queen". It was released amid the tea-and-cake celebrations for the Queen's Jubilee, and while it stirred the teen passion against all that tradition represented, the music was regarded as being so inflammatory that workers in the record plant refused to press it and official chart compilers refused to acknowledge its chart-topping position (Harris, 2004). After punk, rap and hip-hop movements continued the protest against discrimination and poverty: *Grandmaster Flash* ("The Message", 1982), *Boogie Down Productions* ("Stop the Violence", 1988), and *Public Enemy* ("Fight the Power", 1989).

Following in the wake of feminist singer-songwriters of the 1960s and 1970s like Joni Mitchell, Carole King, and Janis Ian, who sang about sexism and sexual abuse, the Third Wave Feminists explored not only sexism, racism, and war but also reproductive rights. Songs included Ani DiFranco's hit "Lost Woman Song" (1990), which was on the topic of abortion, and *Sonic Youth's* "Swimsuit Issue" (1992), which protested against the objectification of women by the media.

In 2017, these protest songs persist, but are critiqued, not least because of the complex emotions created when the celebrities that have been associated with them, often now hugely wealthy and media hungry, offer their names to protest festivals and events in what often seems little more than a branding exercise. Journalist Naomi Klein (2017) has referred to this as "Bono-ization", named after the *U2* lead singer Bono and his role in the Live 8 concert and the Make Poverty History campaign in 2005. Klein believed that celebrity involvement lessened the impact of the protests: the stars were simply present as themselves, while spectators were there to see them and to wave their logo-embossed bracelets. The bracelets themselves have been a further source of critique: these emotion-laden mementos were purchased as a charitable donation at the pop concerts, but were in fact made in Chinese sweatshops by poor and badly treated workers.

The case presented so far might suggest that popular music movements are at the forefront of social and political artistic emotional expression. But this is not the case; less widely popular music artists have also made their impact. Minimalist composer Steve Reich wrote the thirteen-minute-long "Come Out" (1966), which comprised a manipulated recording of a single spoken line given by an injured survivor of the Harlem Race Riots of 1964. In 2012, Australian composer Robert Davidson created an electroacoustic work entitled "We apologise". The piece is created from one second of speech from then Prime Minister Kevin Rudd's historic apology to the Indigenous people of Australia, whose children were forcibly removed from their families between the 1890s and 1970s, creating what is referred to as the Stolen Generation. Davidson has also created a choral work based on a sound recording of Martin Luther King's "I Have a Dream" speech (see Australian Music Centre).

In Estonia, Latvia, and Lithuania between 1987 and 1991, "The Singing Revolution" occurred. Over these years, thousands and thousands of ordinary people gathered regularly in public places and sang national songs and Roman Catholic hymns, sharing the powerful emotional experience of being together in the music. Popular singers joined the trend, using the poetry of nationalist poets as the lyrics of their songs. These people were in revolt against Soviet rule. In this case, song led the revolution, a strong but non-violent resistance, resulting in the restoration of independence to these Baltic countries, and so removing USSR rule (Davidson and Garrido, 2014).

Such acts of communal emotion were not only reserved for political causes. Perhaps the strongest marker of popular culture in the postwar generation is to be found in pop music, sometimes saccharine sweet in its lyrics and melodies, but always present and affecting life at many levels. It is common for the twenty-first-century multi-tasking commuter to be working on a laptop computer, connecting to colleagues globally at the press of a button, while at the same time "self-medicating" using pop music to regulate their mood. Indeed, it is well known that we pump ourselves up with fast tempo music if we want to exercise harder, or conversely listen to slow and lyrical music to calm down and reduce feelings of stress and anxiety (Davidson and Garrido, 2014).

With the production and dissemination of pop music comes a whole mass media industry that does much to shape our emotional interactions with pop stars. Famously, Beatlemania is an iconic representation of such affect. In 1964, the already well-known "Lads from Liverpool" traveled to the USA and appeared on the Ed Sullivan TV show. From that point on, the term "Beatlemania" was coined to refer to the mass hysteria experienced as tens of thousands of teenage girls screamed and cried in ecstasy as they were overwhelmed by the sight and sound of their pop heroes.

This trend predated the Beatles, with Elvis Presley's gyrating hips and sultry, sexy voice producing similar high emotional impact. Another truly global megastar capable of producing such extreme emotions was Michael Jackson, about whom one video-gaming blogger wrote:

> The live show was absolute pandemonium, people screaming like it was the apocalypse and fainting all over the place, ambulances almost couldn't handle it. (www.neogaf.com/threads/is-michael-jackson-the-absolute-king-of-mass-hysteria-at-live-shows.1356555/)

FIGURE 0.4: Beatlemania: police control crowds of fans as the Beatles arrive at the ABC Theatre, July 1964. Photo by Trinity Mirror/Mirrorpix/Alamy Stock Photo.

When Jackson died unexpectedly in 2009, his fans were distraught, mourning in public. In the public realm, it seemed that those expressions of grief and loss that had once been based around international and personal desolation through war were now being shown in response to celebrity. Perhaps the most iconic example of this response was the public grief and mourning at the death of Princess Diana, who was killed unexpectedly in a car crash in 1997. The feelings shared were expressed in mass scenes of public crying and the offering of millions of floral and teddy bear tributes at churches throughout Britain and in huge collections outside Buckingham Palace. The gestures seemed to bring millions of people a temporary sense of community. Perhaps the emotions elicited provided a sense of equality and solidarity as people shared in their common grief (Turner, 2004; Rosenwein, 2006).

The other mass medium of this period has been television, a powerful and pervasive information provider and entertainer, and one that has emotionally connected audiences for decades. It has also relocated the family to the lounge room and given its national transmission, allowing people a focus for shared experiences. Covering all genres of programming, from the mid-twentieth century onwards, TV programs began to create a new emotional terrain. High-rating television programs in the USA included *I Love Lucy* (1951–57); *Roots* (1977); *Dallas* (1978–91), *M*A*S*H* (1972–83); *Cheers* (1983–93); *Seinfeld* (1989–99); *Friends* (1994–2004); *Frasier* (1993–2004); and *Everybody Loves Raymond* (1996–2005). In the UK, the long-running *Coronation Street* (six times a week, since 1960) and *EastEnders* (originally twice a week, but now four times a week, since 1985) have succeeded in giving viewers emotional connections with the TV families and communities. Not all shows were about generating a warm sense of happiness and well-being. The US crime show *The Sopranos* (1999–2007) broke with the convention of crime on television: the emotional relationship of the viewer to the main character, Tony Soprano—a brutal, ruthless killer—is consistently challenged through the depiction of Tony as a family man who sees a psychiatrist. It was edgy, gritty, and challenging television which deftly tested audiences' emotional responses. Significantly, it premiered on cable television, HBO (Home Box Office), which has become a prominent cable channel.

In the past decade, Netflix has transformed television content by producing its own series. It debuted in 2013 with the highly acclaimed *House of Cards*. Starring Kevin Spacey (until 2017) and Robin Wright, it depicts the dark, sinister, and ruthless world of US politics in ways that capture the passion, vanity, arrogance, and manipulative world of the rise to the White House. The emotional rollercoaster ride of the Underwoods immediately connected with audiences. In the same vein, television programs such as *Downton Abbey* (2010–15), *Mad Men* (2007–15), and *The Handmaid's Tale* (2017) have now become part of what has been described as a golden era of television, with their meticulous attention to detail for a given historic period, but above all, by creating for viewers powerful emotional attachments to characters and to their emotional states.

If popular culture defined the postwar generation, in the area of religion and spirituality there were significant shifts over this period. Until the mid-twentieth century, allegiance to established Western religions was seen as part of core individual identity. The Catholic and Protestant Churches enjoyed strong followings in Western societies and even if church attendance began to decline, individuals identified closely with an established religion. The challenge to established religions has come for a range of complex and varied reasons. The winds of change billowing through the Western world in the 1960s eventually touched traditional and established organizations. In 1962, the Second Vatican Council began the process of attempting to modernize the Catholic Church. Pope John XXIII saw the need to bring the Church into a changing world. Further changes were announced in 1963 to 1965 which included conducting the liturgy, including the scriptural readings, in vernacular languages, and allowing churchgoers to drink the consecrated wine from the communion chalice. The aim was to involve the Catholic laity more strongly in the Mass.

Increasingly, alternative forms of spiritualism and religion emerged during the postwar period which drew on Eastern traditions and religions. Most notably the notion of "spirituality" became detached from religion in the 1960s (Anastasia Scrutton, Chapter 2). This referred to emotional aspects of transcendence, in contrast to individual dogmas of religion which were criticized by the counterculture movements. The examples which most dramatically capture the shift in twenty-first century practices include shamanism and yoga. Both these practices have a long history, their appeal seeming to focus on searching for meaning or purpose and a "holistic" view of a person. These mind-and-body practices seem to be at least in part reactions to the fast-paced and stressful lives that people report.

As we established in the opening of this chapter, a distinguishing feature of twentieth-century life was the exploration of the psyche and the inner "workings" of individuals and their emotions. In the twenty-first century, the psychology of well-being has superseded the interior journey that Freudian psychoanalysis initiated. Rather than lying on a couch to have our dreams interpreted, individuals now search for happiness through learning to appreciate such basic pleasures as companionship, the natural environment, and bodily needs. Martin Seligman pioneered this branch of psychology from the 2000s, its significance being in linking well-being to emotion. Experiencing emotions such as hope, compassion, contentment, and empathy has been regarded as the essence of well-being (Seligman, 2011; Webster, 2014).

Well-being, it seems, is very much a construct of the twenty-first century, and is strongly tied as much to emotion and mental health as to definitions of physical health. Positive Psychology has been embraced by educationalists internationally, with researchers Noble and McGrath (2008) discussing how schools help students experience positive feelings such as: (a) belonging to their school; (b) safety from bullying and violence; (c) satisfaction and pride through experiencing and celebrating success; (d) excitement and enjoyment by participating in fun activities or special games; and (e) optimism about their success and/or school. According to this theory, experiencing positive emotions on a regular basis may provide various opportunities for people to feel happiness.

Another element of the Positive Psychology or PERMA model is engagement, which concerns whether a person is deeply engaged with something in life. Among a wide variety of human activities, Csikszentmihalyi (1990) identified arts engagement, such as instrumental playing or painting, as activities that facilitate the experience of flow, or being completely absorbed in an activity. In learning, the more pleasure and satisfaction is achieved, the more the learner's engagement can be experienced as flow, the engrossed focus stimulating its own motivation.

Relationships comprise the third element in the PERMA well-being model, and deal with a person's capacity to build and maintain positive relationships. The fourth and fifth elements of well-being are meaning and purpose: that is, purposeful existence in the world. As lifelong employment opportunities diminish, it is predicted that developing opportunities for pleasure, feelings of accomplishment, and success will increasingly be requisites of good mental health.

EMOTIONS IN THE DIGITAL AGE

The twenty-first century ushered in the digital age and social media, which have created a platform for articulating emotions in an ever-changing way. The Internet, Twitter, Facebook, and Instagram are now the conventional forms of articulating all emotions immediately, at whim, and with an instant response. Ranging over expressions of love, pain, pleasure, anger, and aggression, the digital medium has no boundaries and its reach of emotional impact no limit. It has infused all aspects of life. The strident Arab Spring protests of 2010 drew heavily on social media and illustrated the emergence of forms of political protest facilitated by social media (Stepanova, 2011). The anger and outrage which infused the #Me Too Movement – of women protesting against sexual abuse and assault – emerged powerfully through social media. President Donald Trump uses Twitter as his favored medium to express indignation, anger, and aggression on a daily basis ("Modern Day Presidential"). The use of the Internet by terrorist organizations to recruit members, raise funds, and display the most heinous violence and crimes against humanity is well documented (How ISIS Uses the Internet). Cyberbullying creates depression, guilt, helplessness, and shame and has become a human rights issue ("Cyberbullying: What it is and how to get help"). On a positive note, access to the Internet can create empowerment and social networks for the elderly, providing opportunities for emotional well-being through connectivity, information flow, and entertainment.

As we welcome readers to engage with the rich constructions of emotions that have emerged in the twentieth and twenty-first centuries, we also wish to signal that this digital age is moving so rapidly that it is hard to predict its next development and area of impact on social, cultural, and political life. With the advent of virtual-reality environments, and the new forms of Artificial Intelligence, the move towards an inward and reflective personal world seems to be one potential longer-term trajectory. Yet, as travel technologies develop, concepts taken from science-fiction related to time travel become more imaginable, and in contrast to the movement inwards brought about by personal digital technological developments, travel technology takes us further out into the world, exploring the limits of our emotional lives and what it is to be human.

CHAPTER ONE

Medical and Scientific Understandings

MARK JACKSON

In 1922, the *Report of the War Office Committee of Enquiry into "Shell-Shock"* drew a sharp distinction between physical and emotional causes of psychological breakdowns among British soldiers during the First World War. The Committee had been set up in 1920 not merely in response to concerns about the prevalence of what became known as "shell shock" in front-line troops; it was also the product of anxieties about the impact of traumatic neuroses on military efficiency and the economic burden of compensating large numbers of soldiers who had become sick during combat: approximately 200,000 British soldiers had returned home from the war suffering from some form of psychological disorder, accounting for nearly 15 per cent of all disabled servicemen receiving a war pension (for historical discussions of shell shock, see Bogacz 1989; Bourke 2000; Leese 2002; Lerner 2003; Merridale 2000; Shephard 2002; Winter 2000). Chaired by the civil servant, solicitor, and businessman Lord Southborough, the Committee was tasked with considering the meaning and utility of the term "shell shock", collating evidence from medical and military personnel in order to understand more clearly the causes, manifestations, and treatments of shock, and advising military authorities about how best to prevent traumatic neuroses in future through appropriate military training and education (*Report of the War Office Committee of Enquiry into "Shell-Shock"* 1922: 3).[1]

One of the key points of dispute during the Committee's examination of witnesses was whether shell shock should be explained in terms of "commotional" or "emotional" factors. In his initial descriptions of shell shock in 1915 and 1916, the British physician and psychologist Charles S. Myers had attributed disorders of memory and sensation to the noise and dust associated with shells exploding in close proximity to afflicted soldiers (Myers 1915: 316–20; 1916a: 65–9; 1916b: 608–13). Myers' emphasis on understanding traumatic shock in terms of physical injury to the brain and nervous system echoed earlier explanations of "railway spine" as the product of the damage to bones, ligaments, and nerves inflicted by high-speed travel, as well as contemporary accounts of insanity that stressed the ways in which direct injury to the head could cause "commotion" in the molecules of the brain (for somatic approaches to railway spine and insanity, see Erichsen 1867; Mercier 1890). However, just as somatic interpretations of railway spine and insanity were gradually displaced by an emphasis on emotional factors, so too were physical explanations of shell shock increasingly challenged by medical and military writers who considered the condition to be the product of psychological, rather than organic, disturbances. In an overview of shell shock published in 1917, for example, the anatomist

Grafton Elliot Smith and the psychologist T. H. Pear argued that symptoms of shell shock, including muscular contractures, blindness, deafness, and mutism, were largely due to the continual suppression of emotions, such as fear, remorse, anger, and disgust, triggered by trench warfare (Smith and Pear 1917: 5–12).

Reflecting this growing tendency to read trauma in psychological terms, the *Report of the War Office Committee of Enquiry* was unequivocal in its conviction that shell shock was primarily the product of emotional, rather than commotional, disturbances in vulnerable soldiers. According to the *Report*, evidence suggested that "the purely emotional variety of shell-shock," caused by cumulative physical and mental exhaustion, accounted for "about 80 per cent of all the cases" (1922: 94). Members of the Committee recognized that noise, loss of sleep, fatigue, and the "thousand and one ills of modern warfare" could all precipitate symptoms (ibid.). However, they insisted that distressing circumstances only affected unstable soldiers, those "incomplete men" who were thought to be constitutionally prone to cowardice and ill-adapted to responsibility (on the notion of "incomplete men," see Oppenheim 1991; Moss 2000). "Most witnesses were of opinion," the *Report* concluded, "that the stress of war rarely produced insanity in the stable man, but that it acted, as is commonly observed with other forms of stress, as a factor upon those who by predisposition were liable to breakdown" (ibid.: 97, 144).

As a number of historians have indicated, contemporary distinctions between commotional and emotional causes of shock,[2] as well as the conflation of shell shock with emotional vulnerability, femininity, and cowardice, served military and economic interests.[3] Execution of shell-shocked soldiers was used to deter others from malingering during wartime; and discrimination between the deserving wounded and undeserving soldiers who had broken down emotionally allowed government ministers and civil servants to reduce the payment of war pensions, in Britain at least, by adopting narrow "interpretations of what constituted a war-related injury" (Winter 2000: 9; Bourke 1996; Jones and Wessely 2005). In his evidence to the Committee of Enquiry, Major W. J. Adie, an Australian-born neurologist who had fought in France during the First World War and was working for the Ministry of Pensions, expressly excluded shell-shocked soldiers from compensation for their injuries. "No man who has simply broken down mentally," he argued, "should be given a wound stripe, but the man with an obvious commotional shock who has been buried or blown up deserves one. I distinguish rather sharply between the two conditions" (*Report of the War Office Committee* 1922: 17).[4] In spite of such certainty, the Committee's attempts to separate emotional from commotional shock and to distinguish convincingly between stable and unstable soldiers were confounded by much of the evidence. According to the *Report*, not only did soldiers suffering from commotional shock demonstrate "symptoms of exactly the same type as those who were suffering from the emotional form," but it was also "extremely difficult to say beforehand what type of man is most likely to break down" (ibid.: 92–3).

The War Office Committee of Enquiry revealed, or perhaps more accurately served to consolidate, a set of contradictions and tensions that continued to inflect scientific and clinical interpretations of the role of emotions in disease throughout the twentieth century. At one level, the Committee's *Report* highlighted persistent ambiguities in medical understandings of the interrelations between mind and body, a situation that betrayed the emergent professional and institutional separation of scientific medicine from psychiatry and psychology. At another level, cultural preferences for physical rather than psychological explanations of disease during the early decades of the twentieth century helped to marginalize emotions in personal, professional, and political accounts of patterns and experiences of disease, even though contemporary commentators, such as the historian Caroline Playne (1925; 1928), were seeking to explain the origins and consequences of combat in terms of a collective emotional neurosis generated by the stresses and strains of modern work and warfare. In many ways, shell shock thus serves to capture and anticipate the ambivalence of modern Western societies towards the role of emotions, and their expression or repression, in shaping health.

There has been considerable scholarly interest recently in the cultural history of specific emotional states, most notably: fear and anxiety; the impact of Darwinian theories of evolution and adaptation on understanding emotions; the social and cultural roots of scientific studies of emotion (or what has been referred to as "emotionology") in the late nineteenth and twentieth centuries; the construction of emotional states as psychosocial phenomena; the place of emotions (anatomically and symbolically) in relation to the heart; and the ways in which emotions were incorporated into, or excluded from, scientific investigations of the onset and natural history of disease (Alberti 2006; 2010; Bourke 2005; Dixon 2006; Gouk and Hills 2005; Horwitz 2013; Gross 2006; O'Gorman 2015; Potegal and Novaco 2010: 9–24; Prinz 2003; Richardson 2013; Robin 2004; Stearns 1994; Matt and Stearns (eds) 2013; Stearns and Stearns 1985). Such studies have set the terms of discussion for historians of emotions, urging scholars to pay greater attention to personal and political narratives of emotional distress and to consider more carefully the complex interplay between minds, bodies, and languages across time. They have also challenged historians to recognize the ways in which contemporary understandings of emotions and their pathologies have been informed by gender and class relations, to problematize the apparent stability of emotional categories, and to develop more nuanced historical evaluations of the scientific and cultural drivers of disputes about the role of emotions in disease (Bourke 2003; Dixon 2012).

Emotions have also figured in histories of science. Otniel Dror has drawn attention to the manner in which emotions occupied a paradoxical conceptual space within experimental physiology around the turn of the nineteenth into the twentieth century. Even while physiologists were studying the impact of emotions (as "objects of knowledge") on bodily processes and devising new ways of inscribing and representing emotions within scientific research, they were endeavoring to establish the laboratory as an "emotionally neutral" masculine space, one in which regulating or eliminating the impact of disruptive emotions on experimental procedures became key to producing objective knowledge (Dror 2001; 1999). In an expansive and provocative special issue of *Osiris* published in 2016, Dror and his coeditors further explored the "emotion-denying" narratives of modern science, encouraging historians to expose more clearly the manner in which scientific technologies embodied both a "contemporary masculine emotional culture of self-control and restraint" and a "feminine emotional culture of sensitivity and feelings" (Dror, Hitzer, Laukötter and León-Sanz 2016: 11).

Similarly attuned to reading the modern science of emotions in broad contextual terms, contributors to a recent volume edited by Frank Biess and Daniel M. Gross have argued that, in the wake of what was regarded as the "excessive emotionalism" of Nazism, scientists in Europe and North America largely discarded emotions as objects of scientific enquiry after the Second World War. Instead, they focused primarily on models of rational control and self-regulation, at least until the growth of brain science combined with major social and cultural shifts to reinvigorate studies of emotions among neuroscientists, physicians, psychiatrists, and social scientists during the 1960s (Biess and Gross 2014). Collectively, these authors highlight the need to contest trans-historical and essentialist accounts of emotional states, to recognize conflicting constructions of emotions, to explore the social, political, and cultural specificity of scientific models of emotions in greater depth, and to acknowledge the benefits of more explicitly linking histories of science with histories of emotions.

Taking 1922 as its starting point, this chapter analyzes the shifting form and content of modern Western accounts of emotions and health.[5] The first section explores Walter Cannon's belief in the role of emotions in disease within the context of his conviction that physiological balance and mind–body unity are essential for health. Although not the only theory of emotions, Cannon's model was influential in the development of psychosomatic medicine and physiological studies of stress during the mid-twentieth century. But, as the second section argues, scientists and clinicians who initially adopted Cannon's framework began to dismantle his organismic vision of emotions as performative and embodied, preferring to reduce emotions to the psychological realm and to disregard his emphasis on the emotional origins of many diseases. The gradual disembodiment of emotions and their marginalization as factors in the etiology of disease were accompanied by a propensity for scientists, clinicians, and the media to trivialize emotions. In debates about seemingly emotional life stages, such as adolescence, midlife, and menopause, emotions became objects of ridicule, manifestations of individual weaknesses that once again foregrounded personal responsibility for governing reactions to the stress of life. While scientific medicine reinforced neo-liberal emphases on individual autonomous behavior, rather than structural inequalities, as the key driver of health and fitness, it also displayed a deep mistrust of emotional subjectivity as a causal factor in disease and warned against the physical, psychological, and political dangers of unregulated emotional expression.

THE MACHINERY OF EMOTION

In their analysis of shell shock in 1917, Grafton Elliot Smith and T. H. Pear referred admiringly to Walter Cannon's "striking demonstration of the importance of emotion" in producing the "bodily disturbances" associated in particular with fear (Smith and Pear 1917: 8). Smith and Pear's identification of Cannon's work as critical to understanding the origins and manifestations of shock was apposite. During the early decades of the twentieth century, Cannon was the principal architect of a holistic model of emotions that provided the foundations for psychosomatic and constitutional medicine and shaped early formulations of the health impacts of stress and trauma on both sides of the Atlantic. Having graduated in medicine from Harvard in 1900, Cannon joined the Department of Physiology at Harvard Medical School, succeeding Henry P. Bowditch as Chair of Physiology in 1906. Remaining at Harvard until his retirement in 1942, Cannon pursued laboratory investigations into a variety of physiological and pathological processes: the mechanisms involved in traumatic shock; the organization and function of the autonomic nervous system; the role of the adrenal medulla and its secretions, adrenaline and noradrenaline, in preparing the body for "fight or flight" in the face of danger; and the neuro-hormonal and metabolic pathways and processes by which organisms retained functional stability, or homeostasis, in adverse circumstances (on Cannon's contributions to physiology, see Benison, Barger and Wolfe 1987; 1991; Wolfe, Barger and Benison 2000). Less well known is the fact that much of his scientific work also explored the evolutionary purpose, physiological manifestations, and clinical significance of emotions. (See Figure 1.1 for a portrait of Cannon).

FIGURE 1.1: Walter Bradford Cannon (1871–1945). Wellcome Library, London. Wellcome Images, V0026158. Photograph by Bachrach, 1934. *Copyrighted work available under Creative Commons Attribution Only license CC BY 4.0 http://creativecommons.org/licenses/by/4.0/.*

Cannon was not the first scientist or clinician in the modern era to investigate emotions or to emphasize links between emotion and disease. From the mid-nineteenth century, contributors to the medical and popular press had regularly cited emotional distress as a cause of conditions such as cancer, diabetes, thyroid disease, insanity, indigestion, neurasthenia, and heart disease.[6] Drawing on contemporary studies of physiological regulation and adaptation, these accounts combined an awareness of the impact of personal circumstances, such as grief, financial insecurity, and overwork, on health with a conviction that the increasing pace of modern life was triggering illness in the emotionally unstable. Reflecting a gradual shift away from locating the seat of emotions in the heart towards regarding them as products of the mind, many late-nineteenth-century medical writers believed that the appearance of organic disease in those under emotional stress was mediated by the nervous system. Although there was a continuing emphasis on the function of the brain and nerves in dictating the appearance and manifestations of disease, this approach was complicated in the early twentieth century by evidence that hormones secreted by the endocrine system could also determine health and illness. It was this association between nerves and hormones, which was recognized by the *Report of the War Office Committee* (1922: 100), that led to the development of neuro-endocrinology or to studies of what the English psychiatrist Noel H. M. Burke referred to in 1926 as "the machinery of emotion" (*Report of the War Office Committee* 1922: 100; Burke 1926: 112).[7]

Neuro-endocrine explanations for the impact of emotions on disease were particularly prominent in the work of one of Cannon's contemporaries, the American surgeon George Washington Crile, who, along with Cannon, served in the American Expeditionary Forces in France during the First World War. Crile subsequently corresponded with Cannon, and his work on the dysregulation of the endocrine system in response to emotional shock was also cited by the War Office Committee of Enquiry (1922: 100). Figure 1.2 shows an image of someone suffering from shell shock. In 1914, Crile outlined a mechanistic theory of disease in which both organic and psychological disorders could be understood as the product of physiological attempts to adapt to environmental circumstances. Building on Darwinian understandings of animal emotions as protective reflexes that facilitated escape from danger, Crile claimed that emotions commonly regarded in negative terms, such as fear, anger, jealousy, envy, and disappointment in love, could trigger an "excessive discharge of nervous energy," leading not just to exhaustion but also to histological changes in the brain, adrenal glands, and liver. According to Crile, laboratory studies of the effects of fear in rabbits, as well as clinical studies of patients with thyroid disease, demonstrated the capacity for emotions to disrupt the "control cells of the brain," disturb the coordination and stability of the body, and lead eventually to overt disease: "Chronic emotional stimulation, therefore," he wrote in *The Origin and Nature of the Emotions*, "may fatigue or exhaust the brain and may cause cardiovascular disease, indigestion, Graves' disease, diabetes, and insanity even" (Crile [1915] 2006: 32, 87–8).

Crile's determination to establish a physiological model of emotions and disease was driven by his desire to escape from what he termed "the shackles of psychology," as well as by his belief that it was the brain, rather than the mind, that operated as the organ of control (ibid.: 37). Walter Cannon was no less committed than Crile to demonstrating the physiological, rather than psychological, pathways through which emotions disturbed bodily functions. Cannon's antagonism, however, was directed more specifically at

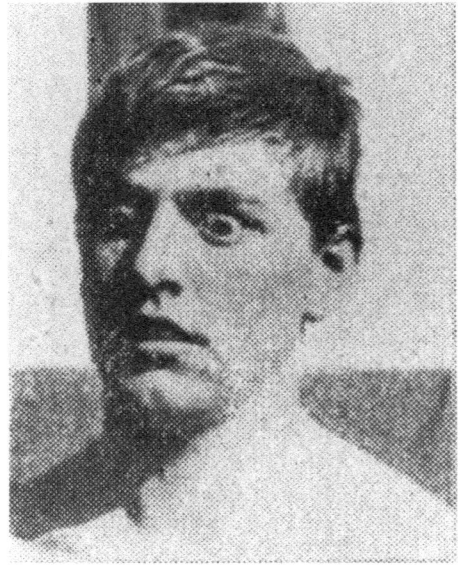

FIGURE 1.2: Patient suffering from war neuroses: shell shock. Wellcome Library, London. Wellcome Images, L0023554. Photograph taken from Arthur Frederick Hurst, Medical Diseases of the War (1918). *Copyrighted work available under Creative Commons Attribution Only license CC BY 4.0 http://creativecommons.org/licenses/by/4.0/.*

"healing cults," including Christian Science and Freudian psychoanalysis. Such approaches, he argued, tended to account for illness in terms of the "ghostly figures" of the id, ego, and superego and to ignore not only the governance of the brain, but also the "considerable role which emotional factors have come to play in the onset of illness, especially among people who are harassed by novel and severe demands on their nervous capacities" (Cannon 1936: 1455). Yet, even though he derided psychological theories of emotion and disease that tended to ignore organic changes, Cannon was no naïve biological reductionist; his vision of how emotions unsettled the body's capacity to cope with stress was also shaped by his opposition to the biological theory of emotions, developed independently in the 1880s by the American psychologist William James (1884) and the Danish physician Carl Lange (1912). According to James and Lange, the subjective experience of an emotion (or "feeling") was dependent on preceding visceral arousal, triggered by the apprehension of an object and manifested in the raised pulse rate, flushing, laughing, and crying associated with emotional states (Lange 1912; Lange and James 1922; for Cannon's objections to the James–Lange theory, see Cannon 1927).

In a series of studies carried out during the early decades of the twentieth century, Cannon developed an approach to the role of emotions in disease that disputed the James–Lange theory, as well as challenging purely psychological models of emotions. Cannon imagined the organism as a coordinated and integrated whole, the functions of which were orchestrated by the thalamus (or archaic portion of the brain) and conducted by the autonomic nervous system operating in part through secretions from the adrenal medulla. Both "motion and emotion," argued Cannon, carried the capacity to disrupt this homeostatic system and cause excessive discharge of medullary hormones (Cannon 1937: 131; see also Cannon 1922a: 1928; 1929). In many cases, this process constituted an adaptive response that raised the heart rate, increased blood sugar and red blood cells, and released the "reservoirs of power" necessary for survival. But if strong emotions persisted or were repressed, prolonged or dysregulated adreno-sympathetic stimulation could disturb the body further, leading to overt disease and, in some cases, sudden death: "the persistent derangement of bodily functions in strong emotional reactions," Cannon wrote, "can be interpreted as due to persistence of the stimuli which evoke the reactions" (Cannon 1939: 261).[8] Cannon's emphasis on tracing the physiological, rather than only the psychological, processes involved in emotional stress and disease was the product of his particular definition of emotion. For Cannon, an "emotion" was a "typical reaction pattern" that comprised a combination (or "storm"—see Cannon 1922b) of instinctive behavior, subjective state, and bodily disturbances, such as palpitations, raised blood pressure, and altered digestion (Cannon 1928: 878). Similarities in visceral changes resulted in some commonality between different emotional states, but Cannon's inclusion of a central cortical, or subjective, dimension to emotional arousal allowed him, unlike James, to explain differences between particular emotions (Cannon 1914). Figure 1.3 presents a graphic representation of the Cannon–Bard/James–Lange theories.

Other early-twentieth-century scientists and clinicians also identified links between emotions and metabolic dysfunction. In 1927, the American physician Rollin Turner Woodyatt, whose work on diabetes was cited by Cannon (1928: 882), noted how "events in the psychic sphere" often accompanied changes in the physical health of diabetic patients: "It is interesting to be able to measure the power of emotion," he wrote, "in terms so tangible as ounces of sugar" (Woodyatt 1927). And yet, at the same time, there was something distinctive about Cannon's insistence on bodily harmony and the role of

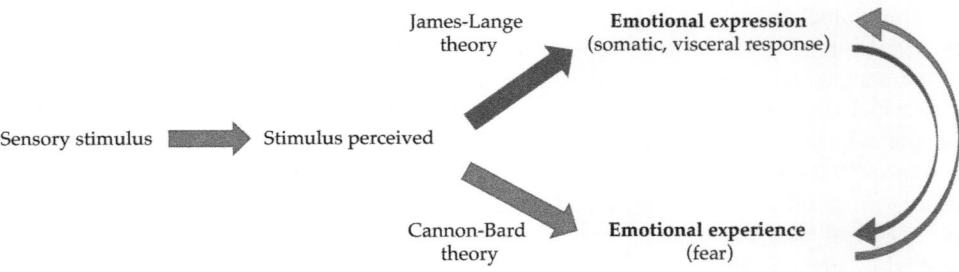

FIGURE 1.3: James–Lange and Cannon–Bard theories.

emotions in disease in terms of its political resonance as well as the brand of scientific investigation and clinical practice that it demanded. In the first instance, Cannon's vision of the body as a coordinated whole regulated by the neuro-endocrine system went hand in hand with his commitment to social democracy and his antagonism to the rise of fascism across Europe during the interwar years. As he argued most forcibly in *The Wisdom of the Body*, first published in 1932, the equitable distribution of metabolites and energy supplies throughout the body in order to maintain physiological homeostasis constituted a model for the effective communication and distribution systems required to maintain social stability and ensure individual freedom and happiness (Cannon [1932] 1939; 1933; 1942a).[9] Equally, democratic political systems (as opposed to the autocracies of kaisers and czars) provided a blueprint for understanding bodily regulation (Cannon 1922a: 92). In a world in which a stable society was dependent on the stability of its members, emotional volatility could disrupt the body politic as much as the body physiologic (Cannon 1941).

Secondly, Cannon's emphasis on the capacity for emotions to disturb homeostasis and cause disease, like the potential for conflict and natural disasters to destabilize societies, necessitated a more holistic and balanced approach to medical practice, one in which the "effects of emotional stress and the modes of relieving it" were to be taken seriously (Cannon 1928: 884). In his most explicit account of the role of emotions in disease, published in 1936, Cannon argued that organisms should be conceived in terms of "a 'mind-body' unity," the health of which depended on the harmonious integration of physiological and psychological processes (Cannon 1936: 1464). To effectively treat disease and promote well-being, he insisted, medicine needed to operate more flexibly "in the twilight zone where physiology and psychology, pathology and psychiatry all meet" (Cannon 1922b: 30). Cannon's search for a theory of health and disease that integrated insights from different disciplines was reminiscent of Victorian beliefs in the unity of knowledge, which continued to inflect models of human behavior throughout the twentieth century, but it was given particular impetus in the interwar years by fears that rising trends in chronic disease were associated with the complex stresses and strains of economic uncertainty, job insecurity, and global warfare (Cannon 1936: 1454). In this context, Cannon's approach to maintaining or restoring "psycho-organismic unity," and his commitment to overcoming rage and hate by promoting "an inspiring and inclusive love," constituted an appealing pathway to emotional health and happiness for the inhabitants of what one of the principal architects of neo-liberalism, L. T. Hobhouse (1915: 5–12, 98), referred to as a "world in conflict," a world that had "lost its heart" and was governed by fear.

EMOTIONS DISEMBODIED

Walter Cannon's formulation of the impact of emotions on health and his emphasis on organismic regulation were eclipsed by more overtly biological accounts of disease and indeed, to some extent, overshadowed by his own physiological studies. Nevertheless, Cannon's model of emotions proved attractive to others seeking to link the emergence of disease to the political and emotional instability of modern lives, particularly clinicians keen to explain illness onset in constitutional and psychological terms. The cultural and clinical roots of psychosomatic medicine are complex. Early proponents of psychosomatic medicine in North America and Europe during the interwar years, such as the Hungarian psychoanalyst Franz Alexander and the American psychiatrist Helen Flanders Dunbar, were influenced by Freudian emphasis on the role of childhood trauma, the psychobiological approaches to illness onset developed initially by Adolf Meyer, the belief of some clinicians that health and illness could not be reduced to physicochemical processes, and Walter Cannon's holistic conceptions of homoeostasis and mind–body unity.[10] These scientific and clinical precepts were embedded in the principles of psychosomatic medicine formulated by Alexander and Dunbar: mind and body should be regarded as indivisible; proneness to disease was established in early life; and emotional distress and repressed emotions could trigger illness by disturbing the neuro-endocrine system. In an early statement of these principles, published in the first issue of *Psychosomatic Medicine* in 1939, Alexander revealed his debt not only to Freud but also to the work of Crile and Cannon on the pivotal role of emotional agitation in disease:

> In other words, many chronic disturbances are not caused by external, mechanical, chemical factors or by micro-organisms, but by the continuous functional stress arising during the everyday life of the organism in its struggle for existence. All those emotional conflicts which psychoanalysis has recognised at the basis of psychoneuroses and recently also as the ultimate cause of certain functional and organic disorders, arise during our daily life in the social contact with the environment. Continuous fears, aggressions, wishes, if repressed, result in permanent chronic emotional tensions, which disturb the functions of the vegetative organs.
>
> —Alexander 1939: 17–18

Although proponents of psychosomatic medicine adopted their own approaches to emotions and disease and aligned themselves variably to orthodox biomedicine in different national contexts, they tended to focus on much the same set of conditions, referred to by Alexander as "the magic seven": asthma, hypertension, peptic ulceration, rheumatoid arthritis, thyrotoxicosis, ulcerative colitis, and neurodermatitis.[11] The clinical implications of linking emotional disturbances to disease onset are particularly evident in Helen Flanders Dunbar's mid-century studies of the role of emotions in asthma, a condition that was subsequently regarded by some authors as the paradigmatic psychosomatic illness, "the clearest demonstration of that complex inter-relationship of body, intellect and emotion" (Pinkerton and Weaver 1970: 81).[12] During the early decades of the twentieth century, allergies were understood largely in terms of altered immunological reactivity triggered by an external agent (Jackson 2006). Dunbar did not deny the role of allergens such as pollen and dust in asthma, but stressed the need for clinicians to pay closer attention to the potential for emotions either to act alone or to interact with allergens to trigger asthma attacks. Asthma, she argued, was a product of psychological trauma in early childhood, defined specifically in terms of a disordered emotional relationship between mother and child:

> There are certain specific emotions which seem to be linked especially to asthma and hay fever. A conflict about longing for mother love and mother care is one of them. There may be a feeling of frustration as a result of too little love or a fear of being smothered by too much. A second emotional conflict characteristic of the allergic is that which results from suppressed libidinal desire, often closely associated with the longing for mother. The steady repetition of this emotional history of "smother love" in the asthmatic is as marked as the contrasting history of hostility and unresolved emotional conflict in the sufferer from hypertension.
>
> —Dunbar 1947: 177

Dunbar's formulation of an etiological link between emotions and disease and her emphasis on the relational and performative dimensions of emotions proved influential in the development of clinical strategies for treating asthmatic children. In particular, it underpinned the adoption of psychotherapy to restore emotional equilibrium and legitimated the removal of children with intractable asthma from the supposedly damaging emotional environment of an "asthmogenic home" or "asthmogenic family" (see Freeman 1950: 158–70). In North America in particular, the practice of "parentectomy" (literally cutting out the parent) became a relatively popular approach to the management of asthma, at least for a short period of time in the 1950s and 1960s: the convalescent home or hospital reduced exposure to domestic allergens but, more importantly, allowed children to escape from any adverse psychogenic factors in the family (Peshkin 1959).[13] In Britain, parentectomy was largely rejected on the grounds that it over simplified the complex factors involved in asthma, but similar schemes operated to remove children with behavioral disorders, anorexia, schizophrenia, and obesity from homes and family relationships that were judged to be pathological. As John Bowlby's theories of maternal deprivation gained purchase in the decades after the Second World War, psychiatrists, psychologists, and social workers in Child Guidance Clinics became convinced that neglectful parents, familial disharmony, and dominant and over protective mothers could all operate as triggers of emotional lability, maladjustment, and disease.[14]

Like Cannon's vision of physiological and emotional stability, psychosomatic and psychosocial medicine were infused with notions of political equity and social justice and used to endorse plans for reorganizing societies and reforming medicine. For Franz Alexander, emotional disequilibrium in response to environmental stresses was analogous to the "social upheavals" resulting from thwarted national "political ambitions" (Alexander 1939: 18). The relatively fleeting prominence of psychosocial medicine in Britain immediately after the Second World War, which highlighted the detrimental impact of social disintegration on psychological health, was encouraged by critiques of Western capitalism, as much as by disillusionment with biomedicine. In his account of what he termed the "sick society," the Scottish physician James Lorimer Halliday, who was influenced by the work of Cannon and Dunbar, argued that rising levels of chronic disease, psychosomatic disorders, sickness absence, and juvenile delinquency were the product of a society struggling to cope with the multiple stresses of economic rivalry, social disequilibrium, and military conflict. According to Halliday (1948: 180), recovery of emotional stability at both individual and social levels lay not only in integrating the insights of psychology and medicine, but also in challenging the growth of the market economy characteristic of Western civilization.

Although advocates of psychosomatic and psychosocial medicine were clearly inspired in part by Cannon's studies, it is noticeable that they gradually distanced themselves from his emphasis on mind–body parity and dismantled his account of emotions and their role in disease. Alexander acknowledged that emotions were expressed through physiological functions, but insisted on the primacy of the psyche in determining health and on the pivotal role of psychoanalysis in understanding the specificity of emotions and restoring emotional stability. "Recently more and more evidence is emerging," he wrote in 1939, "that probably the functions of the ductless glands ultimately are also subject to the function of the highest centers of the brain, that is to say, to the psychic life" (Alexander 1939: 13). The implications of this approach for science and clinical practice became clear. Within psychosomatic medicine, Cannon's "twilight zone" of collaborative investigation and intervention and parallel attempts to develop a unitary concept of human behavior were gradually replaced by more direct emphasis on psychogenic factors in health and disease. Even if the capacity for emotions to disturb the body was acknowledged, the emotional trauma that might trigger disease was reduced to a largely invisible psychological realm.

The tendency for scientists and clinicians to disembody emotions was also evident in mid-twentieth-century debates about stress-related disorders. One of the defining features of psychological studies of stress after the Second World War was an emphasis on personality, rather than emotion, in determining a person's capacity to adjust to the environment. In a study of ulcerative colitis published in 1947, the Dutch physician J. Groen set out what he regarded as the typical "character structure" of patients with ulcerative colitis. Their "outstanding peculiarities," he suggested, included a well-developed intellect, neatness, oversensitivity, feelings of inferiority, egocentricity, passivity, cowardice, and a need for love, manifested in male patients by "a strong fixation on the mother, often combined with fear of the father" (Groen 1947). Groen's debt to psychoanalytic theory and psychosomatic medicine (and indeed to Dunbar's studies of the "accident-prone personality") is apparent. Equally evident are the parallels with descriptions of the infantile dependency and emotional lability of servicemen and -women who broke down during combat or under the stress of bombardment in the Second World War, formulations that owed much to earlier accounts of the victims of shell shock as psychologically unstable (Jackson 2015).[15] Groen was not unique in foregrounding the etiological force of personality. Although discussions of cancer increasingly focused on carcinogens such as tobacco, a number of authors continued—often controversially, it must be said—to cite the ways in which personality factors might govern emotional tensions, hormonal imbalance, genetic mutations, and overt disease (see, for example, Reznikoff 1955; Eysenck 1965; 1991; 1994).

In many laboratory studies of psychological stress, such as those carried out by the American psychologist Richard Lazarus, it was also personality, rather than emotion, that was regarded as the principal mediator of disease in response to environmental stresses. Rather than constituting the basis for an explanatory model of interactions between mind and body, as in Cannon's vision of health and disease, emotion was used by Lazarus and others as a convenient descriptor of the perceived psychological pressures to adapt (Lazarus 1961; 1966; Lazarus and Folkman 1984; Lazarus, Speisman and Mordkoff 1963). Emotionality was only constituted through the objective behavioral manifestations or subjective experiences of psychological discomfort,[16] a form of language used primarily to capture the personality variables that determined the capacity to master stressful situations (Lazarus, Speisman, Mordkoff and Davison 1962: 28). One reason for this may be that, as many postwar psychologists acknowledged, psychological theories of stress were modeled on physiological studies of adaptation, from which emotions were largely excluded, or were intent on identifying physiological markers of psychological distress. The most influential stress theorist throughout the middle decades of the twentieth century was the Hungarian scientist Hans Selye, whose formulation of the tri-phasic "general adaptation syndrome" in response to external stressors was informed by Cannon's studies of the role of the sympathetic nervous system and adrenal glands in mediating stress reaction patterns.[17] Yet, while Cannon emphasized the centrality of emotion as a point of articulation between social stress and individual health, one that united mind and body in an organismic response to the environment, Selye was concerned only to delineate more clearly the physiological and biochemical pathways of disease under conditions of chronic stress. Although he recognized analogies between physiological and social stability, and later developed his own "natural philosophy of life" (set out in Selye 1974) based on notions of altruism and egoism, Selye remained largely uninterested in emotions as determinants of either personal or social dysregulation. There was no reference to emotions in his diagrammatic representations of the pathways of stress, which were expressed simply in mechanistic terms of stimulus and response.[18]

Hans Selye's restrictive notion of stress as a non-specific physiological response to an environmental stimulus was often contested by other researchers, but it influenced many postwar studies of both physical and psychological stress. In the context of this discussion, Selye's work highlights some of the differences between the holistic aspirations of interwar clinicians and scientists, such as Cannon, Alexander and Dunbar, and the biomedical reductionism that began to dominate postwar scientific medicine. During what has sometimes been regarded as a Golden Age of medicine after the Second World War, dramatic advances in biomedical science served to generate models of disease that focused on biology rather than psychology, on bodies rather than minds, and on technical and pharmaceutical, rather than social, solutions to health challenges. This is not to say that holistic approaches to health and disease were entirely marginalized; the principal tenets of psychosomatic and psychosocial medicine, which included some attention to the role of emotions, continued to inflect the work of American physicians such as Harold G. Wolff and George L. Engel, as well as framing British studies of families as sources of stress, emotional tension, and depression.[19] Although we know little about how doctors in everyday practice evaluated the role of emotions in disease, there is some evidence that general practitioners in Britain recognized, and tried to address, emotional disturbances in patients and their families as a means of managing illness (Halliday 1948: 242).[20]

A retreat from emotions may have made sense in the context of striking technological successes and the increased authority of science and medicine after the Second World War. But, as Biess and Gross have made clear, it also had cultural, economic, and political drivers. Declining interest in emotions among scientists and social scientists was the product of an emerging political emphasis on rationalism that held little space for recognizing or endorsing emotionality. The rise of fascism, the traumas of global conflict, the terrors of the Holocaust, and the perils of the Cold War led to widespread condemnation of "irrational and populist impulses" and the promotion of theories of social order and individual behavior that encouraged emotional restraint and self-control. When commentators did call for greater attention to the emotional elements of "political psycho-pathology" (Astor 1962; see the discussion in Biess and Gross 2014: 1–6), the word "emotional" emerged as a derogatory term, employed as part of a reactionary rhetoric to demonize disruptive forms of behavior; denigrate individuals, families, nations, and political parties that embraced radical beliefs and actions; and encourage conformity to domestic, marital, social, and occupational norms.[21]

ENDURING PASSION

Shortly before the Second World War, Walter Cannon emphasized the ways in which effective regulation of bodily function could be compromised by the "pathological ups and downs of existence in an ordinary life cycle" (Cannon 1935: 8). While Cannon was primarily referring to the impact of stress and strain on health, he was also alluding to a commonplace assumption that specific life events such as puberty, pregnancy, and menopause placed significant pressures on minds and bodies. According to a number of writers, the transitional phase from middle to old age—or what the American psychologist G. Stanley Hall referred to in 1921 as "the dangerous age" and others termed "the critical age"—could be especially hazardous emotionally.[22] In a self-styled neo-Hippocratic account of what he referred to as "constitutional medicine," the American physician George Draper (1930: 245–9) identified the "change of life" as a period of glandular imbalance, restlessness, and instability that occurred in both men and women between the ages of forty-five and sixty, and led to dissatisfaction with domestic and occupational routines and the pursuit of new relationships. Prevalent fears of physical decline and emotional deterioration during midlife, or what some advertisements for nerve tonics referred to as "forty-phobia" ("Forty-phobia (fear of the forties)," advertisement for Phyllosan, *The Times*, April 28, 1938: 19), helped to create a market for self-help books that encouraged men and women to believe that life, rather than death, began at forty (or, towards the end of the century, at fifty).[23] At the same time, widely disseminated studies of sexual behavior, including those carried out by Alfred Kinsey and by William H. Masters and Virginia E. Johnson (see Figure 1.4), highlighted the detrimental impact of emotional tension on sexual performance, creating a space for the promotion of alternative techniques, such as yoga, for restoring sexual potency in middle-aged men and women. "*Savasana* and breathing cycles," wrote Nancy Phelan and Michael Volin, "help to relieve the tension that may be contributing to the trouble, and mental exercises leading to increased confidence, inner strength, and a positive attitude should also be practised, since in impotence a negative state of mind can be physically inhibiting" (Phelan and Volin 1965: 73).[24]

American writers such as Walter B. Pitkin, Professor of Journalism at Columbia University, situated their advice for the middle-aged in the context of aspirations for social progress, economic productivity, and sexual and military prowess (Pitkin 1932).[25] By contrast, British authors emphasized the effects of emotional instability on marriages, families, and communities. In her interwar study entitled *Enduring Passion*, Marie Stopes stressed the need to anticipate and address the destabilizing effects of the female and male "climacteric" in order to prevent "happy lovers" from becoming "drabby tolerant married couples": how could couples sustain passion and contentment, she asked, through the psychological and physical changes wrought by aging (Stopes 1928: 2)? Although Stopes was reluctant to use the word "crisis" to describe the emotional transitions of middle-aged men and women, she recognized the profound impact that the change of life could have on health and happiness (Stopes 1936). Figure 1.5 shows Stopes at her desk. Stopes's articulation of the difficulties that many couples experienced in maintaining love and affection throughout marriage energized studies of marital tensions by psychologists and social workers, and facilitated the formation of the Marriage Guidance Council in 1938 and the establishment in 1948 of the Family Discussion Bureau, which later became the Tavistock Institute of Marital Studies and more recently the Tavistock Centre for Couple Relationships.[26] According to Marriage Guidance Council training officer J. H. Wallis,

FIGURE 1.4: Virginia Johnson and William Masters. Photo by Bettmann via Getty Images.

marriage counselors needed to recognize the emotional determinants of marital disharmony and the "turmoil of conflicting feelings" that often obstructed resolution of practical difficulties between couples. In addition to knowledge of the law and the provisions of the welfare state, an effective counselor, he argued, should be able to understand and address a wide range of both expressed and unexpressed emotions, including "unhappiness and jealousy, resentment and anger, misery and altruism, desire and indifference, love and hate, acceptance and rejection" (Wallis 1964: 30–1).

The Second World War and the postwar settlement brought issues of midlife emotional instability to the forefront of professional and political debates about health and welfare. Increased life expectancy, commercial pressures to pursue individual fulfillment, shifting notions of love and romance, and psychological challenges posed by the transition from war to peace placed new stresses on marriages and families, and emphasized the political value of accessing the emotions of postwar populations as a means of evaluating and safeguarding social stability (for provocative discussions, see Beck and Beck-Gernsheim 1995; Langhamer 2013). Describing middle age as a "second puberty," in 1962 Wallis highlighted the biological and psychological readjustments required to maintain health and happiness during the middle years of life and stressed the need to look beyond the menopause, or comparable alterations in sexual potency in men, in order to identify and understand the myriad changes occurring in midlife. Discussions of middle age, he suggested, were marked by a lack of sympathy and a tendency to blame individuals for their inability to deal adequately or rationally with the stress of life, an approach that

FIGURE 1.5: Marie Stopes (1880–1958), Wikimedia Commons.

compounded the problems faced by those struggling to cope with alterations in appearance, vitality, libido, family obligations, and material circumstances. In some cases, such conditions were sufficient to precipitate what Wallis termed a "middle-age crisis," an "emotional typhoon" that was marked by a propensity to reject home and marriage and to engage in "sudden compulsive infidelity" that inflicted emotional shock on partners and destroyed previously secure and happy marriages (Wallis 1962: 89–90).

Reinforced by evidence that divorce rates were rising rapidly after the Second World War,[27] a trend regarded by some commentators as indicative of a postwar "marriage crisis" (Mace 1948), depictions of midlife as a period of emotional risk were taken up by British researchers interested in the specific health challenges of middle age. At a symposium in 1964, Martin Roth, Professor of Psychological Medicine at the University of Durham, suggested that middle age, with its combination of situational stresses and physical changes, was a "great revealer of the emotional imbalance and maladjustment of the basic personality," leading sometimes to overt psychiatric disorders and requiring medication, psychotherapy, and the pursuit of new forms of creativity to restore a sense of achievement and purpose (Roth 1964). Although some clinicians preferred to read midlife affective disorders as the product of endocrine factors alone (Malleson 1953), it was the emotional disruption associated with the transition from middle to old age that dominated debates about the deterioration of mental and physical health in middle-aged women and men.

While historians have begun to explore changing definitions, experiences, and cultural representations of adulthood and middle age, far less historical attention has been paid to midlife in terms of health and emotional stability (recent historical studies of middle age include Gullette 2004; Heath 2009; Cohen 2012; Mintz 2015). Yet, late-twentieth-century discussions of midlife problems reveal a great deal about how emotions were regarded by scientists, clinicians, and the public after the Second World War. Postwar prescriptions for preventing or surviving the emotional upheavals of midlife owed much to psychoanalytical studies of identity formation, personality integration, and spirituality, themes that figured prominently in the works of Carl Jung, Eric Erikson, Rollo May, and others during the middle decades of the twentieth century (for Jung's discussion of midlife transitions, including his own, see Jung 1940; 1945: 109–31. See also: Erikson 1994; May 1953). Psychoanalysis also provided the framework for perhaps the most influential, or at least the most widely disseminated, modern contribution to understandings of emotional distress in middle age. In 1965, Elliott Jaques presented an account of what he termed the "midlife crisis." A Canadian-born social scientist and psychoanalyst, and one of the founding members of the Tavistock Institute of Human Relations, Jaques was best known for his studies of the links between social organization, working conditions, and individual adjustment, and for his attempt to develop a general account of living organisms from the perspective of systems theory (Jaques 1970; 2002). In "Death and the mid-life crisis," first published in the *International Journal of Psycho-Analysis*, Jaques suggested that a crisis of creativity around the age of thirty-five was triggered by growing awareness of personal death and an inability to accept the passing of youth: "The paradox," he wrote, "is that of entering the prime of life, the stage of fulfilment, but at the same time the prime and fulfilment are dated. Death lies beyond" (Jaques 1965). In order to ward off depression and cope with emotional impoverishment and fear of death, Jaques argued, many middle-aged men and women attempted to retain or regain their youth, became obsessed with health and appearance, and engaged in extra-marital affairs that proved to be "as persecuting, however, as the chaotic and hopeless internal situation they are meant to mitigate" (ibid.).

It was this image of emotional chaos, sexual license, and the fragmentation of the family that characterized Western notions of the midlife crisis in the late twentieth century. The personal, social, and political implications of an emotional storm of this nature were not inconsiderable. In a climate of anxiety about the perceived death of the nuclear family, and amid debates about how to preserve marriages while allowing women greater freedom to divorce, the unregulated behavior of middle-aged men in particular, and its impact on the emotional welfare of their partners and children, became a key point of discussion for social and legal reformers hoping to introduce less punitive and more conciliatory approaches to the breakdown of relationships (Chettiar 2016). It also became a recurrent trope in literary and cinematic studies of marriage, fidelity, and the collapse of the American Dream. Sloan Wilson's *The Man in the Gray Flannel Suit* (1955)—and its sequel published in 1984 but set in 1963—explored the dissonance between the exhilaration of combat and the boredom of corporate life, as well as the causes and consequences of marital betrayal. Equally, in Simone de Beauvoir's *The Woman Destroyed* (1967), a poignant diary of a woman struggling to cope with her husband's infidelity, and Ingmar Bergman's *Scenes from a Marriage* (1973), the midlife crisis operated as a critical tool to expose and dissect the emotional vulnerability of postwar populations.

Yet, there was another dimension to contemporary representations of the emotional crises of middle age. While de Beauvoir emphasized the tragic dimensions of midlife transitions, other novelists and journalists highlighted the comical or melodramatic elements of emotional turmoil. Sensationalist and populist media depictions of narcissistic middle-aged men obsessed with fast cars or infatuated by "some golden doll of a girl with a curly head and long legs" (Wallis 1962: 99), as well as fictional accounts of male midlife crises, such as David Nobbs's *The Death of Reginald Perrin* (1975) or John Trent's film *Middle Age Crazy* (1980), not only reinforced negative portrayals of midlife, but also trivialized the emotional and situational stresses often associated with this stage of life. In these cultural contexts, late-twentieth-century accounts of the experiences and understandings of emotional turmoil bore little resemblance to Walter Cannon's examination of the role of emotions in disease, or even to military recognition that emotions could trigger profound psychological and physical disturbances in soldiers under stress. Paralleling the post-Second World War retreat from studying or reflecting on emotions in science and medicine, the unrestrained emotionality of middle-aged men and women became a source of ridicule, seized on as an opportunity to belittle their capacity to exert self-control or cope with the stress of life. Satirical narratives of the midlife crisis intersected with neo-liberal emphases on individual, rather than state, responsibility for happiness and health, providing a potent reminder of the damaging social and political consequences of emotional imbalance.[28]

CONCLUSION

One striking feature of twentieth-century scientific and clinical studies of emotions is their preoccupation with how supposedly negatively-toned emotions such as fear, sadness, worry, and anger destabilized bodies and minds and generated disease. Far fewer contemporary studies investigated the health effects of love, joy, and passion or the possibility that emotional expression might be therapeutic. There were exceptions. In his study of religious experience, William James (1902: 196–8) emphasized the extent to which hope, happiness, security, and resolve could be as powerful as jealousy, guilt, remorse, and anger in generating new ideas and beliefs. In the middle decades of the twentieth century, studies of stressful life events not only recognized that ostensibly pleasurable experiences, such as marriage and the birth of a child, could trigger the onset of illness, but also that emotional stress could be beneficial for health and well-being: according to Hans Selye (1974), it was possible to be stressed without distress, to profit from the physiological and psychological arousal of stressful activities.

Historians of emotion have mainly reproduced contemporary preoccupations with the health effects of supposedly negative, rather than positive, moods and emotional states. Fear, sadness, envy, worry, anxiety, and depression have their clinical histories; the scientific and medical, as well as social and economic, histories of elation, happiness, serenity, pleasure, and love largely remain to be written. This chapter is an attempt to highlight the value to historians of reflecting more closely on how shifting models of emotions and health have shaped the technologies and epistemologies of biomedical science, and vice versa. Emotions have occupied an ambiguous space in modern Western science and medicine. Building on late-nineteenth-century and early-twentieth-century beliefs that emotions were able to trigger disease, Walter Cannon formulated an integrated model of how chronic emotional distress might precipitate ill health by disrupting harmonious operation of the neuro-endocrine system. Cannon's appeal to doctors to take emotions seriously clearly influenced the development of psychosomatic medicine and stress research. But it is noticeable that, even as they drew inspiration from his laboratory studies, initial advocates of Cannon's holism began to reject his emphasis on the pivotal role of emotions. In much of the interwar and postwar medical literature on psychosocial stress and disease, emotions were either ignored or relegated to a psychic realm largely disconnected from the body.

The mid-twentieth-century traumas and tragedies of totalitarianism, global conflict, and the Cold War fractured confidence in global security, reinforced a growing sense of disenchantment with modernity, and revealed the perils of unregulated emotion. The relatively unchallenged authority of science and medicine immediately after the Second World War, and the increased power of pharmaceutical companies to medicate moods, similarly undermined the holistic aspirations of many interwar clinicians. This is not to say that clinical holism was moribund, but simply that it simmered slowly on the margins of Western medicine until it resurfaced, towards the end of the century, in revitalized critiques of biomedical reductionism and widespread rejection of the emotion-denying narratives of modern science. Recent reiterations of Cannon's belief in the role of emotional factors in disease, as well as resurgent scientific and historical commitment to studying emotions, are not merely the products of a "neuroscientific turn," as Biess and Gross (2014) and others have intimated. Rather, they should be seen, like the abrogation and trivialization of emotions in earlier decades, as products of a constellation of interlocking cultural, social, and political factors. Challenges to medical hegemony made possible partly by the Internet, anxieties about the loss of empathy associated with technomedicine, disillusionment with the unregulated economic policies of neo-liberalism that have accentuated rather than mitigated health inequalities, and dissatisfaction with attempts to measure well-being purely in monetary terms—a process exacerbated by the intertwining of emotional and economic relationships (Illouz 2007)—have all encouraged calls for a so-called "fifth wave of public health" (Lyon 2003; Hanlon and Lyon 2011). Expressed in the vocabulary of what some critics have referred to as post-liberalism (Milbank and Pabst 2016), the central tenets of the new wave of public health foreground the importance of subjectivity, lived experience, and emotional well-being in developing more culturally sensitive approaches to health across the life cycle. It remains to be seen whether this shifting ideological context serves to revive or further suffocate scientific, clinical, historical, and public interest in emotions as determinants of health and disease.

ACKNOWLEDGMENTS

I am grateful to the Wellcome Trust (Grant No. 100601/Z/12/A) for funding the research on which this chapter is based.

CHAPTER TWO

Religion and Spirituality

ANASTASIA SCRUTTON

This chapter will consider religion and spirituality through the lens of responses to two of the most striking features of the last century: the medicalization of emotion, and the reimagining of non-Western ideas by the West for therapeutic purposes. Because the medicalization of emotion is a pervasive aspect of Western culture, much discussion in the last century has been concerned with whether religion and spirituality complement, challenge, or conflict with medical approaches to emotion. I will begin by discussing the backlash against the Freudian-influenced negative assessment of religion which is evident in the increasingly numerous studies of whether religion and spirituality are beneficial for mental health, pointing to how attention to a more diverse range of religions and to religions in context might nuance our understanding of the relationships between religion and mental health.

Having considered ways in which religion and spirituality have been thought both to conflict with and to complement mental health, I will turn to ways in which religions and spirituality have been reimagined for emotional healing, initially in "alternative" but increasingly in mainstream popular and medical cultures. At the heart of the reimagining of spiritual resources by Western consumers are not only practical, therapeutic concerns but also some important philosophical concerns to do with the mind and emotion: the relationship between the body and the mind; between the human person and the larger world (or the nature of consciousness); the nature of human well-being and its relationship to experiences of suffering; and the nature, value, importance, and role of emotion. While I am in some ways sympathetic to these reimaginings, I point to some important concerns raised by religious practitioners and religious studies scholars about the appropriation of religious and spiritual traditions for therapeutic ends, focusing on issues of misrepresentation. As with the religion and mental health literature discussed earlier in the chapter, I argue that increased attention to the religious traditions in question is needed, and that this should be combined with a more respectful attitude towards them.

Before beginning, a brief note is needed about the distinction between religion and spirituality. Prior to the middle of the twentieth century, "spirituality" referred to the interior aspects of religious life in religions (such as Christianity) in which interiority is important. In this context, "spirituality" might refer to (for example) the cultivation of religious virtues or the reformation of desires through practices such as contemplation and prayer. A rather different understanding of "spirituality" became popular in the 1960s, when "spirituality" became detachable from religion and began to refer to individual, emotional aspects of experiences of transcendence, as opposed to the perceived institutional, doctrinal, and dogmatic nature of religion which was by and large viewed negatively by the counterculture (see for example Maslow 1964; 1968). Understood in this way, spirituality unadulterated by institutional and doctrinal religion was regarded as a speciality of a romanticized and appropriated East. While this depiction of both "spirituality" and "religion" has been critically regarded by scholars of religion, it nevertheless persists today (see Harvey 2015). Rather than try to evaluate different understandings of "religion" and "spirituality" or to characterize "religion" and "spirituality" in any definitive way, this chapter will simply reflect on the different ways in which "spirituality" and "religion" are currently used by practitioners of the traditions and practices under discussion.

THE MEDICALIZATION OF EMOTION

Arthur Miller's 1949 play *Death of a Salesman* tells the story of Willy Loman, a failed businessman and flawed husband and father who cannot come to terms with the failure of his high expectations. Having been fired from his job and unable to cope with his own and his sons' lack of success, Willy kills himself in a car crash so that his family can claim the insurance. When *Death of a Salesman* was first released, it was interpreted as raising questions both about the nature of the American Dream, which the characters perceive in different ways, and the effect of the American Dream on the lives of those who are subjected to it.

When Brian Dennehy took on the role of Willy Loman in the 1999 Broadway production, the script was sent to two psychiatrists in order to provide fresh insight into the character of Loman. Both psychiatrists said the same thing: Loman was a manic depressive with hallucinatory aspects. *The New York Times* ran an article entitled "Get That Man Some Prozac" in which psychiatrist Peter Kramer reflected, "I think there's definitely people out there saying, 'I wonder what would have happened if Willy got some Ritalin, and maybe got some counselling to get into another line of work' . . . I'm not advocating a clinical lens. I just think it's there" (cited in McKinley 1999). Meanwhile Miller himself remained adamant that the play was not fundamentally about mental illness: "Willy Loman is not a depressive . . . He is weighed down by life. There are social reasons for why he is where he is" (cited in McKinley 1999).

Whether we agree with the manic depressive diagnosis or with Miller, the change in interpretation is reflective of a more general shift that has taken place in the course of the twentieth century. People are more likely to wonder whether negative emotional states have a biomedical etiology, rather than one that derives from the circumstances in which individuals find themselves. Serious and ongoing unhappiness and worry are more likely to be described as forms of mental "illness" or "disorder." Strong negative emotions, and sometimes strong positive ones too, are regarded in no small part as being properly within the medical domain.

FINDING A PLACE FOR RELIGION AND SPIRITUALITY

Given the medicalization of emotion, it should come as no surprise that much discussion about emotion, religion, and spirituality relates explicitly or implicitly to questions about whether religion and spiritualty complement, challenge, or conflict with medical approaches to emotions. Much twentieth-century psychology and psychiatry was influenced by the Freudian assessment of religion as indicative of, or analogous to, psychopathology (Freud 1907). Thus, for example, religion was argued to be guilt-inducing and dependency-forming, with Albert Ellis—probably the most influential psychotherapist after Carl Rogers—arguing in 1980 that religion "seriously sabotages mental health," that "religion, essentially, is masochism, and both are forms of mental sickness," and that religion creates perfectionist and absolutist thinking which is the "prime creator of the most corroding of human emotions: anxiety and hostility" (Ellis 1980: 5, 6, 7). Swimming somewhat against this tide, Carl Jung regarded the mystical rather than doctrinal elements of religion as being important for, and having at their heart, the goal of individuation (the process of being transformed to achieve our innate potential). Jung had a particular interest in Buddhism, since he found it "immensely helpful and stimulating" in relation to his "professional interest as a doctor" and its methods "for the treatment of psychic suffering" (Jung 1978: 236–9).

The last twenty-five years has seen something of a backlash against the Freudian assessment of religion and spirituality, such that arguing for a positive association between religion and spirituality and emotional well-being has become more the norm than the view of a minority. Nowhere is the more positive association between religion and emotion more evident than in studies examining whether religion and spirituality complement medical responses by providing coping strategies in stressful situations and buffers against, or faster recovery from, mental illness (Koenig, King and Carson 2012). Studies that raise these questions were undertaken as early as the 1950s, with one study arguing that religious attendance is positively correlated with personal adjustment in old age (Moberg 1956), a further two finding that religious attendance is positively correlated with reduced anxiety and apprehension of death (Martin and Wrightsman 1965; Williams and Cole 1968), and a PhD thesis finding that church attendance is associated with positive affect among "negroes" but not among whites (Dragastin 1968, cited in Comstock and Partridge 1972). However, over the last fifteen years, such studies have been undertaken in their thousands: in their 2012 handbook on religion and mental health, Harold Koenig, Dana King, and Verna Carson found that, in relation to religion and depression alone, there were 322 studies published since 2000, whereas prior to 2000 the total was only 103 (Koenig, King and Carson 2012: 149; Dein nd). On the whole, most studies indicate that there is a positive correlation between religion and mental health, and that religious belief and attendance contributes especially to greater optimism and hope and less depression and suicide (Koenig, King and Carson 2012).

Concerns about these studies include flaws in the methodology that may invalidate the findings (Sloan, Bagiella and Powell 1999; Sloan 2006), but also that the studies are not sufficiently nuanced or informed in their understanding of religion and spirituality. To give an example of the latter, it is argued that while this research seems to refer to religion as a whole, most of the studies focus on religious attendance and belief rather than (for example) ritual and other aspects of religious practice (Dein nd). This is problematic not least because, as recent scholarship in philosophy of religion and religious studies highlights, the Protestant intellectualizing conception of religion as characterized by belief overlooks other, equally or (in some cases) more important aspects of being religious, including land and place, perception of the sensory world, and relationships with food, sex, and strangers (Wynn 2009; 2013; Harvey 2013). In addition to the focus on belief and attendance, most of the studies also focus on Christianity in the USA. While recent studies of Judaism, Islam, and Hinduism suggest that there is a positive correlation between these religions and mental health, they also suggest that religious beliefs impact in different ways depending on the faith in question (Dein nd). "Religion" therefore needs to be regarded in a less monolithic way, and attention needs to be paid to how (what we have come to regard as) "religions" interact with the communities' identities, narratives, rituals, and other practices (Scrutton 2015b).

What kinds of things might increased attention to different religious traditions in context bring to our understanding of the relationship between religion and mental health or emotional well-being? Here are a few examples. First, in Western society, beliefs and practices to do with spirit possession are often regarded as detrimental to people's well-being (Krippner 2007). This is reflected in psychology and psychiatry discussions about the relationship between belief in spirit possession and mental illness. Thus, for example, while concurring that there is a generally positive relationship between religion and mental health, psychologist Kate Loewenthal states that beliefs in evil spirits and spirit possession are terrifying to those who believe in them, and are likely to exacerbate psychiatric illnesses such as schizophrenia (Loewenthal 2007: 32). This is not so much untrue—in fact there is some evidence to suggest that belief in evil spirits and spirit possession can be pathogenic—so much as one-sided. This is because, as Bettina Schmidt and Lucy Huskinson put it, "More often than not western interpretations of spirit possession have focussed on those instances that imply pain and torment . . . and not on those instances that imply joy and healing, or . . . creativity and comedy" (Schmidt and Huskinson 2010: 7–8). In some contexts, spirit possession is not something that instills fear, but rather something that is regarded as a gift. In other contexts, while it may instill temporary anxiety, it is ultimately a transformative and therapeutic experience (see Smith 2011: 3–17). In these contexts, spirit possession often seems to heal negative and promote positive emotions (see Scrutton 2016).

Increased attention to religious traditions in context can, therefore, contribute to our understanding of religion and emotional well-being because the interplay between religion and well-being often bucks the kinds of trends found in a mainstream Christian or broadly Christianized context. This is relevant not only to mental health literature on spirit possession, but to religion and mental health literature more generally. For example, research pioneered by Kenneth Pargament aims to make religion and mental health literature more nuanced by distinguishing between positive and negative religious coping (Pargament, 2010). Positive religious coping, characterized by (for example) trusting that God will not allow anything terrible to happen, and experiencing God's love and care, is positively correlated with mental health. Negative religious coping, characterized by (for example) believing the stressor might be a punishment from God or believing the stressor to be the work of the devil, is negatively correlated with mental health (Pargament, Koenig and Perez 2000). However, non-Western, non-Christian religious practices and traditions reveal that the picture is not always as straightforward as this. For example, as Jan Platvoet's account highlights, neither the Ju/'hoansi (Kalahari San/Bushman) creator god #*Gao N!a*, nor the lower god //*Gauwa* seem to have been especially benevolent, and the afterlife anticipated is a ubiquitously undesirable state of affairs. Furthermore, the culture's only ritual is not an act of worship of the deities, but, rather, an act of war against them (Platvoet 2001). While (to my knowledge) religion and mental health studies have never looked at the Ju/'hoansi, anthropological literature on them does not give an impression of them having been particularly prone to mental illness. In fact, if anything, the opposite seems to have been the case, and they were certainly a remarkably egalitarian and peaceable people (Katz, Biesele and St Denis 1997; Platvoet 2001). The fact that beliefs in non-benevolent deities do not always result in mental illness or negative affect may be because the way in which beliefs are held and relate to the narratives, rituals, and practices of the life of the community differ significantly from the norms of religious traditions such as Christianity. Thus, in contrast to the serious analysis of the ethically questionable behavior of God in the Hebrew Bible (e.g. Dawkins 2006: 31), Platvoet recounts how stories of *#Gao N!a*'s cannibalism and incest are met in Ju/'hoansi society with raucous laughter (Platvoet 2001: 126).

RELIGION, SPIRITUALITY, AND THE SEARCH FOR NON-BIOMEDICAL EMOTIONAL HEALING

While indigenous ways of healing emotions are in decline, largely on account of land destruction and colonizing activity, modern societies are often returning, or trying to return, to premodern or other-than-modern beliefs, attitudes, and practices in order both to complement and to challenge biomedical ways of dealing with emotions. This is unsurprising when one reflects on the fact that, as anthropological studies highlight, many religious practices (e.g. rituals) are connected with emotional healing. For example, "soul loss," often equated with depression, is cured in Shoshone and Northwest Coast Native American people by healers who entice "the soul back into the body with prayers and rituals," or enter into a deep trance to travel into the other world to retrieve the lost soul (Sandner 1996: 147). "Spirit illness," manifesting in depression, anxiety, and drug and alcohol problems, is treated by the Salish Indians of the Pacific Coast of North America through the Spirit Dance (Amoss 1978). The Ju/'hoansi people cured a number of sicknesses, including those that in the West would be designated emotional or mental, during the community healing dance, in which healers released healing energy through song and dance and the laying on of hands (Katz, Biesele and St Denis 1997). The widows of WeppaWannoland in Nigeria underwent bereavement rituals, which lasted up to one year, and which demonstrated an approach to bereavement that would have met with Freud's approval in that there was a "prolonged, complete and rigorous bereavement and mourning exercise as a way of purging the psyche of the bereaved" (Nwalutu 2012: 316). Sinhalese Buddhists undertake *yaktovil,* sometimes translated as "demon exorcism,"[1] to cure people from troublesome passions, these rituals being described as a kind of "primitive psychiatry" or "cultural psychotherapy" (see De Silva 1994: 203; Ambos 2011: 205).

Anthropological interest in the ways in which emotions are healed in non-Western cultures is not limited to the academic domain. For example, the psychologist and popular writer Andrew Solomon, author of the bestselling book *The Noonday Demon: An Anatomy of Depression*, explains how he moved from the "medical conservative" view that only pharmaceutical drugs and some talking therapies were effective treatments of depression, to interest in the ways in which non-modern cultures treat depression (Solomon 2008). Solomon's own experience of a dramatic ritual in Senegal designed to cure his depression involved asking the sexually jealous spirits who were thought to be causing the depression to leave, telling them, "Spirits, leave me alone to continue the business of my life, and know I will never forget you." Despite not sharing the spirit-inhabited worldview of the practitioners who hosted the ritual, Solomon relates that, following the ritual, "I felt so up. I felt so up." Solomon also relates the perspective of someone he met in Rwanda on traditional African versus Western treatments for depression. As the Rwandan put it:

> We had a lot of trouble with western mental health workers who came here immediately after the genocide and we had to ask some of them to leave.
>
> They came and their practice did not involve being outside in the sun where you begin to feel better. There was no music or drumming to get your blood flowing again.

There was no sense that everyone had taken the day off so that the entire community could come together to try to lift you up and bring you back to joy. There was no acknowledgment of the depression as something invasive and external that could actually be cast out again.

Instead they would take people one at a time into these dingy little rooms and have them sit around for an hour or so and talk about bad things that had happened to them. We had to ask them to leave.

—cited in Solomon 2008

THE SPIRITUALIZATION OF EMOTION: FROM EAST TO WEST

Partly as a result of disillusionment with biomedical treatment for emotional distress, the twentieth century saw a return to a range of religious and spiritual traditions, which has continued into the twenty-first century. Practitioners conceive these traditions, in diverse ways, as forms of emotional healing, and more broadly as conducive to emotional well-being. While the religious traditions drawn on have been diverse, religious traditions from the East have been especially popular. While numerous examples of the religious and spiritual traditions that have attracted Westerners' attention could be given, two examples, shamanism and yoga, will serve as an introduction to some characteristics of new religious and spiritual movements *qua* responses to predominant Western views of, and ways of dealing with, emotions.

Prior to the middle of the twentieth century, "shamanism" was an umbrella term for a number of ancient (and by then declining) indigenous practices, primarily in Siberia and Central Asia, which were thought to share some common features. However, relatively little is known about shamanism in this context, since, as Ronald Hutton explains, the words of shamans were mediated by outsiders mostly indifferent to or opposed to shamanism, and no data survive at all from the period prior to Russian rule when shamanic practice began to decline (Hutton 2001: 43–4). As Hutton argues, the history of "traditional" shamanism can therefore only be approached via the history of European constructions of shamanism (Hutton 2001).

The twentieth century saw the emergence of new forms of shamanism (sometimes called "neo-shamanism") and, concomitant with this, a revival of scholarly and popular interest in shamanism in its historical form. Influential figures in this revival are Carl Jung (see Figure 2.1) and, more directly, the Romanian historian of religion Mircea Eliade, whose 1951 book *Shamanism: Archaic Techniques of Ecstasy* (translated into English in 1964), marked a shift from the (negative) perception of shaman as magician to the (positive) perception of shaman as spiritual healer, common in the spiritual reimagining of shamanism to this day (see Harvey 2015). Eliade argued that "shamanism" describes a collective phenomenon with a shared structure and history, of which Siberian and Central Asian shamanism are paradigmatic but not the only examples—thus paving the way for the popularity of Amazonian shamanism—and characterized shamanism in terms of "techniques of ecstasy" that enabled shamans to journey to spirit worlds (See Figure 2.2 for an illustration of a Siberian shaman). While interest in shamanism was an element of the 1970s New Age movement (for example, through the 1968 work of Carlos Castaneda), it was disseminated beyond this movement in Michael Harner's 1980 book *The Way of the Shaman: A Guide to Power and Healing*, which popularized

FIGURE 2.1: Carl Jung (1875–1961). Photo by Hulton Archive/Stringer Getty Images.

FIGURE 2.2: "Priest of the Devil, Nicholaes Witsen (1641–1717). Amsterdam, 1705. The earliest known depiction of a Siberian shaman." © The British Library Board.

techniques for attaining the "altered" or "shamanic" "states of consciousness" described by Eliade (Harvey 2015).

Today, shamanism is utilized by a broad range of alternative therapy providers offering emotional healing and spiritual development courses and self-help literature, drawing on a range of religious and psychoanalytical traditions, and promising complementarity with any form of religion and none. It is also adopted by people who formally identify it as their religion or spiritual path. Perhaps partly because of the fact that it is impossible to "get behind" Western constructions of shamanism to the historical reality, a striking feature of shamanic scholarship is that a number of more recent shamanic scholars (anthropologists, historians, and religious studies scholars) also identify as shamanic practitioners—a phenomenon Jan Svanberg terms "shamanthropology" (Svanberg 2003). Many recent shamanic scholars are therefore in a good position to represent sympathetically the views of practitioners when they describe the experiences and attractiveness of contemporary shamanism. Thus, for example, Jenny Blain, a shamanic scholar and practitioner, explains the appeal of shamanism for many:

> Within Western "post-modern society" an increasing number of people are turning to construct their own spiritual relationships with the earth, other people, and those with whom we share the earth: plants, animals, and various spirit-beings found in the mythologies of the world. For many, this goes hand-in-hand with a search for roots, authenticity, a quest for meaning that seekers do not find in the hussle and pressures of their fragmented everyday lives.
>
> —Blain 2002: 3–4

Contemporary shamans will often be involved in healing, for example through "wholemaking": working in trance to reconcile people's bodies and spirits (Blain 2002: 119; see also Berggren 1998). As one shamanic healer puts it: "I work with the dying a lot especially Christians, but I work with anybody. My only job is to help" (Bil, cited in Blain 2002: 119). A theme of the shamanic-call narrative is that the shaman-to-be has a period of (what we would call) physical or mental illness prior to becoming a shaman—this is seen as a prerequisite for shamanic practice (Jackson 2001: 5). Thus, as the shaman cited above puts it:

> I went through two years of debilitating illness ... always governed over by the ghosts. ... They told me that they were "remaking me." (I can think of a lot easier ways to get remade though.)
>
> —Bil, cited in Blain 2002: 118, my parentheses;
> see also Berggren 1998

This is related to the idea of the "wounded healer" which has been taken up in the twentieth century by Jungian psychoanalysis, the Alcoholics Anonymous and self-help movements, and Christian spirituality, and which has particularly strong associations with shamanism. As Stanley Jackson puts it, "Shamanism is a realm with a sustained tradition of 'woundedness' playing a key role in a person's becoming a healer, and of that person's efforts as a healer being informed by a personal history of woundedness and suffering" (Jackson 2001: 4). Through healing others, the shaman is also regarded as tending to her or his own wounds: "a sufferer recovers by becoming a shaman, a healer; and some authorities have observed that shamans, in addition to healing others, may be maintaining or reaffirming their own health in the process" (Jackson 2001: 5). Shamanism is therefore seen as a path to the emotional healing of both the self and others.

Yoga has its origins in ancient Hindu practices so varied that Geoffrey Samuel describes precolonial-era yoga broadly as "disciplined and systematic techniques for the training and control of the human mind–body complex, which are also understood as techniques for the reshaping of human consciousness towards some kind of higher goal" (Samuel 2008: 2). As Andrea Jain argues, "the history of yoga evidences that its aims are specific to particular contexts" including carrying warriors to heaven (in the *Mahabharata*), as a multivalent path to liberation from the cycle of rebirth through spiritual practices (in the *Bhagavad Gita*), and as a means of achieving divine consciousness while retaining embodied existence (in tenth-century hatha yoga) (Jain 2012: 3–4).

Modern yoga emerged from the nineteenth-century "mind-cure" movement (for example, New Thought), Hindu nationalism, Romantic orientalism, and twentieth-century conceptions of health, beauty, and well-being (Jain 2012: 7; Altglas 2014; James 1929: 92–3). Nineteenth-century Hindu nationalists such as Swami Vivekananda, keen to reconstruct yoga as a refined spiritual system compatible with modern thinking, adopted ideas from American and European metaphysical thinking such as New Thought, which sought "a modern, holistic approach aimed at the balance of mind, body and soul" (Jain 2012: 5). Postural yoga, the best-known form of yoga in the West, was the result of early-twentieth-century Indian reformers' exchanges with Americans and Europeans interested in health and fitness. As Jain puts it, "Though new yoga systems continued to share with precolonial yoga an emphasis on training and controlling the mind–body complex, postural yoga repurposed yoga for the sake of modern conceptions of health, beauty, and well-being" (ibid.).

Today, postural yoga is practiced in the West as a health and fitness routine independent of any religious worldview; as a form of universal, Eastern-inspired, and holistic spirituality; and even as a technique that can be adopted by Christians in order to strengthen one's personal relationship with Christ (see Jain 2012: 6). In all these forms, yoga is strongly associated with emotional healing and well-being (see Figure 2.3 for an illustration). For example, one fairly typical yoga website article written by a medical doctor includes among (what are regarded as) the health benefits of yoga: happiness, peace of mind, self-esteem, inner strength, and stronger relationships (McCall 2007). Another, again focusing on health benefits, regards yoga as giving an "emotional health boost," and cites a study from Duke University Medical Center that suggests that yoga can benefit people with schizophrenia, depression, and other psychiatric conditions (Myers 2015).

These views are also expressed by Western practitioners of yoga. As Lyn, a London-based yoga practitioner who suffers from depression, puts it in Véronique Altglas's recent study of yoga:

> It just gave me a technique for controlling depression and the ups and downs of the mind. . . . It's this idea of detaching, and just trying to practice calming yoga, trying to be an instrument of the divine, just makes you feel that your life has a purpose. So mentally you feel much happier, and that gives a meaning to life, physically, mentally, because it gives you a framework for that spiritual dimension in your life.
>
> —Lyn, cited in Altglas 2014: loc 3962

Lyn describes yoga as a "technology of spirituality" to address anxiety, promote self-esteem, and control the mind. Altglas notes that many of her interviewees describe yoga as a form of psychotherapy, with one claiming that yoga had "made him less angry and fearful" and another saying that it had helped her "not to worry as much" (Altglas 2014: 211). As Lyn's

FIGURE 2.3: Yoga. Photo by Felix Hug via Getty Images.

account highlights, two important aspects of yoga for these practitioners are promoting positive emotions while diminishing negative ones, and imbuing life with a sense of meaning and purpose. As another of Altglas's interviewees puts it: "There's something I have to achieve or there's more to me" (Lucy, cited in Altglas 2014: 211).

Why are people attracted to these spiritualities and religion-rooted therapies? People's motivations are undoubtedly diverse and complex, as well as being affected by factors such as socialization (Altglas 2014). However, as both Blain and yoga practitioners cited by Altglas have highlighted, one frequently cited attraction is the desire for meaning or purpose. This is often perceived as a difference between scientific/medical and religious/spiritual worldviews. Thus, for example, in their 2010 study of people who hear voices but, rather than being distressed, instead experience it positively, Jackson, Hayward, and Cooke note that:

> Most participants felt that their voice-hearing experiences were meaningful and therefore sought alternative understandings (often spiritual) to an illness-based medical view. Those who had received a diagnosis of mental illness tended to view their voices as more than just "a bunch of symptoms that need fixing" (Rachel). This often conflicted with the medical approach they were offered.
>
> —Jackson, Hayward and Cooke 2010: 149

Gaining a spiritual interpretation of the experience was significant for the voice-hearers; as one put it, it enabled ". . . understanding what was happening for me, giving it meaning and breaking down the fear that I had around not knowing and thinking that I was a complete freak, really different and ill" (cited in Jackson, Hayward and Cooke 2010:

492). In this case, a religious or spiritual interpretation is seen to replace a biomedical one; in other cases, perhaps where the biomedical diagnosis is represented as non-exclusive or non-absolute, religious or spiritual interpretations are seen as supplementing a biomedical diagnosis by providing a sense of meaning that is lacking from the biomedical view (Heriot-Maitland, Knight and Peters 2012; Scrutton 2015a).

A second and related attraction of spiritualities and spirituality-rooted therapies is that, while the biomedical model traditionally seeks to fix a problem (and so construes the aim, health, as an absence of illnesses), movements such as shamanism and yoga typically adopt a broader understanding of "health" that includes a more general and encompassing cultivation of well-being. This fits in well with their roots in the 1960s counterculture—in particular, the anti-psychiatry movement which objected to the dominance of the medical model of "mental illness" and pointed to the inhumanity of many mental illness treatments, and the influence of the humanistic psychology approaches of Carl Rogers and Abraham Maslow which made self-realization the fundamental aim of human existence (Altglas 2014: 204). In some cases, in this view, "well-being" might entail, but perhaps go beyond, the absence of illnesses and other problems, as in the example of the yoga websites, in which yoga is seen to promote health by curing illnesses, including "emotional illnesses" such as depression and anxiety. In other cases, periods of emotional disturbance and distress should not necessarily be regarded as detrimental to well-being, since well-being might include at least temporary problems and diseases. So, for example, as the idea of the wounded healer indicates, times of emotional suffering might in fact be seminal periods of transformation. This is also the case with spiritual-therapeutic movements that emphasize reincarnation as an opportunity to grow and progress. Thus, as one practitioner of (universalized Jewish) Kabbalah puts it, the idea that "what seems to be a problem is actually a gift" is the best bit of Kabbalah because it means that "even the bad times are good" (Arthur, cited in Altglas 2014: 226). A risk with interpreting periods of emotional suffering purely as problems that need fixing, from this point of view, is that the meaningful, transformative potential of the experiences might be disregarded and so lost (see Scrutton 2015a).

A third attraction of these spiritualities and spirituality-rooted therapies is the emphasis on (what is variously called) a psychosomatic or "holistic" view of the person. This reflects dissatisfaction with two views of the human person that dominate modern Western thought: physicalist monism on the one hand, and Cartesian mind–body dualism on the other. The physicalist view holds that what we perceive as mental processes are ultimately reducible to physical realities, and so, for example, thoughts are ultimately neurological states. Physicalists will often hold that, while we cannot currently explain everything in physical terms, this is due to an absence of scientific knowledge: as scientific research progresses, eventually we are likely to be able to explain phenomena ranging from consciousness to schizophrenia by reference solely to physical realities. As this suggests, biomedical treatments for the emotional disturbances categorized as "mental illness" (for example, psychoactive drugs, electroconvulsive therapy) are, all other things being equal, likely to be viewed sympathetically: if an experience has a physical cause, it is reasonable also to seek a physical cure.

This view is often rejected as being overly reductive or mechanistic. In the case of people within a spiritual or religious framework, part of the reason for the rejection may be that it overlooks a spiritual or transcendent element to human experience that suggests a more-than-physical reality. As Colin, a yoga practitioner in the UK puts it:

> There are people writing and researching in fields of psychology whose perspective is really very narrow, they've had no experience themselves of anything transcendent. So they just treat the mind as a machine.
>
> —Colin, cited in Altglas 2014: 215

Mind–body dualism is the primary alternative to physicalist monism available in the popular realm. While physicalism holds that ultimately everything is physical, dualism holds that there are two independent substances: the mental and the physical. Just as there are physical sorts of illness, so there are mental sorts of illness, the two often being regarded as symmetrical and independent of one another. Substance dualism is philosophically problematic. This is in part because, while it is clear from experience that mental and physical things interact with one another (for example, when I think of polar bears, something physical goes on in my brain; conversely, when I drink too much alcohol, I am unable to think clearly and have different emotional experiences than when sober), it is not clear in the dualist view *how* they interact with one another. In other words, it is not clear how two radically different kinds of entity could affect one another in the way we know from experience and from neuroscience that they do.

That (substance) dualism is problematic is recognized not only in philosophy, but also in medical literature concerned with mental and physical forms of illness. Thus, as the *Diagnostic and Statistical Manual of Mental Disorders* (4th edn, text rev.) (DSM-IV-TR) puts it:

> ... the term mental disorder unfortunately implies a distinction between "mental" disorders and "physical" disorders that is a reductionistic anachronism of mind/body dualism. A compelling literature documents that there is much "physical" in "mental" disorders and much "mental" in "physical" disorders. The problem raised by the term "mental" disorders has been much clearer than its solution, and, unfortunately, the term persists in the title of DSM-IV because we have not found an appropriate substitute.
>
> —American Psychiatric Association 2000: xxx

That the distinction between "mental" and "physical" disorders is problematic can be illustrated by the fact that, as a recent study found, it can be difficult to distinguish depression from flu on either neurological or phenomenological grounds (Ratcliffe, Broome, Smith and Bowden 2014). Nevertheless, as suggested by a range of examples in contemporary life, from shower gels that promise arousal for your "body and mind" to the curious disconnectability of the soul from the body in recent fantasy (for example, in the television series *Buffy the Vampire Slayer*), mind–body dualism is alive and well in popular thought. The appeal of the language of the "holistic" may be a modern Western construction that says more about nineteenth-century and 1960s exoticism than it does about the cultures to which "holistic" thinking is attributed (Jain 2012: 5). However, more sympathetically to the people who adopt this language, the emphasis on the holistic reveals a desire to view the human person in a way that recognizes the fact that "mental" and "physical" aspects of human existence are more connected than dualism can explain, but that is less reductive than the physicalist option—resources for which appear lacking in Western thought. In contrast, while the language of the "holistic" is a modern phenomenon, Eastern and other non-modern, Western ways of construing the person are neither physicalist nor (substance) dualistic. This desire for an alternative to physicalism and dualism is played out in the West not only in the language of the "holistic" but also in, for example, embodied ways of dealing with emotion such as that found in modern postural yoga.

SPIRITUALITY AND EMOTIONAL HEALING IN THE WESTERN MAINSTREAM: EMERGING THERAPIES

Spiritual and religious traditions are increasingly being reimagined and appropriated for therapeutic ends, not only in "alternative" (and increasingly less alternative) popular culture, but also in mainstream medical culture. At the time of writing, a vacancy for a "reiki/spiritual healer" has recently been advertised in the UK by the National Health Service (NHS 2015). Far more prominent in mainstream medical care than reiki, however, are mindfulness therapies, which appropriate the techniques, though not the aims, of 1950s Burmese (Theravāda Buddhist) *vipassanā* meditation (Samuel 2014). In the West, mindfulness is advocated as a treatment for an array of undesirable affective states (such as anxiety, depression, anger, and relationship stress) and for the cultivation of desirable affective states (such as happiness and compassion), not only in self-help and alternative literature, but increasingly in mainstream medical, neuroscientific, and psychological literature. Thus, according to the *Mindfulness Report*, "people who are mindful are less likely to experience psychological distress, including depression and anxiety. They are less neurotic, more extrovert and report greater well-being and life satisfaction" (Halliwell nd: 24). In terms of its appeal, the *Mindfulness Report* observes that:

> Some people are strongly attracted to Mindfulness precisely because it appears to offer an "alternative" approach to healing. Holistic, person-centred, "heart-felt" treatments help them feel respected, listened to and cared for in a way that is not always the case in standard medical care. A bonus of Mindfulness courses is that they can be presented and experienced in many different ways, depending on the worldview of the participant. Some people may prefer to regard the practices as techniques that sharpen and calm their minds; others may see Mindfulness as enabling them to reach a level of awareness and meaning that might be thought of as spiritual.
>
> —Halliwell nd: 35

The emphasis on the importance of patients' beliefs, and on respecting and involving the patients' beliefs in treatment, is one that is seen as a corrective to the earlier, top-down medical treatments to which the anti-psychiatry movement was objecting. It is also itself an emphasis that is attributed to religious and spiritual traditions. Thus, one medical practitioner speaks of the relevance of shamanism to medicine in the context of advocating person-centered therapies:

> This model of healing is gaining some momentum in current western mental health practice. For example, recent emphasis by therapists on finding out how the individual views his [sic.] mental illness, what it means to him, and what he thinks can be done to heal him suggests that the individual's world view or context is seen as a critical aspect of mental health treatment. After all, the individual cannot have harmony in his life if the mental health treatment being prescribed for him is not consistent with his world view. Like the shamans, who view healing as coming from within the individual and treatment from external sources, modern mental health professionals are acutely aware that long-term mental health gains can only be sustained by building on the individual's instrumental and spiritual strengths rather than by externally imposed treatments that focus solely on a disease or disorder.
>
> —Singh 1999: 133–4

Relating to but distinct from the theme of person-centered rather than top-down medical care is an emphasis on helping people feel "respected, listened to and cared for in a way that is not always the case in standard medical care," cited in the *Mindfulness Report* as a benefit of "alternative" therapies (Halliwell nd: 35). It is now the case that mainstream medical culture is becoming aware of the damage done by individualism, and of the way in which biomedical treatments, by focusing on the individual as the locus of the person's problems, have exemplified individualism and perpetuated the alienation that arises from it.

The task of overcoming individualism is not a simple one because individualism is an ingrained part of Western culture which "obscures how 'individuals' are constituted by their 'communities'" to such a degree that, even if we wish to, "it is very difficult not to take the separateness of the individual for granted in all kinds of ways" (Martin 2014: 6; Samuel 2014: 572). Indeed, some countercultural appropriations of religious and spiritual traditions are characterized by a radical individualism which is either blatant, or thinly masked by a utilitarian approach to communities that sees them merely as a means to individualistic ends (Altglas 2014; Harvey 2015). Despite this, in part because religious and spiritual traditions can include premodern or other-than-modern worldviews, they may provide resources for non-individualistic ways of viewing the human person, a fact that is being taken up in recent medicine in order to overcome problematic individualistic emphases. Thus, for example, Simon McCarthy-Jones and Larry Davidson have recently drawn on Christian thought to argue that there is a need for "the abandonment of the traditional therapeutic stance of abstinence . . . in favour of a more engaged and compassionate stance which falls under the broad rubric of 'love', for medical practitioners to pay greater attention to the quality and role of patients' other relationships, and for medical practitioners and to employ therapies, such as Compassionate Mind Therapy, which actively involve forms of love" (McCarthy-Jones and Davidson 2013: 376–7). While focusing on love in Christianity, they argue that: "Given the centrality of love to nearly all spiritual disciplines . . . an interdisciplinary partnership between the mind sciences and religious/spiritual disciplines is the most appropriate way to put a consideration of love back at the heart" of the therapeutic process (McCarthy-Jones and Davidson 2013: 370).

As the argument by McCarthy-Jones and Davidson highlights, the shift away from individualism and towards a recognition of the importance of relationships and community relates to a shift in the assessment of emotion's importance, value, and role. This shift in proclivities, from the rationalist and autonomous to the emotional and relational, is beautifully illustrated by Wim Wenders's 1987 film *Wings of Desire*. In the film, an angel, Damiel, ultimately chooses human existence, experience of the sensory world and of human emotion, and the pleasure and pain of a human relationship over the invulnerability of a transcendent, incorporeal angel existence—a decision that is marked by the shift from black and white to glorious technicolor (Wenders 1987). As *Wings of Desire* indicates, the shift away from a negative assessment of the emotional and relational can also be seen as a shift away from a negative assessment of the vulnerable, bodily, temporarily, and spatially located—and, one might add, supposedly feminine—by a culture that has frequently overvalued the opposite of these things: the rational and autonomous, supposedly masculine, powerful, and incorporeal that is capable of escaping the confines of its own time and space (see Martin 2004: 201). Philosophical groundwork for this re-assessment of emotions includes criticism of the idea that emotions are irrational, unintelligent, and morally dubious, and points to the necessity of emotions for human (and perhaps divine) intelligence (Solomon 2001; Damasio 1994; Sarot 1992; Nussbaum 2002; Wynn 2005; Scrutton 2011; Brady 2013; Dixon 2003). In the popular domain, the reassessment of emotion is evidenced not only by the rise of "spirituality" as a category discrete from, and superior to, religion, but also by (for example) the popularity of the idea of "emotional intelligence" in folk psychology (Goleman 1995).

ETHICAL DILEMMAS: WHAT IS WRONG WITH APPROPRIATION?

Thus far, I have indicated some of the discontentments with approaches to the healing of emotion in modern society, in popular culture from the 1960s onwards, and increasingly in the medical mainstream, and indicated the pivotal role of religious and spiritual traditions in providing better approaches. Yet, as with the religion and mental health literature discussed earlier in the chapter, there are twists in this tale. While alternative and medical service providers and users point gleefully to the religious heritage of the approach or practice in question, people belonging to the religious or spiritual traditions, and historians and anthropologists of these religions, are frequently unhappy with the ways in which the traditions and practices in question are misrepresented (e.g. Altglas 2014; Samuel 2014). For example, Samuel notes that the "use of Buddhist-derived practice as therapy, as a way of adjustment to life in the everyday world of *saṃsāra*, is in direct contradiction to the orientation of the Pāli Canon and of the Nikāya period of early Buddhism, from which these practices are often claimed to derive. The Buddhism of this period emphasized withdrawal from the everyday world of *saṃsāra*, not adjustment to it" (Samuel 2014: 5). Relatedly, mindfulness therapies typically aim at not only the diminution of negative emotions but also the promotion of positive emotions, whereas there is no concept of "positive emotion" in Buddhist thought: all emotion is negative, and spiritual practices aim at liberation from them (ibid.).

Given that the intentions are benevolent and the consequences generally beneficial (though see Lamb 2005), why might adopting one culture's practices in order to help people in another culture, while representing the practice as authentic to the originating culture in order to popularize it, be ethically problematic? In part, the answer is simply that it is not generally considered an agreeable thing to be misrepresented—if someone misrepresents my arguments as other than they are, I am likely to feel that an injustice has been done, that I have been disempowered or had my agency denied in some unfair way. Misrepresentation where the misrepresented person or culture has in the past been dominated by the appropriator, for example through colonialism, might be thought to be adding insult to injury. And where forms of domination continue, the romanticization of the culture in question may "assume a pose of innocent yearning" that in fact conceals "complicity with almost brutal domination" (Aldred 2000: 334). Being misrepresented and being misrepresented by a culture that has dominated in the past are both relevant to the case of mindfulness. Being misrepresented by a culture that continues to dominate is more obviously relevant to (for example) appropriations of Native American spirituality, but the fact that the West continues to hold a dominant position globally means that it should not be considered irrelevant to the appropriation of Asian practices such as mindfulness either. As with the religion and mental health literature reviewed earlier, these issues of misrepresentation in the context of the appropriation of religious and spiritual traditions for therapeutic purposes underline the need for a more nuanced understanding of and engagement with the religious and spiritual traditions in question.

CONCLUSION

In this chapter, I have discussed twentieth- and twenty-first-century encounters between religion, spirituality, and medicine as these relate to human well-being and emotional health. Two major themes have emerged. First, that the appropriation and reimagining of Eastern and other religious and spiritual traditions in the West has important practical and philosophical concerns about the nature of mind, consciousness, emotion, and well-being at its heart. Second, that there is a need for a more nuanced, contextual treatment of religious and spiritual traditions in Western (popular and medical) engagements with them. These two themes are in tension with one another, since the former is sympathetic to the desire both to foster human well-being and to make sense of these aspects of human existence, and to the absence of sufficient resources within a mechanistic, biomedical worldview, while the latter is critical of the culpably naïve and colonialist ways in which this has been and continues to be undertaken. Though not logically inconsistent, in practice it is not always easy to fulfill the requirements of the first without succumbing into the pitfalls of the second. There are no easy solutions to this problem, though ultimately it is likely to be in non-romanticizing and therefore more respectful and reciprocal engagements with other cultures and bodies of thought that we find some possible ways forward.

CHAPTER THREE

Music and Dance

WIEBKE THORMÄHLEN

"No musician, no director, no decorator, treating ancient traditions so scornfully, has ever ventured so far in the realm of sound, movement, and colour, or expressed the inexpressible in such brilliant discoveries," a reporter for the French daily *La France* wrote on June 4, 1913. His colleague meanwhile, writing for the *Echo de Paris* described the same music as "disconcerting and disagreeable," turning "music into noise" and creating a truly "a-musical endeavor" (Kelly 2000: 300–31). The event in question is perhaps the most iconic and celebrated, to some the most over discussed, premier in the history of twentieth-century music, and its reception then and now is rife with emotional narratives on a variety of levels. The first performance of Igor Stravinsky's *Le Sacre du Printemps* (*The Rite of Spring*) assaulted the senses with its "frenetic agitation" and with the "senseless whirl of its hallucinating rhythms," that together with "the obsessive insistence of its themes" and its "paradoxical sonorities and daring combinations of timbres" thrust the inescapability of ritual at the audience as the dancers on stage were entangled and enslaved by them. At its first performance, the "ridiculous choreography" (in Giacomo Puccini's words) served to alienate the public perhaps even more than the music itself. Its focus on body over beauty highlighted, in the form of physical strain and pain, the piece's main subject: the sacrifice. Simultaneously, the choreography symbolized the sacrifice of ballet at the temple of innovation as it expressed the subject matter's cruelty in "barbarescent" form instead of disguising it under a mantle of grace and poise as expected of the art form (see Figure 3.1).

The performance's reviews opened up discussion on the music itself, on dance, on the combination of the two, on the expectation of each art form and on the playing with these expectations: on appropriate subjects for art and on the role of beauty, on the role of an art form's tradition and its ability to depict this, and on excess in art. The reviews were rife with emotion-laden language that betrayed the richness and diversity of current debates that this piece had tapped into: a description of the event as "detestable and laughable" latently referenced the debate around art's purpose, while the event's summary as an aberration as much as an ingenuity questioned the role of the composer and the choreographer. The audience's reaction was similarly emotional: there was laughing, shouting, applause, catcalling, astonishment, confusion, and downright anger. The question of music's ability to express particular emotions was raised most poignantly in reports pointing out the diametric opposition between audience laughter and the total absence of humorous content in the piece. Yet, as Jean Cocteau noted, this juxtaposition also highlighted the question to what degree preconceived or prepared narratives determine an emotional reaction to music. For, in rebelling, the audience played the role which it had previously been assigned, as this very reaction had been prepared by reports of initial rehearsals, during which both music and choreography had startled the orchestral

FIGURE 3.1: Members of the Ballets Russes, *The Rite of Spring*, Paris, 1913. Photo by Bettmann via Getty Images.

musicians as much as the previewing critics. The press had subsequently fed the audience particular preconceptions about the piece's outrageousness before any performance had taken place, thereby forestalling any emotional reaction that the music may otherwise have solicited.

Stravinsky's *Le Sacre* polarized audiences and it continues to hold its association with controversy not because of its daring distortion of conventional musical parameters—these conventions have long since become obsolete—but because the piece told a distinct story while nevertheless subverting all expectations of narrative. It exposed the ideology of narrative in music and in dance as a construct that could be undermined. Its significance as a starting point for the developments of the twentieth century lay less in technical innovations than in laying bare conceptual questions about the epistemology of music itself. In particular, *Le Sacre* questioned the idea that music is a narrative, an idea that had long since been recognized as a prerequisite for its ability to speak as the "language of emotions." No other piece so starkly exposed the inherited Enlightenment belief that music is intimately wedded to emotions via its narrative function and structure, and that dance is a lower order of music that ought to be employed to beautify the physiological effects of music. No previous composition had problematized to quite the same degree the dichotomy between sense perception and cognitive processes in the perception of music as emotions, and focused the perceiver's attention on the hierarchy of the eye and the ear in the acquisition of emotional knowledge.

The turns taken during the course of the twentieth century to investigate these assumptions relied on myriad emotion models used to assess music's meaning; they were played out in a variety of discourses, theoretical and practical, conceptual and perceptual. As such, the discourse on music as a social or professional activity (improvised or interpretative) grew increasingly distinct from music's meaning acquired through composition, through listening, and through its combination with movement. In this chapter, I will focus on those discourses that critically investigated music's universally perceived ability to inspire emotional effects, the discourses on composition and its related field of music analysis, and on the psychological and later neuropsychological investigations into music's effects, which focused largely on the process of listening. The discourses are necessarily selective and I refer only briefly to some of the myriad narratives that take the commonly held view of music's wedlock with emotions as given, and that I therefore consider application studies: the use of music in music therapy, in the film industry, in education, in marketing, and later in the gaming industry (North and Hargreaves 2008). I also include in this category the construction of emotional communities through music in the rock and pop era that mirrors patterns set up in the early century's folk music revival, and related dance-based sites of research, such as the techno era of the late 1980s and 90s (Frith 2001; Eyerman and Jamieson 1998; Gaillot, Nancy and Maffesoli 1998).

THE PROBLEM OF MUSIC AS NARRATIVE AND AS THE LANGUAGE OF EMOTIONS

All art forms solicit emotional reactions, yet it appears inescapably true that people report strong emotional reactions to music more readily than they do to the other art forms (Frey and Langseth 1985; Williams and Morris 1996). Affective reactions to music, however, are described variously as anything from general moods via imprecise and undefined or seemingly indefinable feelings, to specific emotions. None of this is news, for the relationship between music, expression, and emotion was already a subject of debate in antiquity and came to the fore during the Enlightenment, yet it formed an unshakable heritage with which twentieth-century composers, performers, and thinkers grappled. Nineteenth-century debates had sought to identify the precise location of expression in music, locating it on one hand at various points along the conception, manifestation, and reception axis, and on the other debating the relationship between the cognitive and the physical in music's reception. The proliferation of musical conception and reception cultures towards the end of the century resulted in a diffusion of segregated discourses that were united only by being marred by the fear of consumerism and its necessarily conventionalized language on one hand, and the role and fear of the physical in a true work of art on the other.

In the twentieth century, then, different types of engagement with music and dance were discussed separately, each within their own disciplines, and any narrative of social or artistic significance was determined by this framework first and foremost. With the emergence of modern dance and its focus on a sense of self, the relationship between performed dance and the music which it accompanied or by which it was accompanied was reconceptualized in myriad ways. Composition, performance, and musicology—as the traditional discourses on music—became separated from the emerging disciplinary discourses in choreography, in education, in psychology, and later in sociology, ethnology, and finally neurology. Narrative, as a result, shifted outside of music to its discourse; the emotional meaning, however, remained firmly tied to narrative.

Each of these disciplines was thoroughly shaken by the mid-century events, forcing each to rethink its rationales and premises and causing a further fracturing of the investigation into the emotions across humanistic and scientific disciplines in the century's second half. The extremes of emotions involved in instigating, rousing, enabling, sublimating, executing, and for decades to come, processing and digesting the events of the Holocaust sparked the vibrant interest in civilizing emotions across disciplines by measuring, defining, and formalizing them. In music, this had a particularly profound effect as musicians, both composing and performing, faced the very real question of what to do with German music, music that accounted for the largest share of the instrumental music canon so far. During the war, programming at the BBC, and programs of London's highly reputable Royal Philharmonic Society still consisted largely of music by the "German masters," the latter even programming the overture to Richard Wagner's Meistersinger *von Nürnberg*, despite the opera's overt celebration of German cultural heritage that includes a celebratory mocking of the undoubtedly (if not explicitly stated) Jewish character's narrow-mindedness. Whereas Jewish composers disappeared from the concert stage and were written out of the canon in Germany, elsewhere even those composers consciously wedded to the Nazi ideology continued to be programmed. It is an interesting yet separate project that compares the emotional narratives with which Wagner's music was endowed during the Third Reich with those that the British used to exonerate that music for the sake of its aesthetic value, its artistic construction, and so as to allow it to move audiences. The question remains puzzling, though, as to what a British audience must have felt when hearing the overture to *Die Meistersinger* on a cold winter evening in December 1942 at the Royal Philharmonic concerts.

While German art music, then, posed its own particular problems post-1945, educational and social engagement with music was similarly tarnished. The Reichsmusikkammer had grouped folk music together with choral music, thereby making a clear connection between German cultural heritage and high art, while bringing all group singing under the control of the German Singer's Union (Deutscher Sängerbund), which in turn promoted the edifying and unifying emotional effects of communal singing, and of folk music repertoire in particular (Levi 1994; Bohlmann 2002). Mass participation in music was linked to mass political spectacles so as to invest the individual emotionally in the nationalist project. The Reich's policies focused on adult music education, on participatory singing in official ceremonies, and on the role of music in youth organizations (Potter 1998; Williams 1994). Similarly, Hitler's focus on the creation of collectivity around the myth of a return to a folk community could avail itself of recent forays into modern dance developed particularly by Rudolf Laban. While the precise nature of Laban's collaboration in Nazi ideology is perhaps debatable, his theories on the parallels of expression through natural movement and the education of emotions through this movement, coupled with his focus on community dance, certainly played into the hands of an absolutism built on ideologies of the equivalence of naturalness with a particular race, moral standing, and rightful feeling (Karina and Kant 2003; Pew 1999). Laban's movement choir choreography formed a significant part of the Nazi Party's edifice of mass communication through the ignition of collective emotions (see Figure 3.2). Here, the Nazis exploited music's ability to shape the individual's sense of self and to cement this through the powerful combination of a physical as well as a mental experience. Those incarcerated by the regime equally used music as a means to affirm their own sense of self, of belonging, of identity, and of a worthwhile subjectivity. This mediation between self and society that music facilitated through the inspiration of emotions, many of which were reliant on associations and memories, was also exploited for the purposes of torture. Research on music in concentration camps has documented both sides: the sharing of music as solace among prisoners, but also the use of music as torture achieved through the distortion of association and practice in the form of forced singing, the use of self-made music during disciplinary actions such as marching but also physical torture, and the use of singing and the associated cultural repertoires for the purpose of humiliation (Brauer 2016).

Much of the socio-emotional manipulation exercised through music relied on music's dual experience located between the cognitive and the physiological, and the subject of

FIGURE 3.2: Rudolf Laban teaching dance, 1931. Photo by Ullstein Bild/Ullstein Bild via Getty Images.

rhythm in music soon took on racial connotations. Dance music, as implicated in the Nazi view, had to occupy a "civilized" middle ground, being physically compelling to spur the body into the appropriate social dance while avoiding the physically distorting rhythms of ragtime and the arrhythmic character of the systematic music of the members of the Second Viennese School.[1] The latter was overtly criticized in the 1938 exhibition *Entartete Musik*, a montage, perhaps, of the most pronounced connection that had ever been made between music and illness (pathology), between body politics and the politics of rhythm and movement; emotions—physically felt yet mentally conceived—were right at its center (Dümling and Girth 1988). The exhibition's name itself implied a physical or mental distortion from the norm, and its effects were framed in terms of emotional aberrations. The musical categories that fell under the umbrella of *Entartung* were music associated with a physically distinctly different race, and music that dangerously infiltrated a Western classical canon with Jewish elements. The formulation of the "de-genrefication" (rather than "degeneration" as it is commonly translated) worked on the basis of the inherited combination of music, narrative, expression, and emotion. In dance, it was similarly the absence of a developing rhythm that could dictate a narrative which deemed it degenerate. Laban's grand spectacle for twenty-two movement choirs, *Vom Tauwind und der Neuen Freude*, conceived for the opening night of the Olympic Games in Berlin in 1936 and commissioned by Joseph Goebbels, was dismissed by the Minister for Propaganda as "bad, contrived and affected."[2] The verdict was formed on the basis that the choreography was lacking in a particular storyline, an emotive narrative that ensured a fixed collective interpretation that went hand in hand with a predetermined collective emotionality.

COMPOSITION, ANALYSIS, AND THE QUESTION OF EXPRESSION IN MUSIC

Early-twentieth-century philosophies of composition mirrored the cognitive turn that was taking place across other disciplines; serious modern music was directed at the mind, not the body. This was the end result of a long ideological trajectory starting with the German idealist thinkers in the early nineteenth century, who rejected the nerves as the site for music's stimulation in favor of ideas (Kennaway 2012). In fact, music's quality came to be classified along the body–mind stimulation axis: lowbrow, trivial music—such as social dance music and overtly virtuosic music—stimulated the body, whereas highbrow music stimulated the mind (Mathew and Walton 2013; Thormählen 2014; Evan Bonds 2006). An emotional reaction to music was considered the result of either form of stimulation, yet only the stimulation of the mind would result in those emotions that were considered healthy, educative, and formative. Experiencing music correctly, in this sense, was tied to the listener's active participation in the grasping of music's form. Abstract form rose to be the determining feature of good music, and a good experience of music was an intellectual–emotional one. Music's emotional impact was paramount for the late Romantics, yet its effects depended on the imagination and the mind's actions, not on a physical stimulation of nerves in the body.

With this, narrative in music became a non-conceptual web of expectations. Music's perceived emotional stimulation was divorced from an external program, in favor of the organic musical form and of the modernist's meta-narrative of a demand to engage with the past while reflecting through art the uniqueness of the present day. The latter ideal demanded a questioning of historical precedents, and modern composers put the connection between narrative and music onto the dissecting table by deliberately subverting the expectations and normative ideas of beauty in music which had rested on the elements of melody and harmony (the traditional keystones of artistic invention), on rhythm, and on timbre. Redefining these key components would subvert the experience of music profoundly.

Different schools of reinventing and reassembling the musical parameters emerged in America and in Europe with the Second Viennese School, and with the school of sound experimentation around the French-born Edgar Varèse and American Henry Cowell. Arnold Schoenberg and his disciples Alban Berg and Anton Webern abandoned tonality altogether before imposing a new structural system on their methods of composition. Both approaches robbed the listener of the expected harmonic tension and release created through the hierarchy of chords within the diatonic system. The intended listeners, however, were culturally conditioned to hear hierarchies that had thus functioned as a safe method to create emotional suspense and reassurance. Abandoning them therefore not only played with expectations but—at an emotional level—forced listeners to question their own expectations and experiences. Music was pulled firmly into a rationalist aesthetic within which its narrative was accessible through intellectual engagement rather than unthinking listening. Schoenberg's atonal music relied on the psychology of musical sensation by creating shapes, phrases, and memorable pitches, but after the mid-1920s, his serial pieces—often criticized as a return to a systemized composition and therefore a retrograde step—were everything but a step back: here, Schoenberg played with musical sensation at a more profound level, as he investigated the physiology of hearing. In his serial or twelve-tone system he replaced the traditional hierarchy of tonal centers. What is more, the rule that no pitch was repeated within the row until all twelve had sounded (while various versions of the row could appear simultaneously) challenged a perception of music that was structured according to the human capacity to memorize, recognize, and thereby possibly empathize.

While Schoenberg challenged the comfort of recognition and limited the sensual perception of music in favor of intellectual engagement, Varèse challenged the narrative conventions at the basis of music's effect by investigating the difference between a musical and a pure sense perception of sounds generally. He focused the listener's perception onto sound per se by writing for unpitched instruments. In works such as *Ionisation* (1931) he placed both timbre and rhythm center stage, but not in a manner that would allow for recognition of narrative. Thus he denied the listener any immediate emotional identification with the music. Instead, rhythmic complexity challenged the mind's habituated desire to hear structure, while the lack of pitches forced the listener away from the search for a musical language and onto the sense perception itself, away from the semantics onto the individual words and syllables.

Varèse redefined the traditional wiring between aural sense perception and value judgment in which certain sounds were perceived as giving pleasure and inspiring positive emotion, whereas others were defined as the cause of discomfort and were central to emerging pathological narratives that were bound up with the changing environment caused by urbanization, industry, mechanization, and science generally (Kennaway 2012; Bijsterveld 2003). Luigi Russolo had long since declared that "we must break out of this narrow circle of pure musical sounds, and conquer the infinite variety of noise-sounds" (1913), and new instruments to create new sounds had been invented in the theremin (1920) and the ondes martenot (1928). The former, in particular, had somewhat failed the modernist project as its performers used it to play famous nineteenth-century melodies, thereby recreating the familiar musico-emotional narratives and co-opting the world of alien sounds into the old emotional sphere (Keil 2003).

In fact, a newly emerging branch of psychology shifted the emphasis fully away from intention and conception to perception. Here, the possibility that music encoded emotions was a given and the onus was on the audience to be educated to read music's universal patterns. These patterns were seen to correspond to principles of organization inherent in the mind itself. Christian von Ehrenfels, an early follower of gestalt psychology, had already used music to illustrate that humans perceive shape rather than specifics by pointing out that everyone recognized a tune no matter which key it was played in, and that its emotional expression would remain unchanged. The gestalt psychologists split an emotional reaction to music into three stages: hearing the music, organizing and recognizing shape (a cognitive process), and mapping meaning onto this (i.e. recognizing it at a psychological level). This formed an extension of earlier models of music analysis that attempted to perpetuate the myth of a scientific branch to musical narrative through textual analysis (Christensen 2002). Music theorists, most prominently Heinrich Schenker, revised the earlier analytical *Formenlehre*, which had placed the onus of understanding music with the audience. The gestalt approach took its place to justify the claim for a universal system of musical construction of works that are "masterful" (Schenker, *Das Meisterwerk in der Musik,* 1925–30). As a return process, of course, the system functioned to stratify music systematically by ascertaining which music exhibited mastery and which types did not. It is interesting that Schenker's theories—like Schoenberg's atonal works—did not rely on the audibility of structure. In both, the value that was once attached to recognition and memory, which in turn determined music's emotional effect, was abandoned. Both approaches presented a critical engagement with notions of collective memory, nostalgia, conventions, and traditions that was paramount to the modernist reflection on the historical situatedness of music, and both stood in contrast with those approaches that consciously invoked memory, recollection, and collectivity.

Choreographers and dancers explored this contrasting pathway: here, the focus lay on the expression of narrative and emotion through an exploration of the physical body and the physicality of space that was divorced from the nineteenth-century stock gestures of classical ballet (Kant 2007). Inspired by Isadora Duncan, Mikhail Fokine choreographed the Ballets Russes de Serge Diaghilev in Paris in 1909 to preexisting music by famous nineteenth-century composers such as Frédéric Chopin, Robert Schumann, and, of course, a number of Russian composers ranging from Mikhail Glinka and Modest Mussorgsky to Sergey Taneyev and Aleksandr Glazunov. These choreographies interpreted the music's narrative as a musically inherent and emotive one without reliance on props or costumes; instead, musical phrases were translated into physical form and expression, an idea which culminated, perhaps, in Léonide Massine's highly controversial interpretation through dance of the musical structure in Brahms's Symphony No. 4 for the "Ballet Russe de Monte Carlo" in 1933. Influenced by his time with Diaghilev, he expanded on Fokine's ideas so as to enhance the balletic narrative through character dances and folk elements which, in his Brahms project, *Choreartium*, resulted in dance styles close to modern dance. His earlier symphonic ballet, *Les Présages*—to the music of Tchaikovsky's Symphony No. 5—was more acceptable, as the work had, since its inception, been shrouded in discussion of its programmatic content, be that narrative, motto-like, or a catalog of emotions. Illustrating the absolute patterns of Brahms's symphony through physical interpretation, however, was attacked as a perversion of music's purity by and through the body.

Modern dance had similarly departed from the traditional narrative of ballet in search of a better expression of the modern condition. Isadora Duncan had turned to philosophical inspiration, particularly to Friedrich Nietzsche's texts, in search of a rationale for dance that highlighted the human condition and that translated the particularly female human state into physical expression. Here, motion was tied directly to emotion as Duncan and her successors choreographed narratives of individuality which were fractured into a series of physical manifestations of emotional states, transformations, and inspirations with nothing but the idea of a "self" at their center (Daly 1995). Rudolf Laban in his *Ausdruckstanz* sought to reconnect to a kind of *Ur-Tanz* that preceded the conventional languages brought about by history and civilization. By studying natural movements and impulses for movement, he saw the body as the return gateway to a discovery and expression of a natural self. Through dance he sought to create communities bound together by their ritualized experience of physicality and physical space (Maletic 1987).

Both modern dance and modern music, then, formulated their critical engagement with and conscious distancing from Western narrative traditions, overthrowing their conventional languages as inapplicable to the modern condition. Yet, their similarities ended with what they rejected as they parted along the emotion axis: while composers sought to eliminate the self as creative subject from the art object, modern dancers placed it center stage. Modern music sublimated the perceived decadence of individual physical and passionate emotion in favor of an intellectual, transfigured emotionality; modern dance materialized feeling by expressing both physical and cognitive elements of emotions through the physical body. Both, in their own ways, aimed to establish communities, yet while both Duncan's and later Laban's dance established sensual communities through the visceral experience of physical ritual and a process of identifying with this physicality by either enactment or observation, Schoenberg and Schenker established a tacit, elitist community of connoisseurs. While dance held emotion high so as to establish collective physical experience, music's community became one of the mind.

ENGAGING WITH MUSIC

The stratification within the art of music into good and bad or high and low, according to its emotional response (and how exactly it solicited this), mirrored wider concerns emerging from a rapidly developing culture, amusement, and leisure industry. Otniel E. Dror has argued on the basis of Norbert Elias's and Erik Dunning's work, that both the medical field and the emerging field of psychology in the early twentieth century investigated these phenomena as sites for emotion control by creating the semblance of decontrolled emotions (Dror 2005; Elias and Dunning 1986; Elias 1982). On one hand, this stratification of leisure activities into different emotional reactions that were located on the axis between physiological and mental reaction created a hierarchy of culture and entertainment. On the other, it dictated myriad appropriate ways to "feel" as one engaged in different activities, and could thus inscribe appropriate codes of behavior that were mapped onto social classes, onto leisure versus work, and affirm a distinction between public and private.

Similarly, the manner of engagement with music and the site for this engagement determined the appropriate way of feeling about music. While the concert hall demanded involved listening—one's ability silently to engage with musical works became a marker for social class—the professional performance of music demanded from the virtuoso a physical display of those emotions felt by the performer in the interpretation of the music. Here, the performer's physiology was supposed to mirror and display theatrically his inner feelings. Domestic music making, as a separate category, acquired a different emotional rhetoric, which presented a gendered opposite to the concert culture as it allowed men to engage in an emotional community that was gendered feminine. Choral societies and other singing clubs were sites to exercise a conglomeration of emotions that resided in the pleasure of unanimity. This spirit was founded on the transgression of class boundaries, since the formalized teaching of singing in the nineteenth-century methods of John Hullah and the Curwen brothers had eradiated the economic boundaries around the learning of music (McGuire 2009). The original connection between the act of making music and moral edification, made in the nineteenth century by expanding the charitable spirit that eighteenth-century choir festivals and large-scale singing had embodied, prevailed; in the nineteenth century, communal singing was further employed for the increasingly explicit formulation of political sentiments. At the same time, music societies and communal singing were sources for local and national pride. In Germany, the Youth Movement celebrated the notion of *Volk* in a revival of German folksongs accompanied by the guitar that were sung in unison at walking and gathering events. The movement was at its core a chance to form an emotional community against the mechanization and uniformity of the modern age, and as such flourished during the first wave of recorded music dissemination in the 1930s (Gilliam 1994, especially contributions by Potter, Hailey and Williams).

Jazz presented a complex nexus of emotional spaces that cut across both the modernist assumption of stability of musical text and meaning exercised in its stable context of the established concert culture, and the social class divide that was implicated in modernists' self-conscious distancing from mass culture. Jazz was from its inception a cultural practice, not an art form that was manifest in a series of artworks. Its close alliance with three musical practices—dance, improvisation, and participation—made it particularly difficult to order into a social hierarchy (Johnson 2003). Jazz was seen less as a form of music than a form of physical enactment; it was a significant tool in the exploration of individual and social identity, yet it occupied a sphere that departed from the mind-centered norms of social engagement in which the physical was purely a representation of the mental. Here meaning, expression, narrative, and emotional stimulation lay in the corporeal act. As Jazz was increasingly popularized over the 1920s and 1930s, a variety of narratives attempted to pull it into the controlled physical environment of the concert hall, but its full power was played out in the counterpart that it offered to ballroom dancing, with its restricted and codified physical movements. The rag involved a whole range of body parts that were codified overtly sexual, and the warnings against jazz clearly betrayed the anxiety that, here, the dominance of mind over body would break down as the physicality of the dance would lead to moral disrepute. Clubs, pubs, and music halls where jazz dance was practiced thus became spaces in which the physicality of emotion and the role of the body in creating emotion could be explored—spaces at the borders of emotional control and disorder. Joseph March expressed this in his 1928 poem "Wild Party," in which he pinpointed that "the rhythm whispered with the fierce unrest of a heart throbbing in a passionate breast." The fear over the transgressive nature of jazz's physicality was expressed by Isadora Duncan, who described jazz in *I See America Dancing* of 1927 as "monstrous," "tottering, ape-like convulsions" that were nothing but sensual, as they emanated from corporeal rhythms created from "the solar plexus, the temporal home of the soul" (Duncan in Copeland and Cohen 1983: 265; Daly 1995). The same year, the

British writer R. W. S. Mendl acknowledged the difficulty that jazz presented within traditional narratives of art, but also within codified spheres of practiced emotion (Mendl 1927). Jazz for him inspired an immediate physiological reaction that brought positive emotions—he described the "instinctive delight in emphasizing with your feet a beat which was not stressed by the players"—while the breaking with conventions that ragtime literally embodied brought a physical-emotional outlet for the anxieties of the modern age, manifest in its speed and noise. Jazz's identity as dance certainly departed from the Western art orientation that had anchored art's communication and evaluation linguistically. This was confounded by the fact that jazz had to be perceived as an event, not an artwork, due to its improvisatory nature. As such, its emotional impact lay in the practice of engagement. The dualistic emotional responses to jazz—fascination, awe, and inspiration on one hand, and outrage and bewilderment on the other—were intricately linked to the locations and occasions in which jazz was practiced. Jazz's emotional narrative was intimately wedded to the emotional communities it formed and to the perceived need to control these within segregated and specified spaces (Crease 2003; Walser 1997).

THE YEAR 1945 AND AFTER: THE END OF EXPRESSIONISM

The idea that music could be a universal language had become suspect by 1945. Its breakdown had been foreshadowed in the diffluence of music's emotional meanings created in the interaction of mind and body across different applications, different engagement or consumption circumstances, and across a variety of audience demographics who came together in different emotional communities that transgressed their social class demarcations. In composition, the modernist aesthetic demand that musical means and meanings reflect the present day now returned to the fore, yet with the sheer impossibility of having to express—post-1945—the deeply disturbing or the utterly inexpressible. As a result, the concept of expression in music per se was investigated and both the notion of the expression of an artist's subjectivity and the stimulation of a listener's feelings came under scrutiny. The result was a critical investigation of the cognitive turn in music that worked in two different ways: one was to make the cognitive so central that even the composer's expression was no longer present; the other was to awaken the senses as objects of perception by forcing listeners to take stock of the expected links between a particular sense perception and their emotional reactions.

Composers around Pierre Boulez took up the serialist stance, developing it into a rationalist system, with the purpose of eliminating the author from the creation of meaning. Boulez suggested a serialization of all parameters of music, not only pitch, but duration, dynamics (or intensity of sound), and timbre, so that the compositional process was governed by charts of tone, rhythm, and timbre rows in works such as *Structures I* (1951–52) (Goldman 2011). In doing so, Boulez responded to the crisis in music by questioning music's validity as a form expressive of an individual's ideas. He undermined the Romantic notion of the genius composer by inventing a system for composition but taking himself as subject out of the compositional outcome (Idom 2013; Campbell 2010). In America, John Cage was engaged in a similar business of resolutely eliminating the artist's ego from the final work, yet in a very different way. In his manifesto "The future of music: Credo" he redefined music as "organised sound," giving the composer the role of the "organiser of sound" (Cage 2011: 3–6). His extension of traditional sounds had emerged from a collaboration with dancers and thus from his engagement with the corporeal manifestation of music. In conceiving his music for prepared piano (championed by Henry Cowell)—inserting objects into the piano to alter the sounds produced by each individual key—he achieved staggering effects for two reasons. As the score now described players' actions rather than sounds, the player's own expectations were discombobulated; the audience would see both instrument and player's action, the sounds emanating were entirely unexpected. Cage, here, focused his listeners' perception on the immediate physicality of music making and on their own unmediated sense perceptions, thus foregoing preconceived narratives.

The elimination of the artist's ego entered Cage's work in a different way, though. Whereas Boulez systematized the composition, Cage, influenced by Eastern philosophies, did the opposite: influenced by the *I Ching*, in his *Music of Changes* (1951) the composer tossed coins that would determine the progress of the music. As such, the composer was taken out of the process of creating a narrative in music altogether. Going further still, Cage took apart the process of listening in the process of receiving music. He described traditional ways of receiving music as analyzing them, whereas he wanted his audience to listen. "I could not accept the academic idea that the purpose of music was communication," Cage explained in an interview in 1973. Instead he posited that "the purpose of music is to sober and quiet the mind (thus making it susceptible to divine influences). . . . The function of music is to change the mind so that it does become open to experience, which inevitably is interesting" (Revill 1992: 30). This break with the concept of communication in and through music and, thereby, with the notion of music as a language of the emotions was a radical departure. In Europe, the compositions emanating from Darmstadt and Donaueschingen were accompanied by philosophizing, rationalizing, and formal justification; they still celebrated the composer and the composer's ways of contemplating music. Cage, on the other hand, sought to celebrate first the material—noise and sound itself—and second, experience.

It is, perhaps, not surprising that this reconceptualization emerged from collaboration with a dancer, Syvilla Fort, who had asked Cage to compose music to accompany a neo-primitivist choreography to be performed in a space too small to accommodate a percussion ensemble. Cage's response was the prepared piano: by inserting everyday devices such as erasers and metal screws into the piano, he tampered with its sonority to turn it into its own percussion space. With every prepared piano the theater of sound emerging would be a different one and Cage used the instrument to defy expectation as much as he articulated the traditional parameter of dance—rhythm—through it. In a life-long collaboration with the dancer and choreographer Merce Cunningham, he continued to explore the boundaries of expectation, eventually upending the traditional relationships between composer, choreographer, and audience as listener and viewer. In their creations, Cage and Cunningham would work entirely independently from each other, preagreeing only a temporal frame. At first, the dancers would only hear the music at the premier, thereby becoming part of the audience, but soon Cage and Cunningham began to conceive of them as part of the soundscape itself by turning them—like the musicians who would operate electronic equipment—into cocomposers as their movements triggered light beams and sounds. Focusing on a chance evolution of the material elements—sounds and movements—replaced a performance with an experience for the one-time performers as much as the audience. *Variations V*, performed in 1965 in New York and then touring, came under attack for its fragmentation which resulted from the chance collage of technological interaction unfolding over the course of the event. In fact, the criticism leveled against the piece was not dissimilar in tone to that leveled against the *Rite of Spring* fifty years earlier, but it focused now on the assault on the audience's senses and sensibilities (Miller 2001). As such, Cage had achieved his goals as audience and critics focused on their own perceptions and their mode of listening instead of searching for meaning in a work of art.

Cage's radical shift away from the work and its processes of creation and onto the listener's experience and emotions is, of course, most pronounced in his most famous work, *4'33* (1952), in which the sense perception of hearing itself takes center stage in a reconceptualization that foreshadows Roland Barthes's 1968 essay *The Death of the Author*. While Barthes still implied that meaning was created as a narrative, Cage went beyond this, as he was not forcing the listener into an active and analytical listening but hoped to focus the listener simply onto the experience of listening. As such, he skipped two steps: from the investigation of the nature of sound via the investigation of the act of listening itself to the experience of listening. Separating the latter two from each other implied an Enlightenment duality of reason and emotions, in which active listening as a rational process was separate from the sense perception itself and Cage classed the experience or emotion-content of music with the latter. Yet the awareness of this distinction relied on the institutionalization of listening in the particular sociocultural-emotional community of the concert hall.

If composer, performer, and listener had once been linked in an unproblematic chain of creation and reception, and music's emotional effect had been merely a matter of details, this chain had now come apart, and its elements were spread around experience as the central concern. As a result, the effect of individual links of that chain—the material itself—came under investigation. On both sides of the Atlantic, composers were increasingly fascinated by the means and effects of technology and by the role it could play in creating meaning. Karlheinz Stockhausen, in his *Gesang der Jünglinge* (1956), envisaged a highly emotive multimedia work: he intended a performance in Cologne Cathedral to an audience who would be using a text to penetrate the degrees of the piece's deliberate incomprehensibility. The contemplation of the text, the visual and spatial setting, and the complexity of the music would inflame the listeners, replicating in them something of the burning fiery furnace to which Nebuchadnezzar subjected the three youths in the accompanying text. In addition, Stockhausen unpicked music's traditional status as a language by reinterpreting words and sung sounds as phonemes: inspired by classes he attended at Bonn University with Werner Meyer-Eppler on information theory and phonetics, he dismantled semiotic sounds into their elements and frequencies, thereby breaking down their communicability and signification. He achieved this by electronically altering a recording of a boy treble singing, superimposing this to create multiple voices, scrambling the parts up, adding reverberation, and electronically distorting the voice by speeding it up and slowing it down. The effect was an eerie mixture of natural and synthetic sounds that held the listener in emotional suspense, less because of the electronic distortion of the voice than because of the absence of a visible performer and the consequent lack of apparent human agency (Decroupet and Ungeheuer 1998).

In works such as this, the ideology of a narrative constructed by the composer and received by the listener to great emotional effect was affirmed rather than undermined, but the normal route of perception was widened into an all-immersive exercise in sense perception. Edgar Varèse's *Poème electronique*, commissioned by Philips for the renowned

Corbusier-Xenakis pavilion at the Brussels World's Fair in 1958, was a similar investigation of the relationship between sense perception, traditional ideas about music, and emotions. Using the relatively new technology of the magnetophone, Varèse's process of composition became visceral as he spliced, mixed, distorted, looped, and added reverb. Played over 400 speakers that had been placed by Xenakis around the walls and ceilings of the pavilion, the piece replaced performers and performance with a spatial sound experience that was described as overwhelming in its pure sensuality (Taruskin 2009b: 175–220). As such, these were perhaps precursors for an entirely different demand on the audience which Cage and Cunningham would explore by posing each individual listener's or perceiver's sense perception at the center of the work.

The degree to which the critique of narrative in music created its own negative emotion communities was illustrated by the first performance of Cage's *Atlas Eclipticalis* in New York in 1962, which caused uproar in the orchestra. Its eighty-six instrumental parts were notated as "star maps" and the *I Ching* determined who would take which line and in what clef to read it. The performers were free to play the whole or part of their lines *ad libitum* and repeat for any duration. Randomness in Cage's eyes was central, yet the performers rebelled: they saw their duties as performers to present a collective, coherent narrative, and to express themselves and the composer so fundamentally undermined as to render their presence superfluous. Cage's *HPSCHD* (1969) avoided the issues caused by the performers' subjectivity by replacing them with a four-and-a-half-hour-long sound installation that was displayed rather than performed. The audience was invited to walk through the sounds, sit down, stand up, lie on the floor, in a process that eliminated the composer for the sake of the individualized experience, created in the moment. Each participant shaped his or her own narrative and emotional journey that was based on a combination of sense perceptions, not only on the aural sense. The relationship of music and emotion had become redefined from one that was product-and-narrative based to one that was based in a physical and mental experience.

An interesting yet altogether different manifestation of this physical and mental experience was presented in the 1970s and 1980s in Germany, in Pina Bausch's newly founded *Tanztheater*. Bausch had grown up in a Germany that had returned to classical ballet as the safe haven that shielded dance from the misuse of the Labanesque *Ausdruckstanz* for politically freighted collective experiences. Confronted on one hand with the formalism of a historical and historicized gestural ballet language and on the other with the experimentalism of American modern dance, Bausch aimed to force the perceiver into a highly emotive physical and mental experience, one not dissimilar from those solicited in music performance happenings at the time; yet Bausch upheld at least superficially the traditional role division between audience and performers, and sublimated the audience's physical experience into the mental as audience members remained stuck—mostly uncomfortably—in their seats. As such, any emotional journey undertaken by a spectator became the journey of the mediation of displayed subjective states with the discomfort of their simultaneous truth and theatricality. Rather than abandon narrative altogether, Bausch aimed to stage the historicity of the gestures that constitute the narrative in a theatrical performance, thereby forcing the audience members to confront their individual and collective pasts, their desire for the abandonment of disbelief, and their continuous search—amply documented in the simultaneous rise of the staging of stock emotion gestures in popular TV dance and pop music shows—for an easy emotional fix through the body in motion (Climenhaga 2012).

MUSIC AND PSYCHOLOGY

At the heart of Cage's, Boulez's, and Varèse's music was a fundamental epistemological question: what is music, and how does a succession of sounds gain coherence in the listener's perception so as to be acknowledged as a musical unit? Composers experimented with the apparent truth that certain harmonic and melodic progressions have particular emotional meaning. It is no accident, then, that this question became a key moment in the development of music psychology in the 1940s and 1950s. With absolute musical values no longer a possibility, performers, composers, and music educators all engaged with this question. Initially, psychological research fell into the two categories of fundamental research and applied research, with the latter published primarily in the *Journal of Research in Music Education*, founded in 1942. The field of music psychology research began to develop in earnest with its own separate publication forums in the 1970s in the form of specialist journals such as *Psychology of Music* (1973–), *Psychomusicology* (1981–), and *Music Perception* (1983–). While the link between music and the emotions was only one aspect of music psychology research, in its early stages it was by far the dominant research area (Hallam, Cross and Thaut 2011).

Prewar analysts and psychologists had retained the idea that physiological sensation, aesthetics, and musical construction formed an inevitable and absolute unity (or at least accounting for "difference" was not their priority as they were concerned with the emotional uses and impacts of a Western classical canon), which was at the center of the emotional and meaning-giving response to music. Postwar music theorists and psychologists presented their universalizing systems with the caveat that cultural conditioning plays a significant role in musical perception, in the recognition of emotions in music and in the naming of an emotional response triggered by music. This distinction in itself was significant, as psychologists recognized that a "musical emotion" could be comprehended without being felt by the recipient.

Musicologist and writer Leonard B. Meyer based his theories of emotion and meaning in music (in his highly influential book of the same name) on "the empirical data, the laws, discovered by gestalt psychologists without adopting the hypothetical explanations furnished by the theory" (Meyer 1956). Instead, he combined the notion that "mental laws (are) formulated upon a wealth of empirical data" with American pragmatist thought, developed by Charles S. Peirce and handed down to Meyer via John Dewey and George Herbert Mead. The latter established that an event's meaning lay in its predicted consequence or rather in the fact that it possessed a predicted consequence that could be fulfilled or frustrated, thereby creating meaning. Meyer's theories were interesting insofar as he bracketed off any music that was "referentialist," which comprised both texted and programmatic music. He separated this from "absolute" music: music conceived in such a manner that "musical meaning lies exclusively within the context of the work itself, in the perception of the relationships set forth within the musical work of art." Both the formalist school that defined meaning in music as a predominantly intellectual endeavor, and the expressionists, who broadened meaning to include the listeners' feelings and sensations stimulated by the music, were absolutists in Meyer's sense as they accounted for music's meaning as a result of intra-musical processes, rather than in the mimesis of natural sounds, in accompanying texts (either in vocal music or in the form of a written program), or in associational effects (as are present in trumpet fanfares). Psychological and aesthetic experimentation were mutually influential, and it is no coincidence that Meyer's work was contemporaneous with the experiments in setting up intra-work expectations within pieces by composers such as György Ligeti and Olivier Messiaen. Messiaen, for instance, notated birdsong but used this referential material within compositional systems that were unique to each piece he composed. Each piece thus built up its own separate pattern of expectations in the listener, casting the original association of the birdsong into the background.

In the late twentieth century, research into the aesthetics of musical expression was replaced in English-language scholarship (in a disciplinary turn branded as "new musicology") by research into the frames within which music was conceived and within which it was now seen to have gained meaning (Fulcher 2011). Instead of seeking meaning intra-musically, as Meyer had so influentially formalized, musicologists—following trends in historical and literary studies—replaced textual analysis and source studies with a wider critical view of sociological, political, and perceptual issues in music, showcasing the particular construction of narratives (and giving rise to a plethora of gender study readings of music, for instance). In these, any universalization of emotional expression was rejected, and both the context and construction of narratives were now seen as the focus of the emotional reception of music by individuals and particular groups of listeners. Music was now investigated as a form of social behavior and social interaction. Any universalization of meaning, therefore, resides in the processes of engagement with music, constructed by the socio-cultural group "reading" that music, and by the conscious application of particular repertoires or practices of music in specific circumstances (Clarke and Cook 2004). Universalism, in other words, was replaced with collectively shared emotional perceptions.

The scientific study of music's effect split into the fields of music cognition, music psychology, and neuroscientific investigations, yet researchers from each field have frequently engaged in interdisciplinary work. Together, the fields have focused on investigating how music evokes emotions in listeners (see Eerola and Vuoskoski 2013 for a survey of the research field). Approaches to this question have grappled with a range of questions, starting with finding definitions for emotions as related to music and investigating the correlation between music as object or practice and emotions. Early on, the need for a nuanced distinction transpired between the gamut of emotions that is commonly at the center of scientific emotion research (survival-oriented emotions such as anger and fear), and so-called "positive emotions" that are the result of engagement with music. While it was clear that music does not trigger survival-oriented emotions, it was less clear which emotions it can in fact induce. Here, scientific research also had to distinguish felt emotions (i.e. those that describe a frame of mind that the listener actually feels as a result of engaging with music) from perceived emotions, those that the listener can recognize as an intended expression in the music without actually feeling them him- or herself.

The studies, then, distinguish themselves by the particular emotion models that they used in order to grapple with these difficulties. Some started from the discrete model, which assumes a basic set of core emotions, yet even here there is no agreement on what these are: some studies assume that only happiness, sadness, anger, fear, and disgust describe core emotions, while others extend this to include guilt, shame, contempt, and embarrassment (Eerola and Vuoskoski 2013: 310). A particular problem encountered in these studies was that they necessarily focused on perceived rather than felt emotions, and the transference to felt emotions remained less clear. Other researchers found that in music and emotion studies it was more useful to leave aside any named emotions and work on a dimensional model that described simply the trajectory from valence to arousal as a scale degree. Here, however, the dimensional model used—most commonly the circumplex model established by James Russell—has been uncritically adopted and left underdeveloped, so that the model does not account for simple things such as ascertaining whether the arousal is perceived as a positive or a negative emotion. Other studies have accounted for the difference between emotions generally and music-related emotions (be they felt or perceived) by developing music-specific emotion models (Asmus 1985; Juslin and Laukka 2004; Zentner, Grandjean and Scherer 2008).

A good deal of recent investigation is still indebted to the computational metaphor of the human mind that cognitive psychology initiated (Sloboda 1988; Neisser 1967). Studies in this field attempt to dissect music into its component parts so as to investigate which elements of music contribute to, or inspire, which effect. The inclusion of text is a particular concern here as texted music is prominent in many social settings (pop songs, etc.). Recently the parameters of sound quality and timbre that were bracketed out in early psychological approaches, as much as in aesthetic investigations, have received much attention. The type of engagement—whether listened to or actively practiced, whether conducted in solitude or in a group setting—has also begun to be taken into account (for example, Clift and Hancox 2001). Yet, overall, the studies still attempt to find universal musical effects, with some attempting to delineate these universals by investigating music in different cultural groups and settings. The central question of these studies, then, remains less focused on the useful application of music's effects—however they may come about in their myriad manifestations—but rather on making universalist, cross-cultural, and ahistoric pronouncements about music's meaning.[3] In the last twenty years, particular strongholds of music and emotion research have been those studies concerned with mood induction and studies in communication accuracy of musical emotions. The latter, interestingly, adopt uncritically the epistemological notion of a piece of music as containing an emotion, measuring the coincidence between groups of listeners. Here, the emotion scales used can look rather too basic when put into the context of the plurality of music in society today, of engagement types with musics, and of contextual settings. Other studies (reviewed by Gabrielsson and Lindström in Juslin and Sloboda 2011: 367–400) focus on acts in the performance of music that would enhance particular expressions of this music in the perceiver.

Methodologically, the studies can be broadly separated into those that deal with the issues theoretically, self-report studies in which participants variously rate or describe both felt and perceived emotions; biological studies that measure changes in heart rate, respiration, skin conductance, blood pressure, and muscle tension; and neurological approaches that also measure brain activity in a variety of ways. Combining these approaches with the music analytical approaches focused on particular musical features, with culturally specific approaches and with studies that take musical expertise and individual educational state into account, has proved highly problematic. The variables are so multitudinous and at times so difficult to control that the results remain somewhat speculative and unscientific. It is extremely difficult to apply results of studies of the contribution of particular music-internal features to actual musical situations, particularly when they work at the level of phrase structure or harmonic progression. Problematically, the separation of music into its component parts negates cognitive psychology's initial starting point (so prominently formulated by L. B. Meyer) that places the creation of meaning on the contextual assembly of musical parameters.

In the early part of the twenty-first century, research into the effects of rhythm and rhythmic entrainment (see Merker, Madison and Eckerdal 2009) have become particularly popular, with studies measuring the commonly held notion that the physical entrainment of rhythm can result in positive rhythmic alignment between people, which facilitates cooperation and allows for the coordination of multiple personalities (Cross and Morley 2009, Dunbar et al. 2012; Kirschner and Tomasello 2010). Others have gone beyond this to assess the positive social attitudes (Lang et al. 2016) that emanate from this, both perceived (Murray and Lamont 2012) and measured (Freeman 2000). The outcomes of social bonding assessed here are fairly traditional and comprise the perception of group identity through identification with a particular piece of music or repertoire, group cognition through the communication of ideas, group catharsis through the synchronization of emotions, and group coordination through the synchronization or harmonization of physical movement. The implications are more interesting: these studies collectively suggest that reactions to rhythm are involuntary and innate. Rhythm appears to influence motor coordination beyond cognitive control, and the emotional reaction to music is therefore, in part, a response to the phenomenon of coordination felt, rather than an instigator of that feeling, as was believed throughout the nineteenth and much of the twentieth centuries. It is debatable to what degree this biologically argued universalism is the narrative of post-modernity's crisis of cultural authority, flourishing on the soil of society's involvement with a vast range of different musics from the Western world and, crucially, beyond. Rhythm, perhaps, becomes the lowest common denominator that may define music; the mode of listening as a cultural construct is taken out of the equation in a claim that human physiology simply reacts to musical rhythm, no matter how, where, and when we listen.

The logical extension of these studies is the investigation of dance. Dance has frequently been regarded as inextricably linked with music and music-related emotions, especially in ethnological approaches; as a result, studies in dance and emotions frequently fall into the bracket of application studies, rather than theoretical investigation. Research, therefore, has focused on dance's sociological and anthropological role, and on its health application, stressing in particular that dance facilitates synchronization between individuals. This approach comes as a result of theoretical investigations into the evolutionary origin of dance. These have variously located it in a biological function in which dance showcases the body over the mind for courtship to aid reproduction, or to inspire social cohesion as a large group of individuals is synchronized and appears to create something collectively. Dance as a form of healthy exercise is also investigated in these contexts.

In these studies, dance is treated as an application—the most natural physiological expression of music's effects—and is seen, in effect, as an extension of the biological processes that music triggers via the perceptuo-motor-system (Murcia and Kreutz 2012). One logical extension of this has been a focus on the study of rhythm in music psychology, another, the study of dance as the physical interpretation of music's automatic and inevitable effects on the motor and somatosensory systems in the brain. Studies in both music and dance and their uses as therapeutic or cathartic tools therefore have focused largely on rhythm. The American Dance Therapy Association was founded in 1966 but dance therapy as a professional discipline has existed at least since the 1940s. The focus lies on the relationship of physical movement to emotion, interestingly a field that in music performance has attracted attention mostly from music educators and has therefore remained empirical and applied rather than theorized.

So far, the twenty-first century's story of the relationship between music and the emotions, and the place of narrative therein, has been an interesting one: while scientific research into music's impact on the brain and the body, and on emotional stimulants and symptoms in each, has operated largely on the basis of a universalism that takes music's effect on the emotions as culturally independent and historically unproblematic, research into music and emotions in the social sciences and humanities has focused on this very cultural conditioning. Post-modern composers, at the same time, abandoned the modernist demand for an intellectualization of music, celebrating and manipulating music's perceived emotional effect instead by self-consciously adopting the conventionalized (and therefore culturally acquired) emotional parameters of music. While film music has adopted these within the narrative framework within which they were deployed in the long since canonized music of the nineteenth century, "art music" composers have called attention to these conventions by rejecting the traditional narrative in which they were couched, assembling them in collage techniques together with musical conventions and parameters of other styles such as rock, pop, or jazz, or of other cultures such as the Indian raga traditions, the principles of Balinese gamelan and of West African drumming. This appears to retain the emotional content as one that can be consciously perceived, yet breaks the emotional identification, calling attention to clichés in the emotional perception of music instead. While scientists often retain a belief in the universal effects of a very small cultural canon, then, frequently reverting to so-called classical music, post-modern composers and cultural historians focus on the degree to which music's emotional power relies on the processes of this repertoire's canonization.

Here, interesting cross-relationships have emerged: while the minimalists of the 1960s and 1970s for instance focused on the processes and effects of a physiology of listening by disturbing any sense of memory through continuous repetition, recent studies on the use of music in torture have focused on the effects of continuous repetition of musical moments and of (culturally associational) musical narratives on the mind. In both, repetition is central, yet their contrasting effect has highlighted the role of a voluntary adoption of particular listening practices in the emotional perception of music: while one type becomes soothing and mesmeric, the other becomes torturous (Cusick 2015; Grant and Papaeti 2013; Potter and Gann 2016). These examples only highlight the key strands in recent research into music and emotions in the humanities, strands that are only slowly beginning to infiltrate the scientific approaches to the issue: how do body and mind interact in the perception of music as a force that induces emotions? What are the effects of different physical and mental listening conditions; what role does the manner of engaging with the music play (dancing, making music, or listening) and to what degree does both actual collective experience and perceived group identity play into these perceptions? And the most significant question arises perhaps from this: what role does a cultural and social belonging of particular musics play in their emotional effectiveness? In other words, whose music is it anyway?

CHAPTER FOUR

Drama

MARY LUCKHURST AND PETA TAIT

This chapter describes and analyses the depiction of emotions in realist and non-realistic drama and theatrical performance from the 1920s to the 2010s. It points to how the emotions of dramatic characters or personae within their enactment reflect but also implicitly influence social behavior and ideas of emotions. An exploration of the seminal realist and non-realist performance illuminates the expansion over the twentieth century from the presentation of emotional relationships and an emotional self to an evocation of subjective feeling and gender, ethnic, and sexual identity.

OVERVIEW

The emotions are intentionally created in drama and theater. The study of the emotions in theater considers the three distinct perspectives offered by narrative, performance, and audience. While the emotions of dramatic narratives have been explored in theater theory since Aristotle, the acting of emotions became the focus of controversy during the twentieth century and, in the twenty-first century, complex theory about the spectator's reception of performance increasingly draws on theories of affect.

The emotions and emotional feelings of characters are often described in the dialogue of a realist play for an audience's understanding, and in the stage directions for the actors to bodily interpret. But the emotions might not be specified especially in non-realist drama or texts, and, instead, the theater director, performers, and other artists create emotional moods. The emotions, emotional feelings, and moods are presented in theatrical performance using words and/or modes of embodied expression, including gestures, together with the other elements of theater production, and performers are surrounded by evocative technical and musical modes that also contribute to the overall effects.

The function of emotions in drama and in its performance corresponds with theories of emotion from other disciplines—including neuroscience. In particular, drama and performance align with psychology and philosophy. For example, there are theoretical and practical differences between the expressive communication of a performer and the evocation of the spectator's subjective feeling, which has implications for analytical approaches. While emotional feeling and affect is commonly described in the first person, and might be speculatively theorized and proposed for others, expressive performed emotion can be framed as, and understood within, a shared system of meaning—that is, theater offers a social language of emotion (Tait 2016a; 2016b). Theatrical knowledge about how actors grapple with the elusiveness of the emotions and a spectrum of possible interpretations corresponds with studies across disciplines, in which the recognition of specific emotions relies on context and language, and emotional display and value varies between cultures.

Realist modern drama and its theater sought to be socially truthful (Cody and Sprinchorn 2007). Modern understandings of the realistic acting of emotional expression were pioneered by Constantin Stanislavsky's "System" of ensemble acting that reached New York with his productions in 1922. The systematic approach to acting evolved into a logical way of reading and staging plays that promoted the idea of an emotionally coherent and consistent character, and it achieved pervasive ideological sway in mid-twentieth-century theater particularly in the USA. Bertolt Brecht invented a theory of estrangement in acting that involved diverting and interrupting both the actor's expression and the audience's emotional responses, with the aim of maintaining a critical distance from narrative and emotions. In Brecht's pedagogical theater, audiences are presented with emotional dilemmas that arise within social and political circumstances. The distinction between an actor inhabiting a character's emotions and an actor demonstrating emotional responses has underpinned important aesthetic and political discourse in twentieth-century and twenty-first-century theater.

The psychologically coherent character constructed in the late nineteenth century continues to be part of much twenty-first-century theater and cinema, although the emotional mappings of that coherence are now presented very differently. This contrasts with contemporary performance in which traditional character constructs are erased, problematized, or replaced by a persona. Both can convey political significance, but emotional connection evoked through realist stories remains especially effective in delivering political messages and stories. From the 1960s, emotion has been characterized and embodied through innovative narratives to do with identity politics and difference, and accordingly feminism and gender studies, post-colonialism and disability studies have generated strong political theater.

These politics of difference and the accompanying explosion in the sheer diversity of theatrical experiment and artistic fusions have increasingly put pressure on the idea that there is a normative construction of emotional response toward characters and other content. They have also problematized Stanislavsky's principles of realist acting, which were developed under particular historical conditions in Russia and in response to the difficulty actors had in addressing the subtle complexities of Anton Chekhov's characters. Contemporary plays often do not psychologically explain or justify their characters in the manner of playwrights such as Henrik Ibsen or Bernard Shaw; dialogue is more elliptical and there is more emphasis on what cannot be said and on what is being evaded. The contrast between the emotional truth of a situation and the abyss that words might seek to veil or deny has been a feature of much late-twentieth-century drama. So too has the gap between material reality and a character's perception of that reality and the terrain of their self-delusion. These features are a cultural commentary on what individual playwrights think their audiences can emotionally bear and not bear and are in themselves political strategies. The interest in setting out the relationship between character, environment, and the character's ability to alter the power structures he or she has to engage with, is as strong as ever in realist forms, but much more emphasis is placed on actors and directors in the negotiation of plotting an emotional trajectory, and playwrights are more attuned to thinking about the cultural adaptability of their texts and their openness to stagings in other countries.

Non-realistic performance might potentially drive debates about emotion in terms of taste, the politics of aesthetics, and the irrationality, mystery, and the danger of human emotions. A notable feature of much non-realist performance is the exploration of emotional limits and the breaching of boundaries of social acceptability or codes of "normality." Many contemporary practitioners are also seeking to change the contract with audiences by experimenting with immersive theaters, one-to-one performance, and by using mobile technologies. Much current rhetoric emphasizes the participatory and the experiential, setting up a false dichotomy with traditional forms of theater that are supposedly offering the opposite. In the current evocation of emotion in contemporary performance, the focus is turning toward the emotional journey of the "consumer" and how he or she might have control over some of the artistic decision making.

LIFELIKE REALISM

Henrik Ibsen and Anton Chekhov—together with Shakespeare—became the most produced playwrights of the twentieth century, their prominence increasing as the century progressed. Realist characters reflected the century's values as "modern drama epitomizes individualistic self-expression" (Krasner 2011: 6). In particular the feminist dimensions of Ibsen's *A Doll's House* made it globally significant. For example, Jiang Qing, who later married Chairman Mao, acted the character of Nora in Shanghai in 1935 in what became known as the "year of Nora" (Holledge and Tompkins 2000: 33–4).[1] Ibsen's drama reflects numerous ideas of modernity (Moi 2006), and *A Doll's House* remains relevant in the twenty-first century because not only is it the classic realist play about the break-up of a marriage and the expectation of gender equality, it also depicts a mother leaving her children. Nora, a mother of three, is married to bank manager Torvald Helmer, and the socially disgraced Krogstad is blackmailing and threatening Nora over a financial debt. Nora's friend, the widowed Kristine Linde, reconnects with Krogstad and subsequently persuades him to rescind his revelation. Nora realizes that the accusatory, angry Torvald is not the heroic masculine figure that she had assumed him to be, someone who would take the blame for her misdemeanor, and she decides to leave the marriage. In the nineteenth century, Nora's emotional realizations overturned what could be publicly revealed about the experience of emotion in domestic worlds.

Theater studies scholarship on *A Doll's House* until the 1980s considered that this is play is about a humanist emotional problem: Nora is an individual trying to become a person. Joan Templeton (1989; 1997) compiles these comments that claim that the play must be considered metaphoric of individual freedom rather than gender inequity. She raises a fundamental question about what types of emotional dilemma can be deemed "universal" as she points out that surely a woman leaving a husband and children constitutes an emotional situation of major social importance. *A Doll's House*, however, presents a second significant relationship: that between Mrs. Linde and Krogstad, who make a mature commitment between equals that reinforces the play's core idea of the necessity of honesty and trust between intimate partners, and the need to comprehend each other's failings.

By the end of the third act, Nora is literally dancing the tarantella and moving, as Torvald suggests, out of madness (Ibsen 1982: 77). Thus the acting of emotion in theater could appear to replicate hysterical symptoms; Nora overcomes her fears and overt hysterical display to appear rational and strong by the end of the play. Ibsen was Freud's favorite playwright, although his plays were written prior to the development of Freud's theories, including on hysteria. The exchange between psychoanalysis and drama continues and intensifies in twentieth-century drama.

Emotion is a performative component in theater and one major criticism made about the character Nora is that she performs socially by acting out false roles to please Torvald—a criticism of theater throughout its history. Torvald confesses that he pretends Nora is his "secret mistress," "my clandestine little sweetheart," and "a huntress and a temptress" (Ibsen 1982: 88). He reveals a sexual dynamic of performative fantasy role playing. These ideas of performative identity and emotions continue to be developed in theater, and in 1922 Luigi Pirandello shocked audiences with *Six Characters in Search of An Author*, in which actor characters speak at length with their emotionally distraught fictional characters—of course, all are actually fictional characters—about family breakdown and incest. In 1958, Jean Genet expressly depicted performances of social and sexual identity in *The Balcony*, in which character types such as The Bishop, The Judge, The Chief of Police, and The Queen perform their roles in order to be recognizable to themselves and others, engaging in a semi-hysterical queer masquerade (Chaudhuri 1986).

The residue of what Deborah Lupton calls the "emotional woman" and the "unemotional man" underlies ideas of an emotional self in realist drama (Lupton 1998: 105), although this gender difference is less apparent in modernist non-realistic drama and performance. Up until the later decades of the twentieth century, it was considered socially unacceptable for men to cry in public but they could be angry, whereas women could cry but not show anger. Modern drama explores how women's emotional experience has traditionally been framed within the domestic sphere and defined by the expression of familial love and related emotions (Lupton 1998: 107–8).

Anton Chekhov's drama became preeminent in England and North America during the 1920s in a series of well-known productions (Senelick 1997). This drama suggests how the arts influence the social explanation and interpretation of emotions, and his lifelike characters quote literary and theatrical works, and draw on what other fictional characters say, to explain their own experience of emotional feeling to other characters. By implication, Chekhov's drama such as *The Seagull* and *Three Sisters* offers a socially realistic depiction of how individuals come to understand and interpret the meaning of their emotions within wider social contexts; they use artistic representation to explain them. Given that Chekhov's characters—and some of Samuel Beckett's characters—quote from theater and literature to explain their feelings to other characters, the meaning of personal emotion is framed in relation to how it is expressed in performance (which expands in the twentieth century to performance on screen.)

Chekhov's characters verbalize their feelings so that the dialogue presents a phenomenology of feeling. This is invaluable for acted delivery in theater and it partly explains why actors welcome opportunities to work in Chekhov's plays. But the increasing popularity of Chekhov's plays globally during the twentieth century can also be attributed to scenarios that are not emotionally deterministic. The open-endedness of emotions in Chekhov's drama prefigures the patterns evident in later realism and non-realism.

ACTING CONTROVERSIES AND POLITICAL EMOTION

Stanislavsky's acting "System" was disseminated through his books from the 1920s, and this made him the preeminent international figure in twentieth-century actor training (see Stanislavski 2010). His systematic techniques are premised on objectives and superobjectives, but the most contested issue among Stanislavsky's interpreters has been techniques for acting emotion. These techniques have become reduced in actor-training vocabularies to the phrase "emotional memory."

Stanislavsky was committed to interpreting plays, and advised the division of a text's dialogue into small, workable components which are then put together again with character objectives for a scene. A Stanislavsky-influenced approach would be: an actor allocates a series of verbs to act his or her dialogue lines, with emotions as adverbs. It is Stanislavsky's principles and techniques that remain relevant to actor training in the twenty-first century, rather than the style of emotional delivery that changes over time. For example, his idea of a subtext involves acting underlying emotions that contradict the more obvious surface emotion of the event or dialogue. Thus a conventional approach might replicate the specified anger of a character—such as that of Treplev in *The Seagull* (Chekhov 1991: 76)—in predictable ways, whereas a Stanislavsky-influenced approach encourages actors to creatively experiment by depicting anger differently, for example, with a subtext of sadness.

Stanislavsky's System was interpreted by leading mid-twentieth-century acting teachers in the USA: Lee Strasberg, Stella Adler, and Sanford Meisner (see Meisner and Longwell 1987). They disagreed about how to interpret Stanislavsky's ideas, and especially about the acting of emotion. Lee Strasberg's controversial "Method" has become well known because of its application to screen performance. In rehearsal and training he encouraged actors to draw on their memories of sensory responses at the time of a personal emotional experience (Gordon 2000: 53). The idea that an actor should draw on his or her own feeling experience in what is called "emotion" or "emotional memory" is usually attributed to Strasberg, even though he was expanding on Stanislavsky's term. Stanislavsky, however, always rejected directly transposing intense personal emotions into acting and he shifted away from the idea of emotional memory with his later emphasis on beginning with physical work (Carnicke 2009). Strasberg highlighted how an actor's emotional self could be applied to the interpretation of a character's emotions. This emphasis on the qualities of the actor's own experience—rather than on the dramatic circumstances of the character—combined with mid-twentieth-century quasi-psychological practices has been widely criticized (Malague 2012). Strasberg has also been criticized for creating a power imbalance between the teacher and student when working with emotions.

Conversely, in following Stanislavsky's later techniques, Adler specified that the play or text should be the focus of the acting and provide the framework for the interpretation of emotions (Malague 2012). This makes the acted emotions more easily accessible but also, importantly, more responsive to socio-historical change captured by scripts.

While there are numerous important twentieth-century realistic and non-realistic acting styles which follow after Stanislavsky and his protégé Vsevolod Meyerhold—who instigated physical theater processes (Hodge 2012)—Brecht challenged the whole dramatic form of realist theater and emotional acting in his theater theory and his ideas for epic theater with a political purpose. Brecht argued against the presumption that audiences forget that they are in the theater, because they should instead cognitively appraise what happens in order to learn about social forces and take this understanding away from the theater. This rejection of a self-contained emotional world had a far-reaching and lasting impact. The issue for Brecht was that conventional realist dramatic theater invited emotional identification with the fictional characters and the dramatic circumstances, and so it forestalled cognitive analysis and remained an experience within theater (or cinema) rather than one encouraging political action.

Brecht's drama—cowritten with female collaborators—focused on the emotional travails of the working classes, and with strong female characters. As Meg Mumford explains, Brecht was exposed to Marxist ideas of production and economic structures (Mumford 2009: 20). While she points out that Brecht sought inspiration for his theater in other non-realistic, popular entertainment forms, despite his focus on spectatorial responses, he did not initially perceive the value of emotional involvement which aligns with, for example, the passion aroused by sport (Mumford 2009: 16).

Brecht encouraged the spectator's detached, objective observation and sought to create theater in which the emotional delivery was interrupted. Mumford argues that Brecht's idea of defamiliarization did not advocate "non-emotional" theater, since thinking and feeling were inseparable. For example, the actor should use a "gest of showing" that externalizes emotion (Brecht 1987: 136). Defamiliarization can be achieved if actors seem to quote, speak the stage directions, and historicize narrative events. This is called the A-effect and it transforms emotion—worry, joy, anger, and disgust—into components of theater like its other elements, such as the lighting and music. Rather than imitating a character's feeling, a performer must dislodge it, and overtly depict emotions as social transactions. Ironically perhaps, Brecht's epic theater can deliver unmistakable and less ambiguous ideas of emotions as actors demonstrate them.

Brecht's ideas did shift more toward those of Stanislavsky over time. As well as developing an emphasis on the spectator, most importantly, Brecht was analyzing the larger function of emotion in theater. Yet this part of his theoretical legacy was far less apparent in the second half of the twentieth century, because decreasing attention was given to emotional delivery in Western theater culture and a greater emphasis was given to directing the visual effects and the physical staging.

LATE-MODERNIST FEELINGS

Samuel Beckett's *Waiting for Godot* is unquestionably the most influential play of post-Second World War theater, for its wide impact, including on artists working in other art forms. It depicts the frustrations and annoyances of two homeless tramps who wait in vain for Mr. Godot (Taylor-Batty and Taylor-Batty 2013; Van Hulle 2015). The play alludes to theater and other performance directly, in the dialogue, and indirectly, in the characters' behaviour. It also provides reminders of theater's purpose in staging emotions as it emphasizes an anti-theatrical dimension with its dialogue about inner experience. The tramp characters reinvent the tramp-clown of popular nineteenth-century entertainment, and Lucky's stream-of-consciousness monologue provides a performance within the play. Chekhov's drama in particular preempts an idea of waiting, the central motif in *Waiting for Godot*, and the dialogue is realist, although the play is also grouped within Martin Esslin's (1968) "theatre of the absurd." The play reached a wide audience globally, with a particularly famous production for prisoners at San Quentin Prison in the USA in 1957 (Phelan 2009).

The two main characters, Estragon (Gogo) and Vladimir (Didi), express the emotional frustrations and physical annoyances of their day-to-day life in excruciating detail, in contrast to drama's usual focus on life's major emotional events such as love or death. Vladimir is pleased to see Estragon, which suggests emotional familiarity and sociability.

They pass their time waiting for Mr. Godot, who does not appear but sends two boy messengers, and they encounter Pozzo with Lucky, who seems to be Pozzo's servant although treated like a slave. Estragon and Vladimir do not recall the immediate past clearly, but minor details in the dialogue reveal that time passes, and the characters impose a type of order on their world through bodily habit and routine. The spoken dialogue is central, and action is transitory, without explanation, rather than theatrically meaningful: for example, Estragon leaves and returns (Beckett 1990: 18). The acts vary through the details: in Act 1, Estragon has a carrot, too-small boots, and a chicken bone; in Act 2, he has a radish, his boots become too big, and the chicken bone turns into a fish bone. Act 2 repeats Act 1 and the play conveys how one day seems the same as the next.

Estragon's first line is "Nothing to be done" (Beckett 1990: 11), which prefigures the whole text. Is this a statement of frustration and hopelessness, or of personal endurance, or of matter-of-fact reality? (The acted delivery might allow for more options.) Esslin writes that *Waiting for Godot* does not "tell a story; it explores a static situation" (1968: 45). But this description does not really convey how the play captures subjective emotions, using rhetorical repetition to verbalize felt experience. As a literary successor to James Joyce, Beckett undertakes the more difficult task of representing subjective experience within dramatic dialogue. While the characters live within the continuous present of the play, emotions arise and dissipate as the substance of the interaction between them. There is doubt about everything beyond what the characters emotionally depict and sensorially describe in the present moment.

The differences between the two main characters arise from emotional nuance. Vladimir seems more nervous and needy, while the slightly reserved Estragon seems to get more exasperated. Esslin summarizes the characters' temperaments: "Estragon is volatile, Vladimir persistent [and practical]. Estragon dreams, Vladimir cannot stand hearing about dreams" (1968: 47). Estragon recounts comic stories and Vladimir gets upset. Esslin claims that while the play is about hope and expectation, the two characters "do not believe in action, wealth, or reason," and Beckett on Proust outlines how the "'*boredom of living*'" can be momentarily replaced by the "'*suffering of being*'" (Esslin 1968: 57–8 [italics in original]). At the core of the text is absence—the absent Mr. Godot. The play depicts characters living out their affective experience and the dialogue depicts short-lived emotional responses to the immediate circumstances as it provides glimpses of long-term underlying moods.

The play is philosophical and it is interesting to note that there is no blame in this play and there is no solid biographical information explaining why these characters feel as they do. While psychology, psychoanalysis, and religious studies are used in interpretations of Beckett's plays, Stanton Garner explains: "Beckett's drama is a theatre 'of the body,' both in the traditional sense that its characters are bodied forth by actors for spectatorial consumption and in a more deeply phenomenological sense" (Garner 1994: 28). The play strips back the action and events to bodily experience—the performer's body is the crucial element of theater. More specifically, *Waiting for Godot* is a play about characters who describe embodied feelings; as Beckett revealed, "'All I am is feeling'" (Graver and Federman 1979: 217). The spoken dialogue depicting bodily sensations and emotional feelings is, in turn, a challenge for actors to enliven in theater. Figure 4.1 shows Beckett in rehearsal with actors.

Beckett's *Endgame* depicts a post-apocalyptic aftermath, with its characters confined to one enclosed room; and *Happy Days* shows Winnie buried to the waist then the neck in an externalization of her inner worlds. There is no self-discovery for Beckett's characters, which continues a philosophical proposition found in Chekhov's drama, and resists a premise that life should be depicted in theater in a neat trajectory toward self-revelation and emotional resolution.

In post-Second World War America, Arthur Miller refines classic realism into finely crafted metaphoric drama to reveal the destructive effects of the emotions underlying shared socio-political beliefs. For example, the deadly social power of an emotional movement that persecuted young women as witches was depicted in *The Crucible*, first produced in 1953 (Miller 1989; also see *The Arthur Miller Journal*). Expectations of social

FIGURE 4.1: *Waiting for Godot*, from left: Carl Raddatz, playwright/director Samuel Beckett, Stefan Wigger in rehearsal at the Schiller. Photo by Everett Collection Inc/Alamy Stock Photo.

success create emotional pressures for the failing salesman father in *Death of a Salesman*, first produced in 1949 (Miller 1989). Emotions continue to be personally and socially transacted in realist drama that remains culturally responsive to socio-historical change.

SPECTATOR RESPONSES

Beckett might have started working in realism, but the way he experimented with breaking up theatrical elements influenced post-modernism and contemporary performance, which is also called post-dramatic theater. Hans-Thies Lehmann writes: "the trivial occurrences in Beckett's works are anything but trivial" because they depict what is real (2006: 101). Beckett's later short performance texts are without characters and fictional settings, and take place in the space in which the actions are executed. Although personal and social emotions have been removed in this type of non-realistic performance, the theatrical mood remains.

Not I, first produced in 1972, presents a mouth, 2.5 meters above the stage, with a hooded, gender-ambiguous figure on a podium as the auditor. In *Rockaby*, first performed in 1981, the voice or voice-over and the visible performer are again separated. A mood of discordant estrangement prevails. Beckett was also influenced by the possibilities of radio and television, and the later performance texts are not plays as such but texts that reveal subjective perception which is fragmented and partial, as if it were not possible to grasp the whole entity of an embodied subject. There is no dialogue in Beckett's 1981 televisual piece *Quad*, as four hooded performers repetitively move anti-clockwise around a square in a triangular movement, as if confined by the pattern of their own movement. In this way, Beckett's texts reveal some of the difficulties of staging emotional qualities in contemporary performance that is focused on spatiality, physicality, and the doing of actions.

These contemporary performance texts strip away theatrical embellishment and the combination of elements that contribute to emotional effects in theater. There are no characters expressing personal feelings, and without the embodied personification of emotions, the emphasis in theater shifts to the responses that the spectator brings to the experience of the whole event.

The divergence in late-modernist theater from the emotional dilemmas of early modernity allowed theatrical performance to explore innovative ideas of fragmented subjective experience. The immediacy of the event opens out the possibility of an unstable performative self as it undercuts theater's former long-standing social function and delineation of rules about emotional expression. It might be argued that this latter function had been superseded by cinema and television in the second half of the twentieth century, reflecting back the emotional relationships on a mass scale in melodrama and popular soap opera. Realist theater continues to develop alongside contemporary performance, enlarging the tendencies of Miller's exposé of individual and social anxieties, Beckett's rejection of emotional resolution, and post-Brechtian political questioning.

EMOTION, DIVERSITY, AND REWRITING THE CLASSICS

From the 1950s the seismic political shifts following the Second World War, and the ideological divisions created by those shifts, were increasingly evident in the constructs of mood and emotion found in realist and non-realist dramas. The ending of European colonization across different African states, the rise of a powerful anti-imperial civil rights movement, the anti-apartheid movement, the Vietnam War protests, the anti-nuclear lobby, and the advance of Second Wave and Third Wave feminism were all major factors in the generation of a greater diversity of playwrights, actors, and directors. A new era of liberalization in the 1960s and 1970s created a momentum for the championing of equality agendas and for change, ushering in unheard stories and previously suppressed perspectives from constituencies who were identifying as different from the cultural majority. Importantly, the burgeoning of politically active fringe theater venues to support and disseminate those diverse voices meant that the worlds represented by modern drama became much more complex.

The emotional registers of this newly galvanized post-1950s realist and non-realist drama were explored in different ways. Brecht's theory and practice of interrupting emotional identification exerted a profound influence but, at the same time, dramatists made bold experiments, mixing formal styles, the real with the surreal, and playing with multiple narratives. The rage of the oppressed was palpable in many plays and theater events. Amiri Baraka, for example, came to be characterized by his poetics of violence and his inversions of the cultural value imposed on a white or a black skin color (See Figure 4.2). The emotional messages in Baraka's dramas *Dutchman* (1964) and *A Black Mass* (1967) manifest in the agenda of the American Black Arts Movement (1965–75), were perceived by the cultural majority of white critics as extreme and unacceptable. However, Baraka's lack of recognition in the wider canon reflects critical prejudices, which have been increasingly strongly challenged (Young 2010; 2013). Who has been allowed to speak on mainstream Western stages and who has not, and which characters have been welcomed or decried for expressing "negative" emotions, is very much under examination by a new generation of academics. The emotional palette of the twentieth-century theatrical canon is more contested than any other.

Particular kinds of education and reference points mattered even in this more liberal post-1960s era, and many dramatists paid homage to the canon while at the same time undercutting it. An education was the route to empowerment, and under imperial regimes too many had forgone that right or had it restricted. Playwrights Wole Soyinka and Derek Walcott, for example, were as influenced by a classical literary English education as by their respective Nigerian and Caribbean cultures, and explored colonial oppression through Greek classical structures and highly formal cathartic conventions that were nonetheless othered by subverting the politics of knowledge, not just through a cultural and textual hybridity but through the bodies of the colonized and their songs, silences, gestures, and rituals. During the apartheid era in South Africa, playwright Athol Fugard and actors John Kani and Winston Ntshona (see Figure 4.3) famously collaborated to write *The Island* (1973). Set in a penal colony resembling the notorious Robben Island where Nelson Mandela was incarcerated for twenty-seven years, two prisoners recover from the days of hard labor by rehearsing Sophocles' *Antigone* at night. One plays the judge, Creon, and the other, Antigone, who breaks the rule of law to bury her brother and is put to death for standing up for her own and her dead brother's rights. The translation of Antigone's story to the continued injustices reported by African-American communities in the United States, and to the abuses that refugee communities in various parts of the world recount, is clear, and *The Island* was performed for over thirty years, into the early twenty-first century, by Kani and Ntshona. Poignantly, the emotional message of resilience and standing firm in the face of injustice is more powerful than ever.

Adaptations of Shakespeare's plays offered fertile political terrain and playwrights went beyond Brecht's Marxist class agenda, remapping Shakespeare's worlds to topical

FIGURE 4.2: Amiri Baraka (1934–2014) speaking at the Congress of African People held in Atlanta, 1970. Photo by Robert Abbott Sengstacke/Getty Images.

FIGURE 4.3: South African playwright Athol Fugard (center) with actors John Kani (left) and Winston Ntshona (right). Photo by *Evening Standard*/Getty Images.

post-colonial and feminist concerns. Protagonists were refashioned to personalize and emotionally galvanize audiences into political self-recognition. Aimé Césaire's 1969 adaptation of *The Tempest*, for example, offered a resonant study of slavery and colonialism (mapped onto Martinique, Césaire's birthplace), in which Prospero is the white master, and his slaves are Arial, mulatto, and Caliban, black-skinned. Césaire's play expressed the anger, injustice, and trauma experienced by many people of color and triggered a spectrum of different reactions among white audiences—from denial to guilt as well as feelings of complicity. The emotional stratification of reactions from different audiences is still a marked feature of post-colonial drama and of plays dealing with racism, but this terrain remains largely uninvestigated.

More recent Shakespearean adaptations have paid less deference to "official" editions of the plays and are more engaged in cocreation by actors, musicians, and dancers in order to deconstruct emotional connections that might conventionally be made with certain characters by reactionary audiences. Indigenous Australian actor Jack Charles's portrayal of King Lear in Liza Dezfouli's *The Shadow King* (2013) has been particularly resonant in a continent where genocide and land rights are inextricably linked. The tragedy is not so much rooted in the classical catharsis of a monarch's self-destructive fall from power but in the overwhelming abuse and cruelty Lear has suffered from the taking of his lands, which, for him, are an innate part of his identity and are neither conceptualized nor understood to be capital. The land owns its people and not vice versa, and the appropriation of that land is not simply theft, it is also a human rights violation of the most grievous kind.

In another rewriting, Toni Morrison's *Desdemona* (2012) undoes the usual construct of Othello's wife as tragic because of her "innocence" and naïvety. Instead, Desdemona,

FIGURE 4.4: Rokia Traore (left) and Tina Benko in Toni Morrison's *Desdemona*, 2013. Photo by Lieberenz/Ullstein Bild via Getty Images.

who appears as a ghost, is recast as wholly complicit with the racist power structures that inform those who want Othello dead. Her greater crime is the dehumanizing abuse she has inflicted on her black slave, Barbary, for as long as she has known her (much longer than she has known Othello). Audiences are given to understand that Desdemona is a product of her environment, but judge her because, unlike Barbary, she is a perpetrator by default, is infatuated by a man of extreme violence, and has failed to engage in any act of empathetic understanding for her maid. Morrison presents Desdemona as politically empty-headed, lacking human sensibility for Barbary, and reprehensibly ignorant of human rights. The tragic figure is Barbary, performed by Malian singer Rokia Traoré (who wrote the music and lyrics in her native language). See Figure 4.4 for an illustration of Traoré and Tina Benko in *Desdemona* (2013). Barbary has an authoritative tragic stance and dignified political understanding, and at the end is still able to find compassion for her ignorantly abusive mistress. For Morrison the humanizing emotion is empathy, and Desdemona's lack of it is a larger statement about the political classes and their hunger for war to satisfy their appetites.

DOCUMENTARY AND THE RISE OF HUMAN RIGHTS

An important feature of late-twentieth- and twenty-first-century drama and theater is their interconnection with the rise of Western human rights discourses since 1945 and the instituting of the United Nations Universal Declaration of Human Rights (Luckhurst and Morin 2015). Drama and theater have a greater relationship than ever to subject matter or human conditions that are considered unspeakable or taboo, and theater has become a significant vehicle for awareness raising, identification, and protest because live performance has the capacity to harness feelings of communal power and collective identity. A strong legacy of Erwin Piscator's and Bertolt Brecht's experiments in the 1920s is the emergence of the post-1960s documentary play, which has proved vital to the telling of many human rights stories and the articulation of collective empathy. Its popularity on mainstream and community stages, in conflict and crisis zones, and as a device for saying the culturally unsayable, is indisputable. Its current prevalence can be traced back to Peter Weiss's documentary *The Investigation,* which premiered on the same night on fourteen different stages in Germany and England in 1965. Weiss's project was an extraordinary affective intervention. In it Weiss took verbatim victim and perpetrator testimony from the Frankfurt Auschwitz trials, begun in 1963, about life in the Nazi death camp before and during the Second World War. Characters in the Ibsenite tradition did not exist. Instead, the real words of victims and perpetrators stood as symbols for a genocide of six million. The stark, horrifying details of clinical experimentation and industrial mass killing, coupled with the perpetrators' lack of connection to their actions and denial of responsibility, needed no fictional embellishment and conjured a world run by humans alienated from themselves. For significant numbers of audience members, it was the first time they had attended a live event about the Holocaust and the first time they learned any details of what had occurred in Auschwitz.

The play was a phenomenon in terms of reach and impact, and audiences found that it tested certain conventions of emotional response. Was it just a performance? An act of rebuke? A call to conscience? Or an act of memorialization? The play cast spectators as witnesses and implicated them both politically and emotionally. This changed the theatrical contract between performer and spectator and therefore the politics of emotion. Was it morally wrong, for example, to take pleasure in the acting, the representation of real victims, and risk deprivileging the actual victims' testimony? What was an appropriate reaction to such barbarism? Was the emotional turmoil and horror generated in many audience members simply indulgent, as well as irrelevant and offensive to victims who had not been helped? The play suggested a much greater implication of guilt in the failure of so many to believe that atrocities were taking place at the time, the failure of many to act, and the continuing failure of many to do anything about the subsequent suffering of survivors or the waves of displaced people in Europe. The most powerful aspect of the play was its mediation of the victims' actual words. The claim to an authenticity of voice and of articulated emotion and the capacity of the documentary form to test the emotional and ethical stances of audience members has made verbatim plays a favored contemporary form. For Piscator and Brecht, documentary privileged the socio-political "epic" over the indulgence of emotion. For more recent playwrights such as Anna Deavere Smith (*Fires in the Mirror* and *Twilight: Los Angeles*), Adrienne Kennedy and Suzan-Lori Parks (*USA*), and Richard Norton-Taylor (*The Colour of Justice*), however, it is the elevation of an individual story to a symbolic plane and the emotional impact of that story as a human rights narrative that is valued.

THEATERS OF EXCESS

Western theater has a long tradition of challenging social and moral codes, but since the 1960s a notable strand of experimentation has challenged the emotional limits of what an audience will tolerate. It is not coincidental that Austria, the country of Hitler's birth, produced two playwrights, Peter Handke and Elfriede Jelinek, who have taken Brechtian and Beckettian experiments to an extreme. Handke's *Offending the Audience*, which premiered in 1966, has become a classic (Handke 1997) "anti-theater" play of its era: in it four speakers, who are indistinguishable from one another, address the audience in a bland manner, drawing attention to audience members' clothes, their stance, their breathing, and the preparations and expectations they have undergone for an evening at the theater. There is no conventional plot or character, and no set, but a continual play on what constitutes spectacle and a refusal to release the audience from the boredom of contemplating their own passive behaviors. The object was to goad the audience into questioning their bourgeois notion of theater as elite and civilizing and to confront them with their own political inertia and ineffectual outrage. In *The Hour we Knew Nothing of Each Other*, Handke describes the actions undertaken by people in a town square and writes a score of movements and actions. A meditative and wordless choreography, Handke shows a debt to Beckett but is interested in sustaining emotional experiments on his audience for far longer periods of stage time than Beckett in the hope of provoking a political stance from a reaction to an aesthetic. Jelinek's plays deliberately test the boundaries of taste, exploring sexual violence, and can be understood as interrogations of patriarchy, sexism, and self-subjugation. *What Happened after Nora Left her Husband; or Pillars of Society* is a late-twentieth-century response to Ibsen's *A Doll's House*, and depicts Nora in a series of domestic and employment roles that demonstrate that the world has changed little in terms of equality and power politics. Jelinek's tactics are to shock, and the grotesque juxtapositions she creates coupled with the masochistic passivity of her female protagonists have forced extreme emotional reactions and walk-outs.

A theater of emotional excess dominated mainstream new writing stages in Europe in the 1990s and 2000s and was spurred by English tabloid press reactions to Sarah Kane's work (see Figure 4.5). Her play *Blasted*, first performed in 1995, showed the behaviors of individuals in a freshly bombed war zone, and portrayed acts of rape and cannibalism. *Cleansed* is set ambiguously in both a university and a death camp, and love is tested by sadistic mutilation, acts of amputation, and mental torture. Kane (2001) argued that she was exploring the theories of Antonin Artaud (1958) in the tradition of the Theatre of Cruelty, deliberately provoking disgust and revulsion in her audiences but doing so because modern warfare and the media have deadened human capacity for appropriate emotional responses. Kane's realist plots yielded to poetic explorations of states of mind as evinced by *4:48 Psychosis* and her portrait of suicidal despair. The refusal of realist plot, and the interest in intertextuality and heightened states of emotion in Handke, Jelinek, and Kane's late work—elements currently masterfully explored by Norwegian playwright Jon Fosse—are all examples of what Lehmann refers to as post-dramatic theater. These works reflect a continuation and a convergence of the avant-garde tradition that eschews behavioral causality and realist logic.

In the twenty-first century, playwrights and performance writers consistently confront their audiences with questions of political apathy and complicity in relation to wars, poverty, migration, identity politics, loss, self-alienation, and climate change. The work of Caryl Churchill (see Figure 4.6), one of the most celebrated playwrights of the age, spans the constructs of emotion shaped by the Cold War, by critiques of capitalist structures, and by leftist discourses of ownership, colonialism, war, and human rights abuses— especially against women and children. Churchill's works investigate the connection between the individual's emotional response to the machinery of state and corporate globalism. What are the individual's political responsibilities? What does complicity mean? Is human capacity for empathy being eroded? Are we more robot than human? Are our emotions genetically or environmentally programmed? Above all, Churchill's most

FIGURE 4.5: Playwright Sarah Kane (1971–99). Photo by Marianne Thiele/Ullstein Bild via Getty Images.

FIGURE 4.6: Playwright Caryl Churchill (b.1938). Photo by United News/Popperfoto/Getty Images.

recent works examine emotional excess and emotional densensitization, social anomie, and the effects of media overload and disaster porn on our empathetic faculties. Many of Churchill's texts explore the ways in which social and political structures create inequities, resulting in individual trauma that has a devastating impact (Luckhurst 2015: 179–82). In *Far Away*, Churchill details a politics of excess through an aesthetics of excess, charting the journey of Joan, who is groomed by the family as well as the state to both tolerate and commit acts of violence. By the end of the play Joan is a savage killing machine, destroying human life and habitat, an active instrument in the apocalyptic end of planet Earth. Premiered in 2000, *Far Away* (Churchill 2000) represents a political system in which human sensibility has been completely annihilated, a theme that Churchill has since repeatedly addressed. *Love and Information* and *Ding Dong the Wicked*, both performed in 2012, suggest the increasing anatomization of human life and the loss of compassion and connection brought about by excess consumption and the normalization of war and extreme violence. One of the most striking dramatic narratives of our times is in Churchill's *Love and Information*, the story of the child without fundamental human attributes. In the scene "the child who didn't know fear," a series of gruesome encounters have no impact whatsoever and the child dies as he has no understanding of risk; "the child who didn't know sorry" represents a narcissist unable to comprehend trauma inflicted on others; and "the child who didn't know pain" depicts a child who can endure grotesque physical damage but feels no pain (Churchill 2012). Neo-liberalism, argues Churchill, is creating a mutant monster species, without empathy or sensory receptors, which will secure human destruction on an unprecedented scale (Luckhurst 2015).

TWENTY-FIRST-CENTURY PREOCCUPATIONS

A feature of contemporary theater is the increasing pressure on the term "theater" itself to describe shows which increasingly fuse art forms, skill sets, and technologies, and blur boundaries between forms, including, for example, burlesque, cabaret, circus, dance, and puppetry, with realist and non-realist text. Many Western mainstream theaters still show an adherence to realism, but mixed media shows with multiple visual and sonic narratives are also prevalent and new audiences are drawn by the use of complex technologies. As the technologies proliferate and the spectrum of experiments increases, it is telling that the debates about dominant actor training in the West still tend to focus on the authentic source of the actor's emotions. This says something about the cultural values associated with the actor in the West and the cultural need to believe in an actor's ability to channel authentic emotional responses through a character or other construct.

Whereas documentary and other forms of realism are aligned with a rhetoric about authenticity of voice and sincerity of emotion, contemporary non-realist forms tend to display a cynicism or skepticism toward veracity or the possibility of authentically felt emotion. A strand of contemporary performance influenced by The Wooster Group since the 1970s focuses on performers doing actions as a construction of what is real, and for spectators there is no linear plot or character coherence. Emotion appears to be generated by the actions of a performer or from an internal source that is not necessarily explained, and the text is not a privileged element. Forms of hyperrealist texts delivered with excessive emotional display have been much explored by Scandinavian directors and by Dutch theater companies such as Toneelgroep, which adapted and performed Ingmar Bergman's *Scenes from a Marriage* in 2005. Toneelgroep depicted the breakdown of a marriage using three couples of different ages, who engaged in extended scenes of intense, overwrought, and exhaustive emotional venting. In one scene, the extended choreographing of anger and insult became blackly comic before descending into farce because the sheer length of the scene caused its emotional meanings to disintegrate. Shows such as this overtly demonstrate the ways in which realism as a style is understood to have limitations and invite interrogation of the discourses of sincerity and of "true" emotion, which continue to dominate discussions about theater, acting, and actor training. In the world of acting, debates about sincerity are especially ironic: while many actors still generate emotion through an imagined psychology of character, many also suggest or enact emotional states through physical action. For an actor, the overriding concern is that the externals of their performance are convincing (which seems to be another anxiety about authentic motivation) and the arguments circle around how that is best accomplished.

The mass global exports of the day are musicals and stand-up comedy. Musicals do not conform to prevalent realist premises but they do borrow from conventions of melodrama and stock characters and notions of the hyperreal in their sung expressions of emotion. Audience mood is intensified by music, and fan bases have powerful relationships to their favorite musicals, expressing a passion for the form that non-musical theater cannot match. Fandom is an important element of stand-up too. A twenty-first-century reinvention of political theater, stand-up is a significant form of theatrical human rights advocacy. In stand-up, as in cabaret, it is the rhetoric of persona, not of character, that holds sway; persona being understood as a more direct means of mediating certain aspects of the performer's own personality and narration of their own life experiences or feelings about living. A stand-up might, in fact, be inventing everything, but the lore is that the closer your act is to your self, the more successful you will be. Again, the performance of an authentic self with authentic emotions is fetishized.

All these developments blur the boundaries of what constitutes theater, and "realism" now has a plethora of manifestations. A recent trend is to market theatrical entertainment not in terms of conventional spectatorship but as an "immersive experience" and to fuse "the real" with particular kinds of audience participation (White 2013). This current trend for "participatory theater" and so-called immersive theater practices has exoticized the participant's emotional experience of a self-directed journey through a site-specific location such as an abandoned warehouse or a derelict hotel. The most famous exponents of immersive theater, Punchdrunk, borrow Gothic horror tropes in their attempt to market the site as the spectral character and the participants as the haunted protagonists who author and star in their own drama. Inspired by gaming, Punchdrunk has rapidly become mainstream and the corporate commodification of "the experiential" is becoming widespread—some see this packaging of experience as a particularly worrying development and a feature of the degree to which theater producers and theater makers have embraced neo-liberal agendas. If in the future the onus is on the emotional journey of the individual consumer and it becomes accepted that each journey can be different, this will challenge understandings of theater as a collective cathartic experience predicated on particular conventions of acting and the performative conventions of signaling certain emotions.

CHAPTER FIVE

The Visual Arts

CHARLES ALTIERI

I was asked to write 9,000 words on emotions in Western art from 1920 to the present. I have persisted because my fascination with the project outweighs my judgment that this topic requires a much larger stage. So I have chosen to limit my topic to painting, with brief excursions into sculpture and performance art. More important, I have decided that the only feasible way to capture the distinctiveness of the affects in art is to deal extensively with only a few works representing the affective consequences of major shifts in artistic orientations. I will pay scant attention to biography or social context or the range of important artists in the period because readers can easily gather that information if they care to.

This task leads me to a conventional story much challenged by those who want to broaden the scope of art history. The demands for concision (and my taste) simply make such coverage impossible. Therefore I will concentrate on how Modernist painting eventually emerges because of one major innovation—the shift from realism stressing what is seen to a spirit of realism that involves the position of the one making seeing possible. Painting came to depend on foregrounding affective forces involved in the act of making. And viewing becomes letting oneself give in to the range of feelings that attention to making can produce.

This shift in realisms occurred for a number of reasons. By about 1860, ambitious painters began working outside their studios, within the actual atmosphere they were attempting to represent. With this, Impressionism was born, and these new perspectives became an organizing force of new work: shadows, for example, were depicted not in chiaroscuro but in the variety of shades that much closer proximity to the image being rendered could reveal.

This realism-stressing painterly perspectival activity turned out to be capable of constant revision and development. Within twenty years a younger generation reared on Impressionist models developed what I have to call the spiritual implications of these moments of material plenitude. Vincent van Gogh, Paul Gauguin, Paul Cézanne, George Seurat, and their followers began to look inward at this new freedom of perspective, so the primary focus of painting became structuring activities reflecting on color and light as states opening into transcendent forces.[1]

Demands for a new art correlating this sense of manifest authorial energies with the range of sensations available from the material properties of the medium, like color, texture, and line, would generate an extensive set of possibilities to be explored by a wide range of modern and contemporary schools of painting (some of which we will study in detail). But before we turn to how particular paintings elicit affects, we need to set two conceptual frameworks. The first will involve how the artists understood the demands they were making on their audience's affective dispositions. The second will try to correlate how we talk in general about the affects with these demands so that we can develop a rudimentary vocabulary for approaching the paintings I isolate for attention.

Modernist painters negotiated the perceived affective dispositions of their audiences in different ways. Their primary concern was to provide alternatives to what they saw as Impressionism's bourgeois acceptance of the constraints of realist representation,[2] and the great adventure thus becomes mapping the affective resources painters can develop for their creative struggle against any kind of fidelity to what seem objective conditions. Second, in order to participate in these affective resources, painters had to distinguish between what Vasily Kandinsky's enormously influential *Concerning the Spiritual in Art* called the "coarser emotions, such as terror, joy, sorrow, etc . . . and the as yet nameless feelings of a finer nature." These feelings involve "emotions that we cannot put into words" (Harrison and Wood 2002: 84). Indeed, the feelings depend on the failure of words in order to evoke a basic difference between retinal experience and states that demand analogies with musical versions of what Hegel called "inner sensuousness."[3] Third, Modernists share a technical interest in developing this plastic consciousness as a condition that does not depend on shapes imitating the natural world. The desired response to a painting has to be based on how the activity in the work takes on visible force as the transformation of matter.[4] Finally, this flowering must be capable of resisting any literary understanding of affect based on narrative or dramatic models of identification. Affect in the new art has to be generated primarily by structural features of the work, stressing relations between shapes, lines, and colors that afford an intimacy not available in the abstractions of language.[5] Where traditional narrative accepts standard Western assumptions about the nature of time, space, and motivation, the new painting treated those assumptions as elements to be reworked by the relationships established in individual paintings.[6]

BREAKING THE CONCEPT OF EMOTION DOWN INTO ITS COMPONENTS

How do we honor these four demands to frame our responses in terms that resist our typical understandings of affect in practical and literary terms? The primary need for affect theory is to break the concept of emotion down into more flexible and mobile components, capable of aligning with what Braque called "a lyricism which stems entirely from the means employed" by the painter (Braque in Harrison and Wood 2002: 214). Let us imagine emotions as essentially narrative forms where some original impulse evokes in the brain an orientation to act on how the person's environment has changed. If what one observes elicits fear, the impulse is to flee, or in fictive situations to identify with the impulse to flee. When anger is represented, we are expected to identify with the urge to strike back or to plot revenge. And when the emotions represented are positive, like love or gratitude or joy, we identify with states like contentment and hope. But this orientation toward action poses a serious risk for painting because it leads painters and audiences to become literary: sensations governed by the painter's labors become less interesting than how the situation fits some recognizable plot.[7]

We need a theoretical framework capable of establishing the affective dimension when the painting focuses on changes in shades of color, or on intricate balances among radiating lines. Then we can isolate conditions of affective excitation from impulses to act upon them. This is why I want to emphasize feelings as an alternative focus for affective experience. All emotions produce associated feelings as responses to details in the situation. But, as we have seen, the concept of emotion structures those feelings into practical attitudes. What if we tried to isolate the domain of feelings themselves as locales enabling us to attend to the qualities of sensations, whether or not they eventually constitute coherent dramatic attitudes? Anger and despair are emotions; vividness and fluidity evoke feelings. So feelings tend to bring out qualities that motivate us to dwell in particular states of attention, even as we observe the feelings changing.[8] Feelings can accompany sensations involving modes of connection to other people, modes of attention to changes in physical states (including states of push and pull), degrees of intensity, conditions of struggle and disruption, shifts from expansive lightness of touch to heaviness of the oppressive, transitions like the emergence of surprise or the confirmation of boredom, and unlimited gradations of how our orientations toward paintings make of the world a more dynamic set of relations than we typically experience.

If we can focus on those particular states, we might even recognize more intricate and immediate modes of felt coherence that do not invite reconstruction into orientations toward action. And to experience such states is to recognize the plasticity of consciousness and to have the opportunity to celebrate how affective states are fundamental to our modes of experiencing the detail of the world. Feelings bind us to a concrete world that we displace when we make action more important than sheer states of attention. And feelings agglutinate rather than submit to any logic of cause and effect, in part because they typically involve states in which there is no past or future. They make vivid only a living present that continually unfolds in a series of relationships among features characterizing what we experience. The key issues in art become attention to shades of thickness and precision of line, or to spatial relations among shapes and contours, or how colors interact, or how the play is organized between mark, sign, image, and event in relation to brushwork. Feelings enliven a world that we see as immediately real, and often more concrete in its multiple presences than any standard notion of object can encompass.

POST-IMPRESSIONISM, EXPRESSIONISM, AND PROTO-CUBISM

The first distinctively twentieth-century heirs of Post-Impressionist versions of spirit were a group of French painters called the "Fauves" (or wild beasts) who ruled the Paris art scene from 1901 to 1907. These paintings by George Braque, Henri Matisse, and André Derain make it appear that colors are simply too lively to brook limitations imposed by nature. Here, the works free sensations almost entirely from practical judgments about what things really look like, demanding the adjustments in affective response that I have been discussing. Key examples of the Fauvist style (such as Matisse's *The Open Window*, 1905; National Gallery of Art, Washington DC) refuse to provide an accurate picture of anything except the free play of sensibility sponsored by nature, but are in no way obligated to it. So vividness of experience replaces accuracy to experience and in the process flaunts resistance to distinctions between inner and outer worlds.[9]

But this linking between psyche and the emergent scene can come to seem too easy, too free of the sense of demand and frightening otherness that is also a significant factor in our experience of the object world.[10] So there emerged two basic painterly ways of adapting Fauvist freedoms to how that object world can push back against the claims of

FIGURE 5.1: Henri Matisse, *The Open Window*, 1905. Photo by FineArt/Alamy Stock Photo.

subjective freedom. The first was a series of Expressionist styles in Germany and Eastern Europe that used painterly freedoms to emphasize tensions between the world outside the window and the agonies of the subject's position, never sure that it sees anything except its own pain and alienation. The subject becomes the object who cannot be at home in any world because of that excess of emotion that Fauvism managed to contain within the space of landscape. Two powerful examples of this Expressionist affective tension are Franz Marc's *The Large Blue Horses* (1911; Walker Art Center, Minneapolis), and, more extremely, Egon Schiele's *Self-Portrait with Lowered Head* (1912; Leopold Museum, Vienna), though for space constraints they cannot be discussed further here.

Cubism, the second development of Fauvism,[11] seems especially animated when it is seen in contrast to Expressionist art. That contrast helps us feel why objects matter as a discipline for freedom and why including perspectival shifts within the painting permits subjectivity to penetrate the space also inhabited by those objects. That is to say, the psyche need not feed endlessly on itself. In developing Cubism, Pablo Picasso turned from color to structure as his basic means of engaging the power of spirit and establishing an impersonal test for the intensities of personality. This is exemplified, for example, in the affective fields produced by *Reservoir at Horta* (1909; private collection).

FIGURE 5.2: Egon Schiele, *Self-Portrait with Lowered Head*, 1912, Wikimedia Commons.

SUPREMATISM AND SURREALISM

The Russian painter Kasimir Malevich insisted that there was a direct line from Cézanne's passion for geometric structure through Cubism to the Russian Suprematist painters, whose elimination of images and reliance on musical structure will have to stand here for all non-iconic abstraction. But there is a quite different heritage for how Vasily Kandinsky eventually developed abstraction by stressing the passions elicited by landscape as ultimately affording their own reality, apart from any objective sources (Kandinsky, 1977). Malevich was a brilliant and inexhaustible defender of the passions and values involved when painting refuses any anchor in representational forms.[12] By denying audiences the crutch that objects provide, Malevich manages to turn a rhetoric based on undoing objects into a rhetoric shaping possibilities for how paintings can establish dynamic forms by which minds can share in the disposition of energy relations that establish life's intensities. Consider, for example, Malevich's construction of intense dramatic aspects of spatial relations and contrasts in size in *Suprematism: Eight Red Rectangles* (1915: Stedelijk Museum, Amsterdam)—all the while keeping color constant.

Vasily Kandinsky's version of abstract painting is much closer to forces directly emerging in landscape. In fact abstraction becomes an impersonal, spiritualizing extension of German Expressionism that I think helps us place the very different dynamics won by Surrealism through its efforts to define how the unconscious manages to find abstraction. Like Kandinsky's abstraction, Surrealist art is concerned primarily with losing control of the will while finding, in something like chance, an intense moment where form takes

FIGURE 5.3: Kasimir Malevich, *Suprematism: Eight Red Rectangles*, 1915. Photo by Fine Art Images/Heritage Images/Getty Images.

hold. This version of Expressionist subjectivity handles its agonies by seeming to give up reflective consciousness so that it can find a satisfying link to natural grounds by yielding to states that relinquish fantasies of mastery. And the painters learn from Kandinsky what ecstasy can be in painting while refusing to separate spirit from nature and religion from pagan absorption in what might underlie our drives for pleasure and relation to other beings. Surrealist art then offers three basic general distinctive models of affect. There are first paintings that establish a sense that the images represent something that should focus emotion, although the painting refuses to give those emotions any coherent place in practical experience. In Giorgio Di Chirico's early work, the main precursor of Surrealism, and then in Salvador Dali's work, we have to shift our orientation from any sense emotion can connect to action to something like moods of disquiet and total alienation from what might be conditions for a decent life. Second, there is the delighted mystification of René Magritte's magic realism. And finally there are the biomorphic fantasies of Joan Miró, Jean Arp, and Max Ernst that I think bring out the fullest possibilities of Surrealist style.[13]

I want to look closely at one painting by Joan Miró because I think he is the best and most suggestive painter of the group. Consider how his *Personnage Rythmic* (1934; Kunstammlung, Nordrhein-Westfalen)[14] is content to dwell in fantasy, without any anxious reaching for a relation to the real. This painting is quite close to Fauvist notions of creativity because there are no constraints imposed by objects; there is only a complex relation between design and figuration that defines the work of imagination as enabling us to share an oddly friendly biomorphic figurative space, shaped by a distinctively human intimacy with vaguely inhuman aspects of sexual attachment. The painting holds out the promise that we can treat sexuality solely in terms of its enticing materiality.

This sense of permission comes oddly from the painting's very strong sense of order—first in its vertical divisions, then in the work the colors do to form a virtual three-dimensional space so that we have the illusion of freely moving around among yielding body parts. The work of the colors leads us to realize that this painting not only represents this hallucinatory space but mobilizes it, and mobilizes the viewer in the process to gain close access to something like a pure sexuality, not confused by other kinds of human intimacies. The reds, the yellows, and the white all create illusions of depth counterpointing the vertical forms. And once we experience this formal construction of a place in which to settle, the rich textures and intricate background shadings come into play, as soft enticements to stay where the image places us. What begins as background takes on a sense of depth, as if one could step into what one's own feelings generate. Maybe our lives could be richer if we could dwell only among yielding body parts without all the trouble of mind and personality.

But what if we could add mind and personality without losing this sense of freedom? This opportunity becomes feasible in the works of sculpture combining Surrealist principles with a strong sense of the work as becoming an expressive object rather than offering interpretations of experience. Such sculpture emphasizes how, in diminishing the role of the creative subject as shaping the object, Surrealism tends to make any kind of intentionality or purposiveness a result of how the object establishes its modes of presence. Such objects become fully living beings that do not comment on experience but define its possible locales.

I stress this connection because I want to account for several of the generative forces that made sculpture an especially vital form in modern culture, from the work of Henry Moore to Tony Cragg and David Smith. And I want to characterize the importance to woman artists like Barbara Hepworth, Louise Bourgeois, and Louise Nevelson of this sense of speaking by creating living objects that function at the limits of rationality. My example will be Hepworth's very large *Figure for Landscape* (1960; Hirshhorn Museum, Tate Museum and Getty Museum). I was attracted first to the surface of the piece. The curving lines have an enticing rhythmic quality supplemented by the intricate balance of the three voids—two centered and vertical, and one an off-center blend of vertical and horizontal. And the texturing of the bronze makes a wonderful supplement to the rhythmic movement. The viewer seems bound to participate in the way the bronze attunes to the space it composes. The surface becomes an endlessly varied experience of what a body might feel like in each of its varied encounters with light and air—this is the life of an object freed to be totally aware of its environment without surrendering its own modes of presence. But then one realizes that the open circles also provide the opposite kind of experience: this figure combines the greed to take everything in and the vulnerability enabling it to risk trying to absorb all that otherness. Here, then, emerges a condition of narcissism defining an ultimate openness and an ultimate willingness to pay the price of that openness, with dignity, majesty, and self-control. This object does not represent these affective states but completely embodies them.

ABSTRACT EXPRESSIONISM

The second half of the twentieth century effectively began with Jackson Pollock arriving at his enormously influential drip paintings after years of Surrealist fascination with how visual art might convey a sense of encountering secrets, and relishing their hold on him.[14] Pollock's movement from paintings like *Guardians of the Secret* to the full action painting of *Autumn Rhythm* shifted from speculating on a secret the artist cannot possess to making the energy and distribution of force within the painting the actual revelation of what had begun as hidden and inaccessible. Pollock then offered another extension of the work of art as a living object. His drip paintings reversed Surrealism's investments in trying to provide images for the unconscious life so that they can pursue a painterly surface that has no secrets and needs no hidden depths of meaning. While Malevich and

FIGURE 5.4: Barbara Hepworth, *Figure for Landscape*, 1960. Photo by Peter Barritt/Alamy Stock Photo.

Mondrian built their non-iconic constructions out of powerful contrasts between figure and ground, Pollock established an all-over design that forced all the elements of the painting to be on the same plane. Line is not drawn on a background but dripped, so that background and foreground offer continually shifting aspects of a single constructive process. This process destroys the possibility of any shape taking on impersonal and universal value. Everything depends on individual creativity and the energy it has the capacity to sustain.

It is easiest to see what is admirable and challenging in Pollock's drip paintings if we compare his two best-known works for the various effects his line and coloring can compose—*Number 1 (Lavender Mist)* 1950 in the National Gallery of Art, Washington D.C.; and *Autumn Rhythm* (1950; Metropolitan Museum of Art, New York). Both paintings are absolutely subjective—but only because they provide a living environment for the impersonal powers of line seemingly free to explore the effects it can compose. Yet the two are radically different in soliciting affect. The first painting seems like an elegant spider's nest illuminated by a sudden burst of sunlight. Its line is essentially loose filament, establishing its own slow temporality as it unfolds through seemingly endless possible variations. Because there is no background, illusions of occasional depth are created by thickenings of line or poolings of paint. So, it seems as if much of the feeling elicited by the painting is produced by the conjunction of light and intricate movement within a quite capacious space—with light and movement each honoring the force of the other as interacting modes of calm expansiveness. There may be no other painting with such

THE VISUAL ARTS

FIGURE 5.5: Jackson Pollock, *Autumn Rhythm Number 30*, 1950. Photo by Peter Horree/Alamy Stock Photo.

FIGURE 5.6: Jackson Pollock, *Number I (Lavender Mist)*, 1950. Photo by B Christopher/Alamy Stock Photo.

generous invitations to linger within its fluid surface movements or to rest in the way line gathers itself into surface units and promises a shallow, but at the same time, infinite sense of resonant recess.

In contrast, *Autumn Rhythm* seems all tumult, all need for the lines to find some kind of peace before some threatened doom takes place. Here there is no generous embrace of various levels of being. There is only the struggle between lines and the shapes they both create and bind in order to occupy the surface plane. Yet somehow the struggle manages to contain itself within relatively open spaces on the vertical edges, as if opposition sufficed to produce effective boundaries. More important, the struggle produces a marvelous blend of shades of tan and black that offers its own efforts to establish rhythmic composure. All four corners of the painting stress heavier black lines, with the effect of releasing and structuring the whites and tans that seem to possess their own light. That light and the kinds of surfacing associated with it suggest within the turbulence why the suffering might be worthwhile.

Pollock had significant peers also struggling to find in Abstraction what their early Surrealist-inspired work could not afford—preeminently Willem de Kooning, Mark Rothko, Robert Motherwell, and Barnett Newman. Their combined influence can be seen in two kinds of work—the color field painting of artists like Morris Louis, Jean-Paul Riopelle, and Helen Frankenthaler, and the ironizing of the entire project of pursuing absolute aesthetic states free from cultural contexts, whose most demanding examples are the quite different attitudes taken up to images by Robert Rauschenberg and Andy Warhol.

Bracket (Triptych) (1989; San Francisco Museum of Modern Art)[15], a large late work by Joan Mitchell, exemplifies the affective power of color field painting because the triptych form elicits complicated structural effects which enhance how brushstroke, color, and space take on agency. The most striking feature of the painting may be how Mitchell uses the contrast between the central panel and smaller adjoining panels to establish different relations between figure and ground. The middle panel emphasizes distinctive brushstrokes of varying textures that construct an overall dynamic contrast between the blues performing an elegant arabesque in the upper regions and warm yellows and gold that recede into a casual lightness. Here it is blue that asserts itself in a relaxed fullness, while the warm colors seem freed to drift into a kind of peacefulness born of lack of conflict. At the bottom edge, the yellows dissipate into an off-white, as if the image were merging with some state of sheer simplicity. But we never forget the blue establishes an amazing push-and-pull structure in both vertical and horizontal dimensions, largely because the white background yields space while also quietly insisting on its powers to frame the whole in a kind of peaceful coexistence.

In contrast, the framing panel on the left does not allow distinctive brushstrokes the freedom to find their own rhythmic place in the whole. Here colors congeal into tangled masses, where warm and cold colors cannot escape one another. Gold and green become especially sinister because their flatness pulls in everything else, including the fluid whites that have such liberating effects in the middle panel. And the white background simply has no power to hold off the colors as they take on density and reflect a force like gravity that has no respect for differences. (We might speak of despair if we dare to offer psychological analogs.) But the right panel is more mysterious, keyed by the more muted and darker residue of the blue arabesque just above the center. This panel has neither the peacefulness of the center nor the loss of freedom to gravity of the left one. Perhaps it presents the kind of freedom that demands struggle but manages to preserve identity. Colors still manage to breathe, but under pressure, as the yellow finally takes on an interactive role within the vital upper half of the painting. Taken together, the interplay among the three panels brings each element of force into complex and shifting relations that make us aware of how much of our emotional lives can take such elemental forms.

I will not comment on Warhol because his characteristically flat attitude is quite well known and I have nothing to add. But this is not the case with Robert Rauschenberg, whose work in the 1950s transformed the future of painting. That work demanded involvement in the messiness of practical life in ways that made it very difficult to maintain the dream that abstract painting could dwell in a timeless world populated by forms and colors.[17] In *Monogram* (1955–59; Moderna Museet, Stockholm), for example, Rauschenberg constructed a sculpture consisting of a standing, taxidermied goat, encircled by a car tire as a kind of halo. The goat stands on a painting, has been eating paint, and has excreted a tennis ball. Such work led many artists to emulate Rauschenberg in shifting from the myth of creative expression as a mode of willing the union of form and content to a kind of dancing within the junkyard that modern visual culture had become.

Consider Rauschenberg's *Bed* (1955; Museum of Modern Art, New York). The title alone provides a clue that much has changed. The title claims universality and it puts us in the material world of generic elements. Gone is anything special about whose bed it is or what formal considerations it might elicit. Yet the impersonality of both title and work confronts the audience with a possible level of bemused irony. This impersonally rendered bed might in fact be more personal than any set of lines or marks like Pollock's. Pollock claims directness, but his marks are mediated by market interests and cultural ambitions—aspects of the personal that he does not want us to see in the work. Rauschenberg can claim that this bed has shared much of someone's life: indeed it is the place where art begins in dreaming. What can be more personal? No wonder the object is in part so passionately rendered, and in part so coolly copied as simply something industrial for which the personal investments are only contingent.

No wonder too that this shrewd ironist would say, "Painting relates to both art and life. Neither can be made. (I try to act in the gap between the two.)" (Rauschenberg 1996: 321). Is this bed a painting? It hangs on a wall. But it has three dimensions like a sculpture. And

FIGURE 5.7: Robert Rauschenberg, *Monogram*, 1955–59. Photo by SuperStock/Alamy Stock Photo.

it is a real object as well as an imitation of a real object offered for reflection. In fact, Rauschenberg's combines have been called flat-bed railroad cars because they seem to invite any actual commodity onto their surface. In this case the bed itself offers a surface soliciting an intense physical process of painting. For the real object would be painfully plain without distinctive colors, with the most intense indicating where the sleeper tosses and turns, and where perhaps dreams or passions or tears find expression in paint, even though the paint only renders the material effect of the dreams rather than exploring their content.

Finally, what passes as mind in this painting, as well as in much of Rauschenberg's work, involves processes of valuing that are very different from the traditions leading to Pollock's work. This painting is as careful in getting right the dull, store-bought pattern of the quilt as it is in marking the site of the sleeper's passions. Just as the work honors the practical status of bed, the labor of painting honors the fact that art's relation to life is probably not something that makes life more noble. Painting is stuck with life because it is always already mired within it. So, art does not dictate to life so much as adorn it or find ways of embracing what is inescapable. Perhaps art's role between art and life makes it possible for us to enjoy both, always with the ironic awareness that there is probably no workable alternative. Life makes our bed; art helps us find ways of sleeping in it.

CONCLUSION: CONTEMPORARY ARTISTS

Rauschenberg's *Bed* could be a satisfying emblem for the kinds of feeling many artworks embodied toward the end of the twentieth century. But this model of feeling could not satisfy artists for long because its blending of irony with sheer acceptance of social conditions does not reflect sufficiently on the horror of many of those conditions or on the difficulties involved in aligning such painting with attitudes useful in actual life. Maybe art could find intensity in facing questions of usefulness, especially with regard to making political judgments and testing alternative approaches to social mores. And maybe artists could develop constructions that actually incorporate the audience rather than insist on the object's own separate space on the walls of galleries and museums.

Consider first the pain and challenge involved in painters having to recognize how the history of their art reflected the racial and gendered exclusions dominant in the larger society. How could visual art produce any significant response to this condition, given the ways in which it seems to demand verbal analysis? I want to discuss how Kara Walker engages the problem because she develops shifts in the medium of painting capable of exhibiting how visual experience might make a difference in our attitudes toward race. Walker usually focuses on the heritage of slavery by working in dark silhouettes against white backgrounds. Silhouette reduces scenes to essentials, to how the shapes memories carry can articulate enduring resentments that the painter can at least hope address visceral memories for her audience. Silhouette also reminds us of children's books. But for Walker children's tales are those that block assimilation into the mainstream society, precisely because of the foundational memories they render in black and white for black and white.

In order to elaborate how Walker deploys contrasts, we will consider one image of her *Emancipation Approximation* (1999–2000; Bellevue Art Museum, Bellevue, WA).[18] Here we find sharp oppositions between white and black, erect posture and bent submission, full skirt with flowing hair versus cropped hair, bent body, and marvelous naked feet, and finally something close to culture versus nature. But the visual fact of sharp contrast is even more important than the particulars. These material differences quickly morph into the presence of painful forces that can only be suggested in visual terms—like which body is above the other, which body has freedom of movement rather than enforced labor, and, most important, which body is likely to take this image to heart as a figure of implacable resentments underlying the enforced subordinations of slavery. So, while this image seems bound to historical circumstances, the abstract structure of differences reminds us of how the scene transcends those circumstances as a vision of why racial relations in the USA are still deeply troubled.

Where racial problems admit stark contrasts, matters of gender today seem more dependent on exposing subtle tendencies that art devoted to these questions has to piece out. The French photographer and conceptual artist Sophie Calle brilliantly responded to this need for subtlety in *Prenez Soin de Vous*, an installation for the 2007 Venice Biennale. This work is introduced by the text of an email from a man breaking up a love affair with her that ends with the words she chooses for her title. Calle does not directly respond to the message. In this case she does not need to express any overt rage or grief because she can simply quote the email, so that its blind vanity and assumptions of male privilege can effectively perform objective judgment upon his character—nowhere more strikingly than when he constantly refers to the difficult heroism of choosing to break up so that he can return to the other women whom Calle insisted he stopped seeing. One sentence should suffice to reproduce the appalling sense of entitlement the writer reveals: "Your gentleness toward me I will miss terribly." One might almost be able to pity the knot he gets into trying to justify himself, were he not so gifted in providing for himself a pity that solicits our ignoring what he makes manifest.

Calle is smart enough just to quote the email without overt response that might drag her into the morass of self-defensiveness he exemplifies. But she does act on the message by asking 107 professional women and artists to comment on the message: "Analyze it, comment on it, dance it, sing it. Exhaust it. Understand it for me. Answer for me. It was a way of taking the time to break up. A way of taking care of myself" (http://cargocollective.com/kathrynlawes/Sophie-Calle-analysis). This taking care is the crucial point of the work. He tells her to take care of herself and he presents the message as necessary for taking care of himself. And although "care" is something woefully lacking in his actual message, she finds a way to care for herself that does not depend on any narrow male pretense to generosity. By asking for the reactions of these women and publishing them as aspects of the exhibition, Calle literally makes the audience of woman active within the work.

In fact, the work defines a kind of care that invites many possibilities for expressing both concern for Calle as wronged woman and rage at the general ways men are likely to stage themselves as caregivers. The personal becomes political because the range of reactions enacts two directions of care—for Calle, and for producing a community among the women without collapsing differences and without demanding any shared rhetoric. The sense of concern, the shared sense of wrong, and the fact that all women are likely to appreciate the range of reactions makes this a community attentive to differences in style and commitment because of a pressing awareness of a shared vulnerability. And art becomes political simply because of what is displayed as emotional content and as more general effects of bonding: there is no need for general rhetoric.

I would love to conclude with these two powerful reminders of how artists can address painful divisions in social life. But I think there is a counter current in contemporary art that also has to enter this story. Even the best artists, or the worst political situations, eventually exhaust the possibilities for fresh imaginative approaches. After all, we know now the depths of our problems, and the work toward solutions is much more a practical matter than a matter of disposing our imaginations. So, artists have to ask what kind of

FIGURE 5.8: Sophie Calle, detail of *Prenez Soin de Vous*, 2007. Photo by Eric Vandeville/Gamma-Rapho via Getty Images.

FIGURE 5.9: Sophie Calle, further detail of Prenez Son de Vous, 2007. Photo by Eric Vandeville/Gamma-Rapho via Getty Images.

presence art can have in the world when it can no longer rely on the idealizations posed by Modernism, or on the modes of overt irony posited by the disillusioned heirs of Modernism? My first figure, the East German émigré Gerhard Richter, is generally recognized as the best painter still working today for his capacity to absorb post-modernist ironies into elegant and sumptuous modes of chilly compassion. The second is the much younger Nicole Eisenman, an American who manages to provide forms of social commentary that nonetheless insist on the complex integrity of pictorial space, thus finding a place for constructivist abstraction within a commitment to representation.

Richter emigrated from East to West Germany in 1961. As he adjusted to the West he had to work through disgust with both systems—with demands for painterly realism in the service of an ideology of cultural revolution and with the West's cynical submission to market-driven values and epistemological skepticism represented by the dominant figure of Andy Warhol. So Richter found himself trying to put all his hope for society into the effort to stage in painting a conflict between his conviction about the value of the particular images he created and an ironic self-consciousness wary of making large social claims for those convictions. What grounds could those large claims have in a world described by Jean Baudrillard as one where "the real becomes not only that which can be reproduced, but that which is always already reproduced. . . . Today the real and the imaginary are confounded in the same operational totality" (Jean Baudrillard, "Symbolic Exchange and Death," in Harrison and Wood 2002: 1019). But while Pop Art played on the manifestations of that confusion, Richter tried to develop an alternative sense of the real based on the power of painting to establish significance for its constructive activity. Painting could have a reality just because of the made thing's capacity to communicate modes of seeing.

Early in his career Richter used two primary devices to deal with how absolutely our world was a world of endless mediation: he would blur paintings so as not to claim representational adequacy and he would derive paintings from photographs so as to claim that any reality effects he established were not claims to represent the real but to bring out features of what were already representations. The artistic consequences of these devices are perhaps strongest in *Ema (Nude on a Staircase)* (1966; Museum Ludwig, Cologne), the second of two paintings he composed as homage to and critique of Duchamp's *Nude Descending a Staircase*. Self-consciousness about dealing with simulacra pervades this painting—from the title, to the photo from which the image of his first wife is taken, to the blurred staircase and the delicate colors for the image.

The image in *Ema* is striking because of the blend of ethereal and concrete achieved primarily by the intricate modulation of color tones. Then there is the marvelous vulva, virtually at the center of the painting and colored as a combination of the brown of the stairs and the modulation of blond hair and slightly shadowed face. (I think of Picasso's alignment of head and hands in his *Portrait of Kahnweiler*, especially because of the strange dark shape in her hair that echoes the pudenda.) Here the prominent vulva seems to echo the way that the concentration on her face seems an effort to resist the blur so that the body might come into definition apart from the stairs. In one register Ema is barely distinct from the stairs, but that proximity also brings out her difference from her

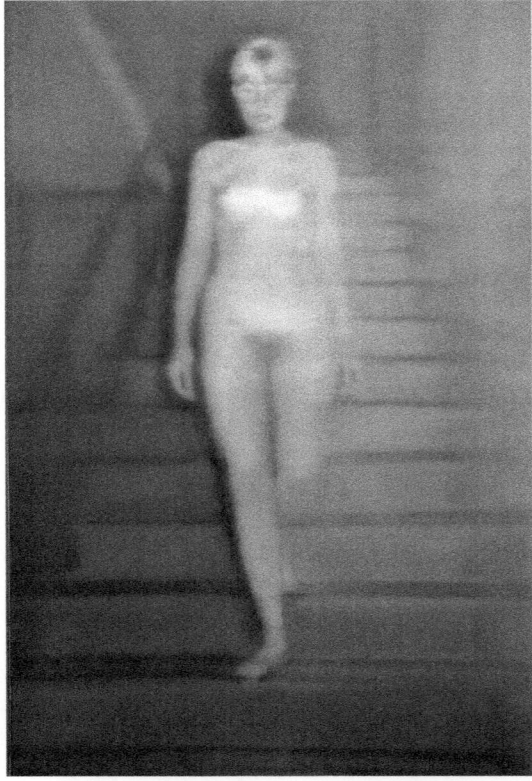

FIGURE 5.10: Gerhard Richter, *Ema (Nude on a Staircase)*, 1966. Photo by Peter Horree/Alamy Stock Photo.

surroundings as well as the painting's difference from its ancestors. Her care in descending the stairs matches Richter's care in modulating flesh tones into a higher key while at the same time binding them to the color of the stairs and of the background. She becomes luminous, as if her concentration were visible in her flesh, and as if the painter himself dared not miss any step in realizing her delicacy. This after all is not just a nude descending a staircase or Richter's own *Woman Descending a Staircase* (1965; Art Institute of Chicago). This is titled *Ema*, his wife. We see from this title that for Richter all of the self-consciousness cultivated by post-modernist sensibilities can become channeled into clearing a space in which painting also composes a testimony for completely direct personal feelings—so long as one can hold off on attempting to put what the painting allows us to see into language. The painter in effect aligns with her care for emerging against this background. In fact this constructivist care brings Richter's self-consciousness through the post-modern back to the best of Modernist ambitions to produce "a lyricism which stems entirely from the means employed" by the painter.

The one feature of Modernism that Richter cannot recuperate is any sense of the freedom from nature and from culture that was celebrated by the Fauves and embraced by virtually all of the painters whom we have considered, even Rauschenberg at play in the dump. Richter sees that deep passion need not and probably cannot be reconciled to a rhetoric of freedom. He makes us recognize this contrast most fully in a non-objective painting, *Ice (2)* (1989; Art Institute of Chicago). I see here significant echoes of Pollock's action paintings, especially the lack of any defined background, the way apparently free color spots emerge within the course of the life of particular lines, and the event of black shapes near the bottom. Yet, as the title indicates, this is as far from Pollock's line as abstract painting can get. Here there is no visible active agency, except for the almost painful sense of carefully self-reflexive composition. It is almost as if the mind were trying to present what it sees without the mediation of any personal traits except the hand. And even the hand wielding a brush makes rare appearances within what seems mostly done by palette knife.

The major effect of this concentration on mind is that it strips the painting of any grounding metaphysical principles or modes of awareness that can claim objectivity beyond the senses. There is no "dynamic balance" (Mondrian) or "inner feeling for the primitive" (Kandinsky) or "real living form" (Malevich). There is in *Ice (2)* not even a projected sense of unity that establishes a synthetic feel of balance and purposiveness. Instead we have to speak with Gilles Deleuze of "assemblages," of tentative and shifting units of attention which do not stabilize a whole but motivate attention to the evocative range of differences possible within a given set of details.[19] Unity is provisional and motivated primarily by particular perspectives. Yet there is an abstract unity on another level, which is simply the totality of the painting as object more than as design. Here I think the totality is given by the title. This painting offers an adventure in a coldness or distance from the proximity of human passions. And as such it can claim both freedom from any particular passion and an inclusiveness capable of sponsoring many quite intense local feelings, especially in terms of the relations between black and red marks in tension with the insistent verticality of the overall structure. But the painting seems to make clear that to concentrate on the local feelings is to miss the force of this totality, simply because of its capacity to solicit and to frame these multiple events. I am tempted to say that Richter's insistence on his work not being about anything in particular reinforces the sense that the affects elicited by his paintings simply prepare our attention to notice resonant differences. *Ice (2)* is not an idealization *of* mind but a realization *as* mind aware

FIGURE 5.11: Gerhard Richter, *Ice (2)*, 1989 (oil on canvas). © Gerhard Richter 2018 (0084).

of its dual roles to register the fascination of different events and to keep its distance from being seduced by anything less than a totality that can satisfy the self-consciousness from which it originates.

Nicole Eisenman cannot compete with Richter's capaciousness of mind. But she can and does revel in the kind of alternative Richter provides to the concepts of freedom deriving from the Fauves. Like Richter, Eisenman cultivates a kind of freedom that is a capacity to trust in the literalness of what imagination produces, without highlighting features that warrant any kind of allegory or interpretive recasting of the image. She cannot keep people from verbal interpretation, but she can make it highly likely that the interpretation will turn out to be painfully inadequate in relation to what the work makes present as a literal condition. Eisenman furnishes this literalness across a variety of typical social scenes, all rendered with biting wit and striking color combinations. But I think she raised her work to another level for a show at New York's Museum of Modern Art in 2014 called "Forever Now: Contemporary Painting in an Atemporal World." The whole show is relevant for extensions of the roles Richter saw painting still capable of playing. But I want to focus now on one image, *Groundsweller*,[20] which I consider the most elegant and intriguing in a series of intensely and variably colored faces she exhibited.

The most obvious feature of experiencing this painting is the simple joy one feels in contemplating its clean lines. But we also have to ask what is the source of this joy, or what specific aspects of joy are we experiencing? A large factor here is the strange geometric quartering of a face into four apparently arbitrary color units. Such arbitrariness done with such a sharp sense of presence produces a sense of contingent completeness—largely because nothing is tentative and nothing grapples with problems of getting an exact likeness. And there cannot be anything wrong here because the primary activity involves playing with the form of a face rather than the rendering of any kind of deep truth or deep feeling. Paraphrasing the poet and literary critic T. S. Eliot, perhaps only those who have sought identification with various kinds of suffering in the face can appreciate fully the category shift by which the face just is what the painter wants it to be. Eliot of course probably did not inhale marijuana, the projected action of the painting. But he probably could have appreciated why the painting presents the colors as both on the face and in the face. The equation between these two intimate phenomenological feelings suggests that inside can be outside and outside inside, with very little difference between these locales.

If "on" and "in" seem compatible or identical, the entire concept of expression seems oddly irrelevant to these faces, again because there is nothing to be expressed but everything to enjoy as surface subject to the whim of the painter, and perhaps to the desire of the represented face if it could imagine this level of interaction with the artist. To deal adequately with this painting we may have to find an alternative to the roles concepts of expression have played in our appreciation of the visual arts. This is a huge task. But Eisenman's painting may make it a desirable one because simply accepting the colors of the moment seems such a satisfying alternative to the anxieties about recognition and misrecognition fundamental to our discourses about expression. Here we feel for the combination of colors as direct information staging the face as a particular state. The whimsical geometrical forms on that face also create a basic aspect of how feeling for the colors might be possible. Perhaps we might enjoy our sensual lives more if we imagined the organs as capable of shifting shapes and colors. Perhaps there are multiple sensations that these configurations might adapt to for which we are now ill-suited. Perhaps painting itself has come to seem on life-support because it has not yet learned to play sufficiently with its materials. If paintings can bring out the possible consequence of changing the questions we ask of them, there may be a very interesting essay in 100 years on the history of emotion in the painting of the twenty-first century.

CHAPTER SIX

Literature

GILLIAN WHITLOCK AND GRACE MOORE

Emotions are not mere icing on the cake—at best a pleasurable distraction, at worst a mystifying spell to be broken so that the work of hard-nosed analysis can begin. Rather, affective engagement is the very means by which literary works are able to reach, orient, and even reconfigure their readers.

—Felski 2015b: 177

The literary critic J. Hillis Miller has written of the relationship between a reader and a text as a "love affair," highlighting the deep affect which can characterize a readerly connection with a text. Miller continues, "Reading, like being in love, is by no means a passive act. It takes much mental, emotional, and even physical energy. Reading requires a positive effort. One must give all one's faculties to re-creating the work's imaginary world as fully and as vividly as possible within oneself" (Miller 2005: 120). What Miller describes here is a total surrender to the world of the text, in which readers plunge into the lives of characters, often abandoning the credulity with which they approach the real world, and at the same time developing deeply affective responses to representations of lives that are totally fictitious.

While today we might think in terms of "fan fiction," identifying lovers of Jane Austen as "Janeites," or imagining Brontë enthusiasts clambering across the Yorkshire Moors to immerse themselves in the world of Anne, Charlotte, and Emily, the connections between reading and love are long-standing and, at times, controversial. Flaubert's Emma Bovary, for instance, developed so passionate a love for romance novels that she was no longer able to distinguish between fact and fiction, racking up debts, committing adultery, and eventually taking poison in a bid to live out the life of a romantic heroine. As the sociologist Frank Furedi reminds us, though, it was Socrates who first observed that "written ideas had the potential to acquire a life of their own," pointing to and, arguably, theorizing the reader's emotional agency. Furedi continues to list the many subsequent authorities, including the Roman poet Juvenal and the Renaissance writer Barnaby Rich, who warned of the dangers of being deluged by books and their imaginary worlds (Furedi 2015: 4–5).

The pleasures of reading have always been a divisive issue, generating emotional responses both from those who approve of reading and those who disapprove. Reading *about* emotions can also arouse extreme affective reactions, since literature plays on and with feelings, and readers respond to characters, plot, and style. Indeed, two independent studies, one by David Comer Kidd and Emanuele Castano at the New School, USA (Kidd and Castano 2013) and another by Dutch researchers P. Matthijs Bal and Martijn Veltkamp (Bal and Veltkamp 2013), have both concluded that exposure to "great" literature can heighten readerly empathy.

This affective identification between readers and texts has long been an object of interest to professional readers who identify themselves as literary critics. Deidre Shauna Lynch has helpfully identified the blurred boundaries between amateur and professional readerships in her study *Loving Literature* (2014). Although literary criticism may purport to be an objective discipline, it is inevitably an emotional activity, with approaches like close reading attempting to capture the aesthetic pleasures of the text, and literary theory becoming ever more politicized as it reflects the arrival in the academy of those who have traditionally been excluded.[1] As the cultural theorist Stuart Hall wisely reminds us, "What we say is always 'in context'. Positioned," regardless of any claims we may make to objectivity (Hall 1993: 392). And, if we follow this remark through to its logical conclusion, we will see that the interpretation of literature can only ever be an emotional, subjective activity.

Neal Oxenhandler commented that, "Affect and its cognates (emotion, desire, the ineffable, the sublime) reappear throughout the history of criticism with seemingly irreducible opacity" (Oxenhandler 1988: 105). Oxenhandler continued to note that, "Although emotive terms serve to locate certain crucially sensitive areas in the reading process, they themselves have never become the locus of a sustained theoretical account" (ibid.). While emotions have thus always underpinned readerly responses, their role within critical approaches has not always been fully recognized. Psychoanalysis, memory studies, and trauma studies all implicitly engage with the emotions, yet it is only recently that these approaches have been identified as aspects of a broader "History of Emotions" methodology, or part of what Alan Palmer has identified as the quest to understand "fictional minds." Palmer's approach, which is informed by the work of the early emotions theorist and psychologist William James (brother of the novelist Henry James), identifies itself as "an interdisciplinary project that is . . . designed to be a source book . . . of some of the ideas about the mind that are current in the various real-mind discourses" (Palmer 2004: 4, our ellipses). Palmer thus captures the cross-disciplinary nature of emotions theory, while at the same time pointing to its applicability to those in "real life," as well as fictional characters.

The "affective turn" which, Jan Plamper argues convincingly, coincided with the aftermath of the terror attacks of September 11, 2001, brought the emotions to the fore of literary and cultural studies, perhaps in an attempt to heighten their sense of relevance during a time of crisis.[2] For Plamper, the event "triggered a tsunami of overwrought communication" arising from the instantaneous nature of electronic media, which for many provided an outlet for instant and raw emotional reactions (Plamper 2015: 60). Furthermore, the "communicative fallout" led to a period of emotional contemplation, emphasizing the need to study how feelings inform action, both in fiction and in fact. In such a context, reading can offer a way to channel emotional extremes, while fiction is also a space through which we are able to rehearse our responses to the wider world.

This chapter will bring emotional engagements with literary texts together with a range of theoretical approaches, the majority of which have emerged since 2001. Focusing on particular novels which adapt nineteenth-century classics, we will consider the emotional dialogue between a reader and a text. The revisionist novel is a particularly useful subgenre for this type of exploration, since the reworking of an historical master text is inevitably an emotional act: sometimes a labor of love, sometimes an impassioned attempt to give voices to figures who may have been silenced, or to chastise a long-dead author for an omission. Responses to these kinds of novels are often extreme, and by tracking the passage of literary texts through acts of reading such as these, we see how novels *move* in and through us intimately, how they now return to enter "inside the skin," enticing readers to become "naked on the page" in experiences of empathetic reading. The chapter will therefore explore how recent research on the emotions understands this emotional entanglement in contemporary fiction, while also addressing the stakes at play in scenes of reading such as these.

"ARCHIVING MACHINES"

In a hut on a beach in Bougainville a teacher, Mr. Watts, reads Charles Dickens's *Great Expectations* aloud to his students, a chapter a day for fifty-nine days, and the character Pip comes alive. "I felt I had been spoken to by this young boy Pip," the child Matilda tells us; "The surprising thing is where I'd found him . . . in a book. No one had told us kids to look there for a friend. Or that you could slip inside the skin of another" (Jones 2006: 21). The children *hear* Magwitch, and they *feel* his ominous presence: "it was like the convict was in the classroom with us" (ibid.); they share Pip's fear and create shrines to him on the beach—with fatal results when the militias arrive. In Lloyd Jones's novel *Mister Pip* (2006), Dickens's text is recreated for the Pacific—literally so as the class laboriously recalls the novel while their island is held hostage in a brutal guerrilla war. The epigraph to Jones's novel is from Umberto Eco: "Characters migrate." In this Pacific migration of Dickens's work, listening and then recollecting the narrative is about faith and belief, about reading to survive. Azar Nafisi's memoir *Reading Lolita in Tehran* is also about reading in order to survive. During the autumn of 1995 a literature professor whose career has been cut short by the totalitarian Islamist republic creates a private class for seven of her best and most committed students. They meet in the living room of her apartment, a highly aestheticized space with its lovely vista of the mountains surrounding the city captured in the mirror, with pastries and good coffee. Her students relish the pleasures of reading empathetically, becoming "naked on the page," casting aside their chadors to enter a space of reading where they encounter Nabokov, Fitzgerald, Austen. At their first meeting they read Nabokov's *Invitation to a Beheading* and the professor introduces them to "upsilamba," a word that captures the pleasures of reading: "a sign of that vague sense of joy, the tingle in the spine Nabokov expected his readers to feel in the act of reading fiction: it was a sensation that separated the good readers, as he called them, from the ordinary ones" (Nafisi 2003: 21). In Bernhard Schlink's *The Reader* (*Der Vorleser* in German: "one who reads aloud") a boy reads literary classics—Tolstoy, Homer, Schiller, Lessing—aloud to his illiterate lover in bed, beginning a life-long practice of reading and auditing literature in an intercourse that is entangled with questions of guilt, shame, and responsibility in Germany after the Holocaust, where the legacies of genocide remain haunting and unresolved. "The geological layers of our lives rest so tightly one on top of the other that we always come up against earlier events in later ones," the narrator tells us, "absolutely present and alive" (Schlink 1997: 216). Here, reading is at the heart of this vivid "absolute" presence of the past in the present.

As readers of contemporary fiction, we encounter scenes of reading such as these repeatedly, where literary "friends" such as Pip, Magwitch, Lolita, and Gatsby (among others) return once more, with feeling. Novels recite their precursors to create feedback loops, becoming little "archiving machines" (Clough and Halley 2007: 3) animated in and through experiences of reading in volatile networks of affect.[3]

ETHICS OF READING

A central concern here is of the *uses* of literature now. In the epigraph to this chapter, Rita Felski turns to aesthetic experience and argues that we are sorely in need of critique that nurtures richer and deeper accounts of how selves interact with texts at scenes of reading, and descriptions of "the affective attachments and cognitive reorientations that characterize the experience of reading a book . . ." (Felski 2008: 11). Reading, Felski argues, "fuses both cognitive and affective impulses": a logic of recognition, an aesthetic experience of enchantment, the creation of social knowledge, and the experience of being shocked by what we read. For Felski, the affective turn in theory in the recent past has created an opening to explore "reflective reading" and to develop accounts of why texts matter to us, what energies, pleasures, and enthusiasms they inspire in readers. Those powerful narratives of passionate reading in Bougainville, Germany, and Tehran resonate with Felski's questioning of how literary texts are mobilized in and through practices of reading, inspiring intense responses and inchoate emotions. Reading itself, she suggests, can be a possession, an invasion of the self by a text in ways we cannot fully control or explain. Most particularly this affective force and experience of literary works eludes the training in reading "against the grain" that Felski describes as a "rhetoric of suspicious reading" that has become powerful in literary pedagogy (Felski 2015b: 187). In turning to the emotions, Felski sets out to map how texts move in and through readers, how they latch on to receptive hosts, "sticky" with affect.[4]

Elsewhere the emotions are evoked differently in debates about literature, and its social value in public life. The value of the humanities more generally has been called into question in these times when the instrumental uses of disciplines in terms of "value" and "impact," and their pedagogies and institutions of learning, enter public discourse, and the reading public for literary texts continues to decline. The value added by literary studies in particular has been a focus of debate (see, for example, McDonald 2015; Small 2013; and Brooks 2014). "Very often," Peter Brooks argues, in writing on this marginalization of humanistic thought and analysis and the public value of the humanities, "humanistic interpretation starts from a specific act of reading—of a document difficult to decipher, a word needing to be glossed . . . and moves from there to larger interpretive theories and structures. Insofar as the humanities are an interpretive enterprise . . . they cannot do without interpretive reading of a careful, analytic, self-conscious kind" (Brooks 2014: 3).[5] This characterization of an ethics of reading and a defense of close, intense, disciplined reading may seem remote from the erotic and emotional charge of the reading that we find in Nafisi, Schlink, and Jones. Yet the case for the defense, and why the humanities "matters," frequently turns to the emotions: "Literature may be able to diminish real world injury, and the three attributes of literature—empathy, dispute, beauty—can perhaps be credited with that outcome" (47), claims Elaine Scarry (2014) at a forum in response to Brooks's remarks on an ethics of reading. Empathy—the recognition that there are multiple points of view, and the chance to practice and deepen and strengthen that recognition—is at the heart of an ethics of reading for Scarry, beneficial to the reader herself and to other, often unknown, beneficiaries of reading and its cultivation of an openness to others. Here a connection across the remote and dispersed scenes of reading that begin this chapter is evident: all of these are scenes of reading where novels come alive with feeling amid suffering and social injustice. Scarry invokes other recent research on narrative ethics that focuses on empathetic reading. Steven Pinker (2011), for example, argues that increasing literacy, the acceleration of book production, and the rise of the novel in the seventeenth and eighteenth centuries were instrumental in the expansion of imagination and responsibility for suffering others—women, children, the poor—in the course of the Humanitarian Revolution. Lynn Hunt connects the novel and its cultivation of empathy to the invention of human rights: "Novels made the point that all people are fundamentally similar because of their inner feelings, and many novels showcased in particular the desire for autonomy. In this way reading novels created a sense of equality and empathy through passionate involvement in narrative" (Hunt 2007: 39).[6]

In her book *Cultivating Humanity. A Classical Defence of Reform in Liberal Education* (1997), the American philosopher Martha Nussbaum makes a powerful case for the importance of narrative imagination in the cultivation of cosmopolitan citizenship. The capacity to empathize with others and grasp the reality of different lives with historical and cross-cultural understanding, to understand their emotions, wishes, and desires, and to reach out to others through the use of the imagination is, she argues, vital to the cultivation of intelligent citizenship. In times when the discipline (and the humanities and curricula of a liberal education more generally) has been under pressure to demonstrate its instrumental value, this association of literary pedagogy and ethical citizenship draws the emotions into the center of debates about why literature matters, and the value of the humanities more generally.

Nussbaum takes care to separate her argument about the narrative imagination and the value of literary texts from the debate about Great Books, and its privileging of a Western canon of classic texts—for example, she argues for a literary education that adds new books to the well-known canon of Western literature, and she uses Ralph Ellison's novel *The Invisible Man* (1952) as well as Socrates' *Philoctetes* (409 BC) to suggest the ways that literary texts cultivate capacities for perception and recognition.[7] She recalls the nursery rhyme "Twinkle, twinkle little star, how I wonder what you are" as an example of how even the most simple narrative forms teach children to attribute life, emotion, and thought to a form whose insides are hidden and unknown, a training of the imagination that occurs through storytelling. This literary imagination, she argues, is essential to the cultivation of compassion and empathy:

> This is so because of the way literary imagining both inspires intense concern with the fate of characters and defines those characters as containing a rich inner life, not all of which is open to view; in the process, the reader learns to have respect for the hidden contents of that inner world, seeing its importance in defining a creature as fully human. It is this respect for the inner life of consciousness that literary theorist Lionel Trilling describes when he calls the imagination of the novel-reader a "liberal imagination" – meaning by this that the novel-reader is led to attribute importance to the material conditions of happiness while respecting human freedom.
>
> —Nussbaum 1997: 90

We can separate several strands of the argument here. Firstly, Nussbaum makes a connection between literary imagining and the cultivation of empathy (that she defines as the moral capacity to imagine what it is like to suffer pain and misfortune) and compassion (a sense of one's own vulnerability, and the shared vulnerability of humanity more generally). Secondly, Nussbaum attributes to devices of characterization in fiction, an attachment to the novel in particular as the literary form that develops these emotional and moral capacities. It is the novel, Nussbaum argues (drawing on critic Wayne Booth's metaphor of the literary work as a "friend")[8] that leads us to have sympathy with characters of many kinds, although sympathetic reading always needs to be critical reading as "we ask how our sympathy is being distributed and focussed" (Nussbaum 1997: 101). The novel, after all, can elicit empathy and compassion unevenly, directing our attention to some human beings and not others (for example, Nussbaum points out, the novels of Virginia Woolf rarely recognize working-class people, while the novels of Charles Dickens have little sensitivity to the lives and experiences of women). Thirdly, Nussbaum not only privileges the novel, but follows the American literary critic Lionel Trilling (and the novelist and critic Henry James before him) in the association of the novel as a genre with liberalism, with "the individualism and privacy of each human mind" (Nussbaum 1997: 105)—like the hidden being of that little twinkling star. In practice, this cultivation of humanity tends to privilege highbrow canonical novels in English. Identity politics is an anathema to Nussbaum's argument, as she fears it risks a withholding of compassion and empathy. Although she is sympathetic to revising and expanding the literary canon to reach out to represent the experiences of silenced people, Nussbaum's turn to the liberal imagination and narrative ethics appeals to a classical and Stoic conception of world citizenship that recognizes the worth of all human beings, and to an expansion of the imagination that is the gift of literature and the realist novel in particular as practiced by George Eliot and Harriet Beecher Stowe, as well as Dickens and James. Why this particular genre, narrative fiction? It engenders identification with fictional character, a feeling with and for another that extends to egalitarian and altruistic ideas and action—that cultivation of empathy that Elaine Scarry (2014) identifies as a fundamental attribute of reading and the emotions.

In "Righting Wrongs," an argument in defense of literature and the humanities that takes a very different tack on the ethics of reading and the work of the emotions, the post-colonial critic Gayatri Spivak contests this turn to empathy and the liberal imagination as what she identifies as a "metropolitan Humanities pedagogy" (Spivak 2004: 533). Nussbaum's argument for the virtues of literary education in the cultivation of a sympathetic imagination and an altruistic recognition of distant others remains firmly embedded in metropolitan privilege, in Spivak's view: "like many academic liberals she imagines that everyone feels the same complicated pleasures from a Dickens text" (Spivak 2004: 567). Spivak's principal concern is the cultivation of pedagogy appropriate for the disenfranchised in those "other worlds" of the Global South. Her comments on literary pedagogy advocate a "habit of literary reading" that cultivates a "suspending of the self" in the text of the other (rather than the narrative imagination that cultivates a "bringing of the other into the self" through empathetic reading). The first condition and effect of literary reading, Spivak argues, is cultivating humility: "a suspension of the conviction that I am necessarily better, I am necessarily indispensable, I am necessarily the one to right wrongs, I am necessarily the end product for which history happened, and that New York is necessarily the capital of the world" (Spivak 2004: 532). Spivak's defense of literature and reading presents a post-colonial critique of the liberal humanism and the legacy of the European Enlightenment and its rational autonomous subject, precepts that are foundational to the ethics and politics of Nussbaum, Scarry, Pinker, and Hunt. For Spivak, Western liberal understandings of subjectivity and humanity consign the colonized to the space of the self-consolidating other—the "strange people" who become "fellow sufferers" in the narrative imagination of metropolitan readers (Spivak cited in Mansfield 2000: 126). These arguments invoke very different understandings of subjectivity and the emotions; they are embedded in radical differences on the uses and abuses of empathy, and the value of the liberal narrative of compassion in particular. Yet Spivak and Nussbaum both affirm the importance of literature, and the potential of reading to *move* readers and cultivate more expansive understandings of subjectivity—our own and others'.[9] Either way, as we see, Dickens and the pleasures of reading the novel offer a touchstone for thinking on these questions of literature and the emotions.

EMOTIONS IN OPERATION

These debates on the cultivation of emotion and the ethics of reading present a compelling and influential example of how literature in general and the novel in particular become attached to the emotions, most particularly the cultivation of empathy, in recent debates on literature, reading, and the emotions. In *The Cultural Politics of Emotion* (2004), Sara Ahmed, a prominent critic associated with the affective turn, questions how some emotions (such as compassion and empathy) are elevated and attached to moral cultivation and virtue and worked on in this way. How are they defined against others (e.g. fear, disgust, hate, shame, anger) that are considered uncultivated or unruly, and unworthy of the competent and cultivated self? This cultural politics approach in contemporary research is less interested in emotion as an organic and authentic or spontaneous feeling (and certainly not a biological phenomenon) than the social and aesthetic dynamics that cultivate, move, and elicit emotion, and attach it to notions of personhood and subjectivity that are historical and social.

A cluster of emotions gathers under the auspices of "compassion" and the plural "compassionate emotions," and these include empathy, pity, and sympathy. The differences among these are important. The problem with compassion, argues Marjorie Garber, as she carefully parses out its different modes and expressions historically, begins with its history and etymology. In early modern usage, the word "compassion" (deriving from Latin *com*, together, and *pati*, to suffer) described "fellow feeling," *suffering together with one another* and an emotion felt *on behalf of another who suffers*. Of these it is the second, compassion felt not between equals but at a distance, which has remained in use. Particularly in religious contexts, Garber suggests, there was an emphasis on the emotional benefits attached to feelings of compassion, and compassion "quickly tipped in the direction of inequality, charity, altruism, or patronage" (the non-sufferer showing compassion to the sufferer), whereas "sympathy" was associated with "fellow feeling," and suffering shared by equals, "persons with similar feelings, inclinations, and temperaments" (Garber 2004: 23). As Garber's clarification of the different associations of feeling, relation, and status across the compassionate emotions suggests, the very uses of these terms are subject to change. "Compassion" can be tainted by associations with benevolence, a feeling that benefits those with privilege (as we see in Spivak's post-colonial critique), or its affinity with "pity" and "sentimentality" that also suggests self-indulgence, and the pleasures of compassion for those who look upon the suffering of others, often distant strangers. "Charity" similarly carries implications of patronage, bestowed upon others.

"Empathy" is an associated and modern term, a twentieth-century neologism that frequently emphasizes personal agency and individual emotion, and it is at the focus of recent debates on literature and the emotions:

> A person who displays empathy is, it appears, to be congratulated for having fine feelings; a person who shows or expresses sympathy has good cultural instincts and training; a person who shows compassion seems motivated, at least in part, by values and precepts, often those learned from religion, philosophy, or politics.
>
> —Garber 2004: 24

These distinctions among the compassionate emotions are themselves volatile; however, the differences Garber draws out here suggest why "empathy" is privileged as the morally improving and emotional response associated with "the narrative imagination" by narrative ethicists in the recent past. From its beginnings in psychology and German aesthetics early in the twentieth century, "empathy" has been associated with a feeling for others made available through experiences of reading, although, as Keen points out, the aesthetics of high modernism along with the dominance of New Criticism and its critique of "the affective fallacy" marginalized the cultivation of narrative empathy in literary studies in the postwar academy (Keen 2006: 210).[10] It has been the influence of feminist criticism, queer theory, and post-colonialism (and identity politics more generally) since the 1970s, as well as the philosophical and ethical turn to the narrative imagination and affect, that has renewed interest in the cultural politics of reading, embodiment, and emotion.

An understanding of the compassionate emotions as political and historical opens the way to consider how literary texts, and the novel in particular, play a role in the cultural politics of feeling. In *Compassion: The Cultural Politics of an Emotion*, Lauren Berlant, a critic whose work has been formative in theorizing reading and affect, calls for new genealogies and archives of compassion, "seeking to understand the concept as *an emotion in operation*," that investigate the compassionate emotions, "their aesthetic conventions, their place in political theories, and their centrality to modern subjectivities" (Berlant 2004: 4–5). From this perspective, which is useful in thinking about the Nussbaum/Spivak debate, the turn to literature and empathy and the work of the novel is one powerful example of the compassionate emotions "in operation." Sentiments of compassion are fueled by good faith, kind intentions, and the desire to ameliorate pain and suffering, but, Berlant argues, there is nothing simple about compassion apart from the desire for it to be taken as simple, as a true expression of human attachment and recognition. The cultural politics approach to specific and historical "scenes of compassion" questions what kinds of obligation are entailed when readers and viewers witness scenes of suffering, and what moral demands are made upon us: "sentiments of compassion . . . derive from social training, emerge at historical moments, are shaped by aesthetic conventions, and take place in scenes that are anxious, volatile, surprising, and contradictory," suggests Berlant (2004: 7).

Recently, Robin Bernstein's research (Bernstein 2011) on the relations between children's literature and the material culture of play has focused on children's emotional responses to Harriet Beecher Stowe's *Uncle Tom's Cabin, or Life Among the Lowly* (1852), the novel that is widely recognized as a powerful force in the cultivation of empathy for the enslaved and the abolition of slavery in the United States. Bernstein's study suggests how volatile, surprising, and contradictory scenes of reading can be. This novel, widely recognized as the "ur-text of the liberal narrative of compassion" (Woodward 1998: 62), led to a fashion for black dolls, and there are numerous autobiographical accounts by white children who read books about slavery and then used dolls to act out their responses to the narrative. Bernstein argues the material culture of play offers insights into how children's literature engenders complex emotional and psychological responses, and so for example black dolls were used to reenact scenes of antebellum personhood that included performances of racialized violence and forced labor—which is to say they were used to reproduce culturally inappropriate responses, and to reproduce the perverse pleasures of these feelings. Abolitionist literature such as *Uncle Tom's Cabin* challenged the definition of some human beings as things, as commodities (its original subtitle was "The Man That Was a Thing"). By focusing on white children's performative play and questions of race, Bernstein argues that the association of dolls and slaves indicates the complexities of those boundaries between human and thing, boundaries which are perpetually in play—especially so in children's literature. Studies of material and textual cultures of childhood reveal scenes where the close relations of compassion to aversion, human to thing, are played out, quite literally.

It is Berlant who suggests a connection between literature and the emotions and the transit of texts via "recitation," that return of books as "friends." In "Poor Eliza," her essay on *Uncle Tom's Cabin*, Berlant questions the effectiveness of the moral responses it evokes, focusing on the ongoing "emotional quotation or affective citation" (Berlant 1998: 647) of Beecher Stowe's novel—its capacity to return once more, with feeling. Berlant turns to the Rogers and Hammerstein musical *The King and I* (1949), which stages a scene from *Uncle Tom's Cabin*, and invites the spectator to empathize and bear witness to the suffering slave, to feel her pain, understand her suffering, and connect it to the social injustice of slavery. For Berlant, like Spivak, the political effects of the emotions engendered by empathy are limited, and so are the beneficial effects for suffering others: "the ethical imperative toward social-transformation is replaced by a civic-minded but passive ideal of empathy" (Berlant 1998: 641). But Berlant does not dismiss the possibilities that ur-texts like *Uncle Tom's Cabin* might return to inspire radical reworkings and citations that create more complex emotional responses to social suffering, that she calls "postsentimental" narratives. For example, in her reading of Toni Morrison's novel *Beloved*, Berlant identifies both citation and reworking of Beecher Stowe's novel that disrupts empathetic identification with characters, and conjures the ongoing presence of traumatic and genocidal pasts (as Schlink's narrator reminds us, "the geological layers of our lives rest so tightly one on top of the other that we always come up against earlier events in later ones . . . absolutely present and alive" [Schlink 1997: 215–16]). This turn to recitation has inspired other approaches to *Beloved* and the "exercise of empathy" that becomes available through scenes of reading evoked by this "postsentimental" novel, for Morrison "stages an experience for readers, inviting their intellectual, emotional, and aesthetic engagement with the subtleties of human interaction and relationships. She doesn't redefine empathy as much as she allows it to unfold in time" (Jurecic 2011: 19). Berlant's notion of "emotional quotation or affective citation" that ripples through adaptation and appropriation across novels and beyond the page to stage and screen, suggests that some novels have an enduring capacity to move in and through readers, "little archiving machines" that can spring to life unexpectedly, and unfold in time to "represent, stage, elicit, disrupt, or block empathy" (Jurecic 2011: 22).

CUEING READER RESPONSE

But why is this so? What does current research have to say about the cognitive and emotional effects of reading fiction? What evidence is there that reading novels produces changes in feelings, behavior, and beliefs? Recent neuroscientific research on the emotions has introduced new possibilities for studying empathy at a cellular level by exploring the mechanisms underlying empathy, and for measuring mirror neurons in the brains of readers in response to literary texts using fMRI imaging of the human brain. This subjects the association of empathy with altruism—changed attitudes, improved motives, better care and social justice, and good world citizenship—to empirical scrutiny: for the first time we might investigate whether human differences in mirror neuron activity can be altered by exposure to literature.[11] In her survey of empirical scholarship on narrative imagination, including social psychological studies of reader response and reading habits and cognitive approaches to literary studies, Suzanne Keen concludes that the evidence for a causal relationship between reading, empathy, and prosocial action remains weak: "the set of links among novel reading, experiences of narrative empathy, and altruism has not yet been proven to exist" (Keen 2006: 207). Research in psychology also identifies the significance of differences of temperament, environment, gender, disposition, and cultural background that may promote or inhibit emotional and empathic feeling in individual readers at scenes of reading.[12]

Empirical investigations of reading practices raise questions about the hierarchy of types of reading that recur in discussions of the narrative imagination: about distinctions between literary interpretation and other kinds of reading, and the qualities of literariness that might engender empathetic response. Nussbaum (1997), for example, suggests characterization in the novel is a cue that triggers empathetic response, but there is little empirical evidence to support this. The assumption that the quality of literature (the preference for serious and more discontinuous texts rather than popular literature such as genre fiction, for example) promotes empathy more effectively is not empirically verifiable, and the connection between fiction and the compassionate emotions is not a given. Suzanne Keen (2006) observes an inconvenient truth: the middlebrow novel and genre fiction move and inspire readers powerfully, yet the privileging of canonical highbrow fiction endures in academic literary and cultural critique. Gender politics is alive here too, in the enduring refusal to engage with middlebrow reading and its particular appeal to women readers in studies of literature and empathy.

As Keen (2007) argues in her collection of hypotheses about narrative empathy—an invaluable appendix in her authoritative study of the novel and empathy—reader response is variable and unpredictable, more unruly and unresponsive than the narrative ethicists would have us believe. We cannot assume that social good comes out of empathic reading, and evidence of the empathy-altruism connection is the exception rather than the rule (Keen 2007: 67). Reading is a private transaction between a reader and a book, and readerly empathy differs from social empathy, and the impulse to social action (Jurecic 2011: 15). Nevertheless, the absence of empirical evidence for a causal relation between empathetic reading and prosocial behavior proposed in the empathy-altruism hypothesis does not preclude readers' desire for empathetic reading experiences, and extensive qualitative evidence connects empathy as a pleasure of reading novels in particular. Readers testify persistently to the power and pleasure of empathy; booksellers and publishers appeal to the compassionate emotions to promote novels; and authors create imaginary worlds that appeal to the emotions. Readers, concludes Keen, value empathy and actively seek out novels that enable immersion in vividly rendered fictional worlds and allow them to "feel with fiction." Despite an absence of empirical verification in recent research, a faith in the relationship between reading narrative and moral or social benefits for the individual and the community endures, a faith so strong and pervasive "that it remains a bedrock assumption of many scholars, philosophers, critics, and cultural commentators" (Keen 2007: 100). Strong normative expectations privilege empathetic reading, and a failure to feel moved in this way may seem to reflect on the character and emotional competence of the reader, rather than on this cultural politics of emotion.

In contemporary literary culture, empathetic reading is marketed to both middlebrow and highbrow markets, and ingeniously so. Broadcast media and social media are now powerful conduits in the cultivation of empathetic reading. The major case study on this issue in recent research is Oprah's Book Club, a book discussion segment of the *Oprah Winfrey Show* that began in 1996 and ran for fifteen years, during which a selection of seventy books (mostly novels, mainly contemporary but some historical) were the focus of attention, introduced to a middlebrow reading public.[13] Schlink's *The Reader* was an early choice, while Toni Morrison's *Beloved* was another, and the final selection was Charles Dickens's *Great Expectations* and *A Tale of Two Cities* in 2010, a sign of the enduring association of nineteenth-century novels and empathetic reading—and another return to Pip and Magwitch. Oprah Winfrey (like Nafisi's passionate literature professor) presents an inspiring public performance of empathetic reading, and her approach is keyed to nurture the literacy of middlebrow readers outside the academy: open to storytelling with heart and mind, *moved* by literary fiction to feel for others and bear witness to their suffering, and to advocate social justice on their behalf. The pleasures of reading are visualized on the Oprah site; for example, a feeling for books is promoted in the deluxe trade paperback "keepsake" edition of *Great Expectations* and *A Tale of Two Cities* published for Oprah's readers, with her distinctive badge on the cover.

"When was the last time you read a Dickens classic?" Oprah's Book Club producer "Jill" asks, conjuring a compelling scene of reading: "there's no better gift to yourself than

FIGURE 6.1: Charles Dickens with two of his daughters, c.1865. © National Portrait Gallery, London.

to take the next few weeks and curl up with some hot cocoa and Mr Dickens."[14] Oprah confessed she had not read Dickens, and commentaries on her site prepare her readers for a fiction that was "required reading" at school, but can now become an "unforgettable" reading experience, supported by the extensive paratextual commentary on the Oprah's Book Club site. In times when the reading public for literary texts has declined significantly across Anglo-American markets, the impact of Oprah's Book Club as a strategy to promote reading fiction has been impressive (for more extensive discussion of Oprah's Book Club see Illouz 2003; and Farr and Harker 2008).

In Azar Nafisi's *Reading Lolita in Tehran*, which is keyed to highbrow rather than middlebrow reading skills, literary imagining through empathetic reading is presented as a learned and "cultivated" response, rather than spontaneous feeling (although many readers might experience emotional responses to reading fiction that way). While the connections between the novel and empathy are often naturalized in contemporary literature and criticism, there is almost no empirical evidence that novels move their readers to empathy "naturally," or that reading narrative produces the alterations in readers' norms and values that narrative ethicists suggest. *Reading Lolita in Tehran* demonstrates a key point: pedagogy and social training are critical in creating scenes of reading that cultivate an empathetic response, and the influence of books and the heightened moral and social understanding associated with an empathetic response is facilitated by teaching and active discussion in association with reading (Keen 2007: 146). This training may well occur in book clubs and reading circles, through blogs and chat rooms, and readers need not be institutionalized in any formal way. Azar Nafisi's memoir is a celebration of highbrow taste and competence, that experience of "upsilamba," and it is a brilliant example of how timing and the context of the reading experience matter one of Keen's key hypotheses about narrative empathy (see Figure 6.2). Originally

FIGURE 6.2: Author Azar Nafisi (b. 1948). Photo by Steve Pyke/Contour by Getty Images.

scheduled for a limited print run, in the wake of the September 11, 2001 attacks, Western readers' empathy for autobiographical accounts of women in Iran—suppressed by mullahs and liberated by canonical novels in English—created an immediate and receptive reading public. *Reading Lolita in Tehran* is, we have argued elsewhere, one example of how memoirs, autoethnographies, and autographics accrued value as "soft weapons" in the wake of 9/11, and how accounts of empathetic reading have accrued value in the literary marketplace in the recent past (Whitlock 2007).

"CHARACTERS MIGRATE"

Suzanne Keen's theory of narrative empathy identifies "cues": narrative techniques that facilitate empathetic reading. Character identification is critical (as Nussbaum argues in her approach to the narrative imagination), but Keen's empirical research using testimonies of readers' experiences of reading novels suggests this requires only minimal elements of identity, situation, and feeling; realistic or complex characterization is not necessary. Negative affective states (persecution, suffering, grief) promote empathetic reading, and so do plots that involve suspense and episodes of conflict or irresolution. Narrative situation is significant: readerly identification is facilitated by modes of narration that present a single, focal center of consciousness and point of view located in a main character. All of these "cue" scenes of reading that invoke strong empathetic emotion. Although empirical evidence for the empathy-altruism hypothesis is lacking and, Keen points out, nearly always exaggerated in favor of the beneficial effects of novel reading, there is no question that readers feel empathy with, and sympathy for, fictional characters and fictional storyworlds, and that reading fiction resonates emotionally for authors and readers.

The most beloved fictional narratives and characters do not rest undisturbed; they migrate to populate contemporary fiction: Pip and Magwitch, Crusoe and Friday, Jane Eyre, and Antoinette Cosway to mention a few. Fictions that invite empathetic reading are the most popular revenants. Recitations of classic texts reroute and rewire established readerly affections; they return to earlier emotional transactions, and often with disruptive intent. These treasured "friends" return as unfamiliar characters, and minor characters command presence in the first person. Adaptations and appropriations of literary classics seek out those we love, and return us to them once more, with feeling. Part of the pleasure of adaptation, argues Linda Hutcheon, is the repetition with variation, the comfort of recognition and remembrance of a familiar text with the piquancy of surprise (Hutcheon 2006: 4). An example of this kind of piquant surprise occurs in *March* (2005), Geraldine Brooks's prequel to Louisa May Alcott's *Little Women*. The pleasure of the prequel depends on a familiarity with the original, which is transformed in this first-person account by the elevation of two relatively minor characters in the original: the absent father, Captain March, and the wife and mother, Marmee. Readerly cues are altered significantly as Brooks alters narrative temporality, point of view, and setting: the Civil War, a distant suffering in *Little Women*, moves center stage; and the domestic focus of Alcott's novel is transformed. Hitherto, debates about responses to *Little Women* have focused on empathetic engagement with the girls—Jo or Beth?—but Brooks's prequel is now a new and proximate fiction that coexists peacefully with its precursor.

When adaptation becomes appropriation, a dissident reoccupation of a canonical text, preceding and pleasurable "piquant" scenes of reading can be disturbed, and earlier transactions with the narrative are disrupted and estranged. In *Jack Maggs* (1997), for example, Peter Carey (see Figure 6.3) appropriates one of the disreputable characters of *Great Expectations*, Abel Magwitch, and one of the beloved characters of nineteenth-century fiction, Pip, and transforms them to create the characters of Jack Maggs and Henry Phipps, his ungrateful and elusive heir, to set in motion a new fiction as Maggs returns from exile as a convict in the Australian colonies to the streets of London in search of his adopted son, Phipps. Carey reengineers multiple cues for empathetic reading to elicit identification with a villainous character, and excise Pip as the focus of empathetic attachment. Narrative point of view and perspective, character traits and names, and the narrative situation are transformed in *Jack Maggs*. There is a struggle for ownership of Maggs's story in the novel, as Tobias Oates, a character modeled after Charles Dickens, elicits Maggs's life story even as Maggs writes his own account, in invisible ink and backward script. The inclusion of Oates in the narrative as a figuration of Dickens's authorship introduces a new meta-narrative that questions the role fiction plays, as it elicits accounts of suffering and shame for the pleasure of a metropolitan reading public. The copresence of *Great Expectations* and *Jack Maggs* is not a peaceful coexistence, for Carey has created an agonistic fiction that disturbs scenes of empathetic reading where readers "curl up with Mr Dickens and hot cocoa." Lloyd Jones's *Mister Pip* (2006), another contemporary Antipodean appropriation of *Great Expectations*, hovers on the horizon here too, and this has produced some critical commentary, on neo-Victorianism in contemporary literature, for example, and the relocation of Dickens to Bougainville (Taylor 2009). By appropriating a canonical novel from an age when an appeal to sympathetic imagination was germane to narrative fiction, both Carey and Jones call into

FIGURE 6.3: Author Peter Carey (b. 1943). Photo by David Levenson/Getty Images.

question the earlier, empathetic reading and the ethics and politics of pleasurable immersion and identification in the novel. Cues that Keen identifies as triggers that set empathy in motion as scenes of reading are targeted, rerouted, and rewired by these appropriations.

Suzanne Keen's qualitative research on empathy draws on reader testimonials as well as social psychology, and these accounts confirm that, for the sheer intensity of readerly relationships she inspires, the character of Jane Eyre stands alone (Keen 2007: 69). We can see why this is so in terms of those "cues" that inspire empathetic reading: there is an account of childhood suffering and persecution narrated in the first person and a single focus of consciousness, there is a suspenseful plot and romance, and the final famous intimate direct address to the reader as a confidante: "Reader, I married him" (now the title of an edition of stories inspired by *Jane Eyre*). This does not necessarily meet with an affectionate or even amiable readerly response: there are unruly and resistant readers, but the response to Brontë's novel is overwhelmingly empathetic.[15]

A rewriting of Brontë's novel, Jean Rhys's novel *Wide Sargasso Sea* (1966), now coexists alongside *Jane Eyre*, as a brilliant example of how readerly empathetic engagement can be rerouted to create powerful and new emotional transactions with the narrative. Rhys's novel haunts its precursor, uncannily drawing out what remains unsaid in the original, and the latent racism and prejudice of Brontë's novel and culture (Sanders 2006: 102). This is a piercing appropriation that reengineers those elements of characterization, plot, and mode of narration that cue empathetic reading. Like Dickens's much-loved protagonist Pip, it is perhaps the intense empathetic engagement with Jane that renders the novel available for (or vulnerable to) appropriation. In Rhys's appropriation of *Jane Eyre*, the "life" of the first Mrs. Rochester, Bertha Mason, the mad wife in the attic, is center stage, and the historical and social setting is transformed as the narrative begins in Jamaica in the immediate and violent aftermath of emancipation in the 1830s. In her *Letters* Rhys observes that the Creole in Brontë's novel is necessary to the plot, yet unseen and unknown, and inaudible: ". . . but always she shrieks, howls and laughs horribly, attacks all and sundry—off stage" (cited in Sanders 2006: 101). As both Antoinette and Rochester become first-person narrators, the intensely pleasurable and intimate association with Jane, the first-person narrator who addresses the reader directly and intimately, is lost, and narrative point of view and characterization are transformed, as the plot is extended with Antoinette's own history that moves inexorably to the story we know from Brontë's novel: her incarceration and violent death at Thornfield Hall.

In her writing on *Wide Sargasso Sea*, Spivak points out that when Jean Rhys, born on the Caribbean island of Dominica, read *Jane Eyre* as a child, she was *moved* by Bertha Mason, and thought she would "try to write her a life" (cited in Spivak 1985: 242, our emphasis). Rhys's novel begins with an act of dissident reading, of reading Charlotte Brontë's novel against the grain to identify with a minor character, who is presented in the original as less than human. The point is an important one, a reminder that readers have the capacity to be what Keen calls "unruly," to empathize with minor characters, or to resist and disconnect entirely. There is now an extensive secondary literature on *Wide Sargasso Sea*, and one of the earliest critical readings was by Spivak. Her critique of "metropolitan reading" and liberal individualism anticipates the later debate with Nussbaum on empathy and canonical literary texts, with that memorable comment that not "everyone *feels* the same complicated pleasures from a Dickens text" (our emphasis). Spivak's interpretation of *Wide Sargasso Sea* is informed by her experiences of teaching Rhys's novel in tertiary institutions in the USA and Europe, and the gaps in her students' reading in class. She draws attention to the beginning of *Jane Eyre*, as a dramatic scene of reading: "The reader," she suggests, "becomes her accomplice: the reader and Jane are united—both are reading" (Spivak 1985: 239). As another reader at this scene, Spivak sets out to "wrench oneself away" from the "mesmerising focus" of reading (and feeling) *with* Jane Eyre, and observe the enduring colonization (or "worlding") of the Third World as "distant cultures" waiting to be "recovered, interpreted, and curricularized in English translation" (Spivak 1985: 235). Rhys's novel invites its readers to return to *Jane Eyre* and feel for a character who is something less than human in the narrative: "What it was, whether beast or human being, one could not . . . tell" (Brontë cited in Spivak 1985: 240). Here, as with *Uncle Tom's Cabin*, boundaries between the human and the thing come into play.

In her hypotheses about readerly empathy, Keen points out three key elements that draw attention to the fickle and unreliable nature of readers' emotional engagements with fiction: empathy with characters does not necessarily occur as a result of reading an emotionally evocative fiction; the capacity of novels to invoke readers' empathy may change over time (and some novels may evoke the empathy of only their first, immediate audience); and empathy for a fictional character need not correspond with what the author appears to set up (Keen 2007: 136). Contemporary literature exploits the mutability of empathetic transactions in these brilliant and innovative returns to books we know and love, fictions that are charged by multiple scenes of reading. Through the lens of research on literature and the emotions we discern networks of intertextual relations that mobilize contemporary and canonical texts in fluid and uncertain emotional transactions, where the currency of individual fictions is subject to change, and texts resonate unexpectedly across time. More than this, we can propose a further hypothesis: fictions that elicit a powerful empathetic response may be more open to reengineering, as little machines that possess an enduring capacity to "reach, orient, and even reconfigure their readers" (to return to the epigraph that begins this chapter, and Felski's compelling characterization of the agency of affective engagement inspired by literary texts).

PASSIONATE READING

Current research on literature and the emotions generates hypotheses on narrative empathy that significantly advance on the "untestable generalizations" of earlier broad assertions about reading, empathy, and altruism. This research informs, for example, the work on readerly "cues" we have used as devices for reading here, and the substantial critique of the reading empathy-altruism thesis that is a classic defense of literature and the humanities. Now, more than ever before, new technologies enable quantitative and scientific research that can map emotions in and through the body, charting cognitive responses in and through reading. There is a growing interdisciplinary field on emotional responses to literature that draws on developmental and social psychology, philosophy, reader response theory, and cognitive literary studies. Recent research on empathy and the novel affirms the value of empathetic reading. While this eludes quantitative methodologies, it thrives in qualitative analysis that draws on readers' testimonials (e.g. Keen, Jurecic). Arguments about why the humanities matter frequently turn to literature and the emotions, as we saw at the beginning of this chapter. What exactly would be lost if we lost the humanities? "Only in the grey early morning light, when a lover departs in the taxi for the last time, are we suddenly aware of the depth and intensity of our passion," Rita Felski suggests (2015a). The intimate and passionate pleasures of reading recur in this chapter: Azar Nafisi's turn to reading as becoming "naked on the page"; in the crumpled bed where the lovers in Bernard Schlink's *The Reader* begin an enduring intercourse through books; and in J. Hillis Miller's "love affair" between reader and text, where each brings the other into being. Even the banality of cocoa with Dickens and Oprah's "Book Notes," though lacking in intensity perhaps, promises sensual comfort at least. Debates about empathy and reading have a long history, beginning with sentimentality three centuries ago.

This chapter has set out to both review and inhabit the contemporary ideoscapes and sensescapes of research on literature and the emotions, and to practice ways of reading open to the ongoing migrations and agency of fictional characters, settings, and plots that touch, move, and pleasure us. It has reflected the impact of thinking on literature and affect that is producing interpretations open to speculations about novels as little "archiving machines," non-human actors with the agency and the power to move in and around us. The affective turn expresses new configurations of bodies, technologies, and matter that shift thinking about critical theory toward networks of bodies and things (Clough and Halley 2007: 3). This networked thinking is open to citation and recitation, to feedback loops that challenge chronological literary histories and canons. The turn to affect is opening literary critique to models of textual attachment and trans-historical mobility across boundaries of period and nation, to ways of reading open to the "transtemporal liveliness of texts and the co-constitution of texts and readers" (Felski 2015a: 154). It draws us into scenes of reading and emotional transactions where novels are rewired and reengineered, to return "once more, with feeling."

CHAPTER SEVEN

In Private: The Individual and the Domestic Community

PETER N. STEARNS

Trends in twentieth-century emotional standards, applied to private interactions, involve a number of developments. First, key patterns visible in the nineteenth century, often associated with Victorian middle-class culture, continue to apply. An emphasis on happiness and cheerfulness, emerging well before 1900, gains new attention and becomes a growing marker, encouraging, for example, a more decisive distinction between negative and positive emotions. A number of currents, however, encourage changes away from the Victorian precedent. New kinds of expertise, deriving from psychological and medical research, expertise and popularization, directly attacked a number of earlier conventions. The growing interest in consumerism, while it built on the idea of happiness and cheerfulness, also promoted change—for example, in a more restricted realm for grief. The reduction in birth rates and infant mortality rates shifted emotional standards in childrearing. Patterns of change can be explored in particular emotions: not only grief, where nineteenth-century conventions were directly attacked, but also in a redefinition of the value of envy and a surprising degree of concern about jealousy. Friendship was also revisited, and here and also in courtship Victorian conventions were directly reshaped. The language and conventions applied to these kinds of relationships were adjusted—in the case of friendship, in part because of new concerns about homosexuality. Other changes deserve attention, even as they developed somewhat more recently: examples include a fascinating reduction in privacy and reticence, in favor of more public disclosures of personal experience, and an intriguing increase in private fears and anxieties in the United States by the 1980s.

Finally, however, two larger approaches to twentieth-century emotional patterns suggest some larger coherences, though always subject to careful analysis including comparative criteria. One approach stresses a systematic reduction in formality, beginning with manners but extending to emotional rules. A more relaxed approach, from dress and posture through emotional styles such as the new phenomenon of "social kissing," contrasts with Victorian conventions but demands the capacity to learn a set of subtle constraints. A second development, which may well be complementary to the informalization model, stresses a systematic concern about emotional intensities, from anger or grief on the one hand to love and jealousy on the other. Here, causation highlights the new role of psychological and medical advice along with new public awareness of health risks associated with degenerative disease. Both informalization and the efforts to reduce intensity modify, without eliminating, the Victorian interest in highlighting emotions that would support and justify family life.

A variety of factors conditioned private emotions from the 1920s onward, both in Western Europe and the United States. Some applied to specific emotions, as with the impact of declining child mortality on grief. Others were more general, including shifts in gender relations in work, school, and socialization, and a move toward greater informality. The intensification of consumerism and new patterns of sexuality also had an impact.

A key approach to the combination of changes and continuities in patterns of private emotion—always granting great variety by individual or social group—involves comparison with a well-established and meaningful framework created during the previous century. Often labeled "Victorianism," nineteenth-century standards for private emotion in the middle class aimed at supporting the family and intensifying its role as an emotional unit. Private emotions after 1920 maintained this framework in part, and rising levels of nostalgia also reflected an appreciation for real or imagined nineteenth-century family virtues. But the Victorian framework was loosened in many ways, and the results capture some of the significant changes in private emotional expectations and behaviors.

THE VICTORIAN MODEL, IN AND AROUND THE FAMILY

In broad outline, Victorian emotional standards sought to counter the declining economic importance of the family with new emotional functions. Claims that the family constituted a "haven in a heartless world" (Lasch 1977) reflected a belief that an increasingly harsh and competitive external environment needed a familial alternative, where children could be raised in greater tranquility and where even men of affairs could repair to alleviate external stress. Courtship was increasingly redesigned around emotional criteria, at least in part, rather than the property arrangements that had traditionally governed parentally organized matches in the middle and upper classes. Children, now at school rather than entering early into the labor force, could be treated differently as well.

Changes in the economic functions of families were supplemented by two other factors. First, particularly on the childhood front, middle-class couples began reducing their birth rates, in some cases as early as the 1790s. The result arguably, on average and over time, intensified the emotional attachment between parent, particularly mother, and individual child. Second, changes in private emotionality also reflected the huge ideological shift introduced into Western culture by the Enlightenment. A host of new emphases emerged as a result. Shame was newly attacked, both in society at large and within the family, as incompatible with personal dignity; most obviously, older shaming rituals like the public stocks were abolished outright, but within the family efforts to develop alternative disciplinary forms, and even references to the importance of self-esteem, surfaced as well. From the Enlightenment also came a new emphasis on happiness as a measure of social and individual progress, enshrined in documents like the American Declaration of Independence (McMahon 2007). Enlightenment individualism was supplemented, however, by the implications of early Romanticism, as evidenced in the new genre of the novel, which valued sentiment and lingered fondly on the mysteries of love and grief (Campbell 1987).

Victorian emotional culture, then, built on some crucial structural changes, particularly around the role of the family, but also reflected new ideological influences that stressed new standards for a variety of emotions including at least a hint of a new division between valued emotions—that would help the family and provide individual pleasure—and more negative emotions, like shame, that should now be minimized.

This framework had a number of specific expressions in the realm of private emotion. The high valuation of love was obvious, with some sense, now, that women might be a particularly loving gender. Childrearing manuals, from the 1820s onward (with hints earlier), emphasized the importance of maternal love in raising successful children (Mintz 2004; Stearns 1994). Children should of course respond in kind, contributing to the affectionate family environment. Love in courtship gained increasing attention, maintaining earlier momentum but also reflecting the Victorian hope that emotional intensity could both draw a couple together but also allow them to avoid the temptation of premature sexuality. Several historians have documented the almost religious-like intensity with which courting couples, both male and female, could express themselves during the second half of the century (Lystra 1989).

There were other implications as well. A loving family should keep anger and, if possible, fear at bay. In contrast to earlier formulas, parents were now urged not to use fear in the discipline of children, now held to be innocents who should not be spoiled by this kind of encounter. Anger should be checked as well. Men might be urged to use anger as a spur in public life, to combat injustice or fuel the competitive instinct, but they should refrain at home. And women, sometimes regarded as the natural emotional agents in the family, were not supposed to be quick to anger in the first place. In fact, women often worked hard to live up to this image, but it was quite real nevertheless; and anger standards for men were complicated as well by the public–private differentiation (Stearns and Stearns 1986; and David Potter 1954 discussed emotional tensions in Victorian manhood). Grief played a strong role in the Victorian family, an outgrowth of intense love combined with what was still a fairly high rate of child and maternal mortality (Rosenblatt 1983). Happiness was emphasized of course, including injunctions to present a smiling countenance. While a happiness criterion was only gradually applied to childhood—not traditionally seen as a particularly joyous life stage—children were increasingly urged to be cheerful. The idea of cheerful obedience raised the stakes for children, and then by the late nineteenth century cheerfulness itself increasingly replaced references to obedience outright. A new word, "sulky," began to apply to family members, particularly children, who could not measure up to the expected standards (Stearns 2010).

Intense, positive emotions also applied to friendship, in some senses providing training for later family life. Female friends used an elaborate vocabulary to declare their devotion, and often maintained positive relationships throughout their life. Middle-class men, for their part, developed strikingly fervent friendships in early adulthood, writing letters proclaiming their devotion, and even referring to embraces and other physical expressions. Here, however, contacts tended to loosen once courtship and marriage became possible (Smith-Rosenberg 1975; Rotundo 1993).

Emotional intensity, and a hope to moderate some of the harsher emotions, were not the only components of the Victorian framework. Great emphasis also applied to good manners and appropriate restraint, possibly extending the earlier trends which Norbert Elias (1982) has described as a post-Renaissance "civilizing process." Grief rituals included careful dress and visiting arrangements, increasingly facilitated by the new profession of funeral director. Manners should also help people manage their anger, as well as combining with love to help organize appropriate courtship (Kasson 1990).

The Victorian framework faced a number of challenges and qualifications. It embraced men less fully than women, even in principle, for men had an external life that was not so carefully circumscribed. And even many women might find Victorian standards undesirable or impossible. The standards applied particularly to the middle classes, who were often inclined to view urban lower classes as widely undisciplined and unrespectable. Working-class families developed their own norms—for example, a characteristic courtship pattern might involve love but more frequently included sexuality as well (Seccombe 1993). Some, for example among aspiring artisans or former domestic servants who had assimilated middle-class ways, might extend elements of the Victorian framework into their private lives. There is no claim, however, that Victorian standards had any uniform applicability.

The standards were, however, quite powerful, pushed strongly in family manuals and in mainstream religious texts. They were, as we have seen, hardly accidental: they responded to some very real needs in a changing family and urban environment. And they surely served as guides in many actual private lives, as many diaries and family memoirs attest. Many people hoped to find the kinds of love and happiness that the standards suggested, and to avoid the darker emotions, and some appear to have achieved these goals.

CHANGE AND CONTINUITY

By the 1920s, elements of Victorianism began to make less sense as guides to appropriate private emotions, and in some cases segments of the middle class, headed by venturesome youth, actually rebelled outright.

Advice literature altered, as one component of change. Most emotional advice in the nineteenth century came from moralistic authors, often female, whose writings, though usually non-denominational, retained a strong religious element. By the 1920s, advice and popularization increasingly emanated from psychologists or other scientific experts, including the new breed of marriage advisors. This shift, which encouraged authors to claim that older standards were erroneous or perilously out of date—hence the need to buy their wares—inevitably called elements of Victorianism into question. Changes in the media, with the arrival of movies and the radio, introduced other new signals into the emotional realm. One historian has argued that, as a result, attention shifted, at least in the United States, from developing character to encouraging personality, as a means of "performing" successfully in the new popular culture (Susman 1984).

There were other important shifts as well. Whereas the nineteenth-century middle class had depended heavily on sexual restraint to effect birth control as well as support respectability, twentieth-century standards loosened. Dating—where couples enjoyed commercial entertainments outside the home—replaced home-based courtship, and while outright sexual intercourse was still reproved, new latitudes developed as part of standard behavior: as one historian put it, activities of this sort moved from front porch to back seat (Bailey 1988). Adultery was still frowned upon, but sociologists like the Lynds began to note that it drew less criticism by the 1930s than had been the case just a decade earlier (Lynd and Lynd 1937). Above all, though initially particularly among middle-class adults, the availability and acceptability of birth control devices created greater opportunities for recreational sexuality. All this, in turn, inevitably spilled back into some reconsideration of Victorian emotional values.

Gender relations changed even beyond the sexual realm. Huge divisions continued in effect, but young men and women increasingly interacted in schools and universities.

Offices and shops now benefited from the expansion in the numbers of women workers as clerks or sales personnel, at least before marriage. Insistence on the innate domesticity of women's emotional apparatus declined at least in part, and there was a modest movement to discuss some new emotional roles for fathers in the family at the same time (Benson 1986; Griswold 1993; Strange 2015).

Consumerism expanded, as the introduction of dating suggests. Parents spent an increasing amount of money buying toys for their offspring. A debate occurred at the outset of the twentieth century as to whether it was really appropriate to buy commercial items for babies, but this was quickly resolved in the affirmative: teddy bears (copied from earlier German models) became one of the first commercial successes. Birthday celebrations became more elaborate; in 1926 the lyrics to "Happy Birthday" were introduced, winning widespread acceptance during the ensuing decade. Escalation also applied to Christmas giving. Attachment to "things" and to the process of acquisition, though launched earlier, became increasingly significant, inevitably affecting emotional interactions (Jacobson 2004).

None of this—a few self-proclaimed rebels aside—necessarily repudiated Victorian standards completely. New factors did however require some serious adjustments. Nostalgia for Victorian values—for example, a common tendency to identify the turn-of-the-century years as the "good old days"—reflected both change and the continuing hold of the Victorian image (Matt 2011).

In what follows, I will first highlight elements of Victorianism that on the whole persisted, though sometimes with new levels of intensity. I will then turn to a few significant specific adjustments, for example in grief. Larger changes—including some unexpected redefinitions of friendship—form a third category. A final section sums up the overall trends—change and continuity alike—and also discusses some possible overall frameworks that may have substituted for Victorianism overall.

THE CONTINUITIES

Emotional standards in the twentieth century clearly maintained, and tried to enhance, the concerns about shame and shaming that had begun during the Enlightenment and affected both public and private conventions during the nineteenth century. The idea that shame was inappropriate and counterproductive in various emotional relationships advanced in some additional territories, at least to some extent. Schooling was one domain. Concerns about using shame in the classroom had lagged behind other areas in the nineteenth century, but now it gained new attention. Teachers were urged to find other means of discipline and motivation, and while subtle forms of shaming persisted, a number of nineteenth-century conventions were undone—for example, use of the dunce cap (see Figure 7.1) or other devices that brought classmate derision on an errant student (Stearns forthcoming; Stearns and Stearns 2017).

Furthermore, expert research began to catch up with the other sources of concern. Psychologists and others in the twentieth century—though particularly from the 1940s onward—began highlighting the ill effects of shame, the extent to which it damaged individuals and might actually lead to counterproductive reactions (Lewis 2000). This new expertise in turn helped motivate wider attacks on shaming in more private settings. Women were urged to resist shaming in family contexts, for their own self-respect. Behaviors that were once kept secret because of shame were now revisited, with the hope that the individuals involved could benefit from professional help. Thus, sexually transmitted disease, drug use, and a host of other problems deserved support and

FIGURE 7.1: Classroom with boy wearing dunce cap (1906). Stereo photograph by Underwood & Underwood, 1906/Everett Collection/Bridgeman Images.

remediation, rather than shame-based concealment. Newer issues, like obesity, generated additional occasions to urge against shaming as both unfair and unconstructive. Under the leadership of popularizers like Brené Brown, a major movement emerged to help people bring private shame out into the open, to reduce its burden (Brown 2004; Brown 2012).

All of this extended emotional standards that had already developed: what was new was the range of applicability and the increasing effort to root out shame in a greater number of private settings. Some new debates also emerged, particularly in the United States after the 1980s, with conservatives urging that shaming might be appropriate after all; and new technologies, such as social media, would also create new opportunities for shaming. The most significant trends, however, saw the earlier distaste for shaming traditions amplified as a key element in twentieth-century emotional standards.

The most obvious and important continuity, however, between the nineteenth-century heritage and twentieth-century emotional goals involved the ongoing emphasis on happiness. This Enlightenment-based theme not only maintained its hold, but gained new outlets. To be sure, events could overtake happiness in some places and periods—as in the clearly uncertain and disoriented post-First World War atmosphere in Europe; American commitments were more straightforward. On the other hand, happiness could gain additional sources of support; for example, from the purveyors of consumer goods and entertainments. It was no accident that the new Disney film company, set up in Hollywood in the mid-1920s, took the provision of happiness as its core mission.

The happiness theme translated, in terms of private emotions, most obviously into a heightened expectation of cheerfulness. Childrearing manuals expanded their insistence that parents find ways to create cheerful personalities, as in the injunction "children should be helped and urged and joked into cheerfulness." Parents should modify discipline as needed to promote this quality; a bit of indulgence was often called for. Again from a 1920s manual, under the heading "How to Have Cheerful Kids": "Making success sure and rewarding it with warm approval isn't coddling. It is, rather, building the attitudes of succeeding and the habit of cheerfulness" (Stearns 2010). Popular advice givers were not entirely sure about whether children were naturally cheerful, so that parents need only protect this quality, or whether more active efforts were required given temperaments that might otherwise be less sunny. But there was wide agreement on the personality goal, now seen as necessary not only for a warm family environment but for adult success as well.

Not surprisingly, pressures mounted on adults as well. Cheerfulness was increasingly emphasized as a desirable quality at work, whether the goal was a smoothly functioning management team or effective salesmanship. Industrial psychologists worked on systems that would reduce tensions and promote at least what one called "superficial friendliness" at work. Dale Carnegie, the relentless salesmanship trainer whose career began in the 1920s, insisted on the importance of a cheerful demeanor as a means of selling goods—no matter what the mood of the targeted customer. It was no accident that smiling poses became increasingly common and expected in photographs, as opposed to the sober poses of the nineteenth century; improved photographic techniques played a role here, with less time required for poses, but the larger environment was even more important (Carnegie 1998).

Emphasis on cheerfulness had other consequences—and here, a basic continuity actually encouraged additional change. For example, childrearing experts now cautioned parents not to rely excessively on guilt, because while this might correct undesirable behavior, it could also constrain the sunny personality that children should develop. More positive corrections, including reasoning and, a bit later, appeals to the child's self-esteem, were more appropriate.

More widely still, the push for cheerfulness—enhanced by the promotion of consumer satisfaction—created sharper distinctions between negative and positive emotions. Whereas nineteenth-century standards had found some cautious use for emotions like anger—not of course in the family, but potentially in public life—anger was now increasingly dismissed as dangerous. American childrearing manuals, by the 1930s, began substituting the word "aggression" for "anger," further clarifying the undesirability of this emotion in personal interactions (Stearns and Stearns 1986).

In the workplace, insistence on a cheerful approach toward customers or colleagues, often promoted in formal training sessions from the 1920s onward, could create a sense of manipulation in the employees involved, which could spill over into life off the job. What sociologist Arlie Hochschild has called "managed" emotions might affect a variety of private encounters, where some of the individuals involved became uncertain about what their "real" emotions were. This possibility became more vivid as training methods became more sophisticated in the decades after the Second World War, but the seeds were planted earlier on. Flight attendants, for example, were carefully taught how to subjugate any instinctive reactions to nasty passengers. Later training programs, like the Total Quality Management movement popular in the 1980s, pressed further to teach middle managers to shake off any negative emotions—and again the result could spill beyond the workplace (Hochschild 2012).

RECONSIDERING GRIEF

A new approach to grief was a striking innovation in emotional standards, again from the 1920s onward. Whereas Victorian culture had indulged, indeed expected, considerable grief as an inevitable and desirable family emotion, recommendations now shifted sharply, making prolonged grief undesirable and problematic.

The shift reflected the preference for cheerfulness, obviously. Prolonged periods of mourning ran counter to this larger goal, and what had been an implicit tension in nineteenth-century standards was now resolved in favor of downplaying grief. Other factors entered in, however. By the 1920s, for the first time in human history, the decline of infant mortality throughout the Western world created a situation in which the average family no longer needed to expect at least one child to die. This huge change almost necessarily promoted a reconsideration of this aspect of family emotionality. Indeed, particular emphasis was now placed on trying to shield children from grief, as many experts urged that this particular emotional experience might prove overwhelming for a young person. Accompanying the objective changes in the encounters with death was the fact that, increasingly, deaths occurred in hospitals rather than more private venues and that doctors, trained to give top priority to maintenance of life rather than management of death, now gained the lead role in dealing with major illness—replacing religious personnel (Stearns 2007).

The attack on grief showed in many ways, including the hope that cheerfulness could quickly be restored. Mourning customs were progressively revised, as distinctive costumes and markings were often abandoned. Etiquette shifted. By the 1940s etiquette manuals placed a higher premium on urging quick recovery from grief (now seen as an unwelcome burden on others) than on comforting the bereaved (Vanderbilt 1952). Most tellingly, prolonged or unduly intense grief now became the province of psychiatry, with individuals urged to "get help" from professionals skilled in what now began to be called "grief work."

The result was a new and interesting dilemma in the realm of private emotions. Occasions for grief did diminish in most decades, given the decline in death rates and increasing life expectancy. Rituals that might express and manage grief declined as well. In all probability, as the etiquette books suggested, tolerance for the grief of others diminished, though of course personalities might vary on this point in reacting to the emotions of a friend or family member. But expressions of grief hardly disappeared, and the reduction of death rates could make death even more poignant when it did occur. Several situations deserve attention:

- In contrast to the nineteenth century, when deaths of some children had to be anticipated whatever the pain involved, now the much rarer death of a child could occasion almost unbearable anguish. Many people would feel not only grief but massive guilt. Many marriages dissolved as a result, victims of an emotional intensity that now had no easy outlet.

- By the middle of the twentieth century, a variety of grief groups took shape in many cities, helping adults cope with their grief by surrounding them with other people who had faced similar loss. These were clusters of strangers, bound only by their participation in an unwanted emotional experience—replacing earlier reliance on friends or family members who were now less likely to be tolerant and supportive.

- Emotions even at the death of an older parent may have become more acute, again because of the absence of accepted grief standards and the medical emphasis on fighting death. Certainly many relatives fought hard to maintain life-support arrangements as long as possible, even when the individual had earlier expressed a desire for a more dignified death, and certainly despite the huge costs involved.

- Particularly from the 1980s onward public grief on the occasion of certain kinds of death—the premature passing of a celebrity, certain kinds of mass shootings— elicited an interesting outpouring of emotion and insistence on public memorials. New customs of marking these occasions with masses of flowers and also teddy

FIGURE 7.2: Kensington Palace after Diana's death. Photo by Sally and Richard Greenhill/Alamy Stock Photo.

bears suggested another kind of adjustment in the emotions surrounding death, in which private reactions blended with new types of impromptu public displays (Stearns 2007). See Figure 7.2 which shows floral tributes outside of Kensington Palace after Princess Diana's death in 1997.

ENVY AND JEALOUSY

If changes in grief bore some relationship to the ongoing but intensifying emphasis on cheerfulness, important innovations in several other emotions, focused primarily on private life, responded to other factors. Neither jealousy nor envy had received great attention in the Victorian emotional model, but they now drew new comment.

Redirection of envy was significant, though ultimately unsurprising. While not a huge target in the nineteenth century, envy had continued to elicit fairly conventional religious criticisms as an undesirable emotion suggesting greed and vanity. This approach hardly comported with a growing emphasis on consumerism and a rising emotional attachment to the acquisition and enjoyment of goods and, often, the growing attention to the importance of personal appearance. Envy now might be acceptable, even desirable at least in small doses, in promoting appropriate commitment to consumer standards (Matt 2011).

Reconsideration of jealousy was a more complicated issue. This had long been a somewhat problematic emotion in the Western tradition—open to criticism as petty and demanding, but also potentially a praiseworthy sign of deep love and devotion to honor. Victorian emotional commentary had not singled out jealousy, even as part of the focus on family life. But the 1920s saw a new rush of concern.

Several factors promoted the new and negative approach. Smaller family size may have created new tensions among siblings, competing for parental attention without the buffer of larger cohorts of brothers and sisters. At the adult level, changing patterns of socialization, mixing men and women without traditional chaperonage, almost certainly created a greater need for restraint, lest interpersonal relationships be complicated by possessiveness. It was revealing that, in law, jealousy was no longer regarded as an acceptable justification for violence, in most Western countries. Finally, psychological research and commentary began to emphasize that jealousy could be a real problem in certain situations, as well as a sign of personal immaturity that could tarnish career and family life alike (Stearns 1989].

A particular focus was now given to the phenomenon labeled "sibling rivalry." Experts warned that toddlers could pose a danger to a new baby because of excessive jealousy, while developing personality traits that might spoil adult life. Active measures were essential to provide diversion and teach greater self-control. For adolescents and adults, recommendations for dating and for marriage emphasized the importance of keeping possessiveness in check.

In fact, over time, the new concerns about jealousy had some measurable effect, always granting the variety of personalities and situations involved. (Indeed, comparative studies suggested interesting national variations, with jealousy prompting sadness in the Dutch, anger in the French, but a desire for concealment among Americans [Salovey 1991].) Many people clearly sought to claim that they were either not jealous by nature, or were capable of control; polls of teenagers, as early as the 1930s, showed a recognition that jealousy was a sign of immaturity. By the 1960s and the "sexual revolution," declining concern about virginity in choosing female partners or spouses showed a significant redefinition of private emotional expectations (Stearns 1989).

LOVE AND FRIENDSHIP

One of the most striking changes away from Victorian emotionality involved friendship—though the subject warrants further historical attention. The intense same-sex bonds that marked middle-class life in the nineteenth century, at least before marriage, faded in a number of respects. The florid letters that seemed normal into the early twentieth century, particularly among women, now appeared only as odd or slightly shocking remnants of a bygone era. Patterns of male friendship, involving not only verbal but physical expressions of affection, were replaced by greater restraint. Individuals, of course, might well continue the earlier kinds of emotional experience, but the larger patterns clearly changed (Rosenzweig 1999).

Several factors contributed. Most obviously, new attacks and psychological claims concerning homosexuality played a huge role. Encounters that in the nineteenth century seemed normal now could be taken as dangerous signs of homosexual leanings, particularly among men, but among young women to some extent as well (Chauncey 1994). Margaret Mead, among others, wrote of the concerns she and her classmates felt, in college in the 1920s, about any possible signs of homosexual leanings (Bateson 1984).

Greater attention was now devoted to heterosexual activities, from dating onward. Emotional energies that in the nineteenth century had applied to friendship, at least for a period before marriage, were now often devoted to the opposite sex, often from later adolescence onward (Modell 1989).

More broadly, at least in some circumstances, shifts in standards encouraged a greater interest in being what in the United States was called "pals," than in forming a smaller circle of intense friends. Advice about work relationships promoted wider but often more superficial friendships, as part of acceptable management teams, over more targeted friendships. Even parents (particularly fathers) often saw themselves as "pals" with their children, sharing consumer pleasures and games and obviously promoting cheerfulness.

Changes in technology—greater reliance on the telephone for social encounters, and certainly the much later rise in the ubiquity of mobile phones and social media—in all probability promoted similar trends, maintaining a wide range of social encounters but often inhibiting the kinds of intensity that had marked nineteenth-century expectations.

Did similar developments affect love? The answer is a tentative yes, though the subject is surely more complicated than the changing patterns of friendship. Certainly Victorian standards of familial love continued to have some impact and appeal, both in parent–child relations and among couples.

But there were changes. As with friendship, the intense outpourings of some nineteenth-century courting couples now became less fashionable, though the decline of letter writing reduces the comparability of evidence. Without any question, marriage experts, from the 1920s onward, began warning young people about the dangers of excessive emotional investment and about the need for more rational assessment of potential marriage partners (Popenoe 1943; Coontz 2006; Bailey 1987). Intense love could mislead, encouraging both bad choices and expectations that would be doomed to disappointment. For experts and ordinary people alike, the steady increase in divorce rates during much of the twentieth century could itself promote somewhat greater emotional circumspection.

Most obviously, Victorian-style love was frequently modified by more open and frequent premarital sexuality, even in the 1920s but certainly from the 1950s onward. Elements of nineteenth-century intensity that had reflected sexual sublimation and provided emotional alternatives to sexual activity (with some individual lapses) increasingly no longer applied. Love remained a goal. By the 1990s it was an increasingly open aspiration among many same-sex partners as well, validated by the surprising expansion of public approval of same-sex unions throughout the Western world. But the nature of love may have become somewhat different (Chauncey 2004).

OTHER SHIFTS

Many changes that began to take shape in the 1920s carried through for many decades, though often with additional modifications as in the case of grief, or the methods of communication among friends and acquaintances, or the virtual sea change in responses to homosexuality. And we will return to the subject of overall twentieth-century patterns momentarily.

Yet several important adjustments emerged somewhat later as well, and without pretending a complete canvass, two seem particularly worth noting, significant in themselves and indicative of the ongoing process of change in the emotional standards applicable to private life.

The first began to emerge if not in the 1920s, at least in the 1930s, and has expanded fairly steadily since, though it has been studied particularly in the United Kingdom and the United States (Cohen 2013). Large numbers of people became increasingly comfortable, even eager, to blur the boundaries between private and public in aspects of their personal life. This reflected, in part, the ongoing effort to reduce the shame associated with certain kinds of behaviors, but it went beyond this. British newspapers began, for example, to promote stories about personal behavior and even indiscretions, generating surprising responses from people who seemed to relish wider attention. Issues that were once kept rigorously private—as part of Victorian culture and possibly earlier honor-based cultures as well—such as illegitimacy or infidelity, might now be almost proudly revealed. And, equally obviously, the public began to crave and welcome revelations about the private lives of other people, beginning with celebrities of various sorts. See, for example, Figure 7.3, a photograph of the American reality TV celebrity Kim Kardashian who came to media attention through being a stylist for socialite Paris Hilton (a member of the Hilton Hotel family dynasty). Fame is ironically her claim to fame.

The trend would obviously escalate. Journalism became increasingly intrusive. A variety of television shows, later in the twentieth century, encouraged guests to discuss topics ranging from infidelity to mental illness. Still later, slightly beyond the bounds of the twentieth century, new opportunities such as Facebook both promoted and revealed the widespread interest in disclosing various aspects (or claims) concerning what used to be regarded as one's personal life. The pattern was intriguing.

It embraced two elements. First, of course, was a reconsideration of standards. Behaviors that had once seemed at least slightly shameful were now recalibrated, making it easier to talk openly about psychological problems or sexual behavior. "Taboos" were loosened. Second, the blurring of public and private emotional topics suggested an interesting new effort to use a wider public to validate the self. Increasing familiarity with mass media made many people, otherwise remote from show business, actors of a sort, eager to perform for a somewhat anonymous audience (Cohen 2013).

A second, still later change applied particularly to the United States, but it is well worth exploring in comparative context. Fear increased—well before the advent of the most recent outcroppings of terrorism—and it arguably developed particularly with regard to

FIGURE 7.3: Celebrity Kim Kardashian. Photo by London Red Carpet/Alamy Stock Photo.

community settings—in other words, especially in the realm of private emotional interactions. In 1982, the American custom of allowing children to go "trick or treating" on Halloween, seeking candy from neighbors, was shattered by reports that some children had received apples with concealed razor blades, or candy that had been poisoned. In response, and to this day, trick or treating has been restricted, and when it occurred it has almost invariably been accompanied by parental chaperones who would then dutifully check the neighbors' offerings to make sure they had been properly sealed from harm. Neighborhoods, now, were scary places. But the most compelling aspect of the shift was the fact that the reports that occasioned the reconsideration were simply false: there had been no actual attacks on children's loot. Yet such was the new uncertainty about community relations that the reports were instantly, and durably, credible. And it was in the same period that wildly exaggerated beliefs about strangers abducting children took hold in the American public, again prompting new measures to make sure that children were carefully monitored, no longer allowed to travel freely on public transport. Here, too, decreasing casual contacts among neighbors and a decline of other kinds of informal associations—the kind of isolation Robert Putnam would describe as "bowling alone"—created an emotional environment in which new kinds of emotional anxiety took easy root (Fass 1999; Stearns 2006; Putnam 2001).

New kinds of television news reporting, that fastened on disasters such as a child snatching even on the other side of the country and made them seem immediately real, measurably promoted the sense of danger. A fascination with fictional portrayals of crime and violence may have distorted reality as well. Actual changes in neighborhood relations resulted from women's new patterns of work outside the home and reduced informal connections. Other factors deserve consideration as well. Americans developed a number of beliefs whose emotional significance outweighed reality: beginning with an insistence that crime rates were going up when in fact they were rapidly declining (Glassner 1999). And the result was not only a set of fears that might readily be exploited politically, but some anxiety-induced changes in parental satisfactions that stood out as well. By the end of the twentieth century the pleasure claimed in parenting (particularly by mothers) was declining according to most polls, and even more revealingly married people without children were displaying greater happiness than their parental counterparts. And this disparity was unusual: similar data from most other Western countries showed either scant happiness difference between parental and childless couples, or even a slight margin for the parents. There was something distinctive about some private emotional evaluations in the United States, and it was clearly novel (Glass, Simon and Anderson 2016; Stearns 2003).

The larger points here, obvious enough, are twofold: first, further historical work on changes in the emotions of private life, and particularly greater attention to comparative developments, is highly desirable, even for recent years. And second, while significant changes in emotional experience do not occur every decade, they do crop up recurrently, and they must modify, at least in contemporary history, any effort to claim a simple or clear-cut periodization. Patterns exist, continuities definitely require attention, but complex changes can intrude as well.

A TWENTIETH-CENTURY STYLE?

Two efforts, at least, have sought to make larger sense of the various changes in private emotional standards and experiences of the past century. Neither approach refutes the need for ongoing attention to change or to comparative challenges within a larger Western framework. Neither explicitly contradicts the other—the two frameworks overlap in many respects. Both, however, try to suggest some coherences that warrant comparison with the misleadingly tidy Victorian context.

The first approach emphasizes what a Dutch sociologist calls "informalization" (Wouters 2007; de Swaan 1981). In contrast to the nineteenth century and perhaps an even earlier "civilizing process," middle-class manners visibly began to relax in the twentieth century. Codes of politeness became less rigid. Dress styles emphasized greater informality, for both genders but particularly for women. Posture recommendations changed, reducing stiffness again in favor of a more leisurely appearance.

Even beyond the domain of manners per se, the informalization model embraces of number of the developments central to the changes in private emotional standards from the 1920s onward. Informalization reflected the impulses of consumerism and the growing interest in—and emotional commitment to—the enjoyment of material goods and professional entertainment. It captures the growing emphasis on cheerfulness, which linked directly with the other signs of a more relaxed self-presentation. Casual cheerfulness and the impulse to smile explicitly illustrate the more informal social style. Parents could spend less time urging children to internalize a complex set of behavioral rules, which reduced the need for disciplinary measures or the invocation of guilt. Informalization certainly fits the changes in the manifestations of grief, where rigid ceremonies and defined decorum increasingly melted away. Attacks on jealousy suggest another dimension in which greater informality may apply. The range of applicability is considerable.

The informalization approach, however, has an essential twist. Greater informality does not mean that any possible behavior or emotional impulse becomes acceptable. A capacity for restraint and selectivity remains vital. But the "rules" now are much less clear, because they are no longer defined by codes of manners. Thus, to take an obvious example, jealousy is in fact more rigidly confined than before; it requires more attention, at least for some people, to present a cool and informal demeanor than was the case previously, when behaviors were more formally regulated (Wouters 2007).

The challenge is particularly obvious in the sexual domain, as the jealousy complexity already suggests. With informalization, men and women mix more readily, in a variety of educational, social, and professional settings. Gender distinctions do not disappear, but they are reduced. Clothing styles overlap in some cases, and on the whole become less concealing. All of this, however, actually enhances the need for personal restraint, and a subtle understanding of emotional propriety no longer defined as clearly by more rigid codes of conduct. Clearly, this aspect of emotional informalization remains a work in progress. Recent efforts, including legal efforts, to define breaches of the new decorum, through attacks on sexual harassment or other forms of non-consensual contact, show the difficulty of clearly defining, much less enforcing, the new rules. But the result highlights the complexity of informalization, the need to learn new emotional standards that are inherently more amorphous.

One study drives home the positive side of the advent of greater emotional informalization—the extent to which the new system can function and at the same time contrast with Victorian convention—through exploring the nature of the "social kiss." The social kiss, between a man and a woman, was an innovation in the Western world that began to take shape in the 1920s and 1930s, though the precise date varies a bit by country. It expresses the greater intimacy now possible in social and even professional settings, for it is obviously independent of courtship or other forms of emotional depth.

But it also highlights restraint: it does not involve bodily contact and demonstrates the capacity to greet an acquaintance of the opposite gender with a casual and clearly asexual interaction. It is, in fact, a small triumph of the rules that make informalization work (Wouters 1995).

The second approach toward defining a larger framework for many of the changes that separate twentieth-century emotional conventions from their Victorian counterparts focuses more directly on emotions themselves than the informalization model does: it stresses, quite simply, a rather sweeping effort to reduce emotional intensities. The move against intensity shows up in family life—with parents, for example, urged to divert their children from sharp experiences of anger, or fear, or jealousy. But it emerges in other private domains as well (Shields and Koster 1989; Stearns 1994).

The idea of fairly systematic deintensification obviously applies fairly readily to the new standards developed not only for jealousy but also for grief. It extends further. Where Victorian standards urged boys, at least, to learn the quality of courage in facing up to fear and danger, recommendations by the 1920s were more muted, suggesting that children might not be up to the task and urging more parental intervention instead. Friendship intensity declined, in part because of the new fears associated with homosexuality. And possibly, as we have noted, intensity expected in love dropped off as well. As with informalization, the idea of a widespread effort to reduce intensity has wide applicability. And the two approaches may directly interrelate: it may be easier, and safer, to be informal when simultaneously one has learned to keep the lid on too-vigorous emotion.

The big question about the claims about intensity involves causation: why the new, and fairly general, attempt to constrain? The pattern is compatible with growing consumerism, particularly to the extent that, from childhood onward, acquisition and material enjoyments draw emotional commitments and help shape interpersonal connections. But the more obvious spur involves the role of new kinds of psychological and medical advice. Experts of various sorts, after all, were busy by the 1920s warning about the dangers of undue intensity not only in jealousy but in love: intensity could lead to a host of bad decisions and misleading expectations. But medical doctors played their role as well. As attention shifted from contagious to degenerative diseases, and particularly to the dangers of heart attack and stroke, intensity was an obvious target. One historian has in fact claimed that the transformation of fear in the early twentieth century toward a focus on unseen forces within one's body adds up to a significant, and very private, exacerbation of this emotional tension (Delumeau 1990). Certainly, the interaction between emotion and new health concerns and advice deserve attention, and may help explain the move toward deintensification across the board, for "positive" and negative emotions alike.

Obviously, some people would ignore the new complexities of informalization or brush aside the advice about intensity, including the implications for health: the new frameworks were not uniformly accepted. Nor will they last forever: the new manifestations of deep public grief, for example, might be a recent sign that some people seek new outlets for intensity that private rituals no longer provide. There is ample room for further inquiry into the adequacy of each of the two models, and into their mutual relationship.

Both models, further, play against the lingering Victorian image. Victorian standards for private emotion were strongly focused, as we have seen, on supporting and even giving new purpose to the family unit, or through friendship training for or supplementing family ties. Neither informalization nor the new concerns about intensity dethrone the family, but on the whole they dilute the focus at least to some extent. Informalization calls attention to a wider array of relationships, in which the family has less pride of place.

Concerns about intensity focus somewhat more on the individual, and the need for restraint in the interests of physical health and psychological balance. Both patterns are compatible with the actual decline in family focus and family stability in the twentieth century; they may reflect the changes, but they may also help explain them.

Both models, finally, caution against a common popular belief that somehow, by the later twentieth century, emotional rules had been cast aside, that any emotional outpouring became acceptable—that contemporaries simply "let it all hang out." It was true, particularly as part of deintensification, that people were encouraged to discuss emotions more openly, even to "ventilate" them in order to reduce their burden and avoid unwanted emotional behaviors. The decline of reticence also increased the public display of emotional claims. But actual emotions were still subject to controls and standards even if, with informalization, the rules were no longer clearly codified in manners.

CHAPTER EIGHT

In Public: Collectivities and Polities

EMMA HUTCHISON AND ROLAND BLEIKER

In the past decade, research on emotions in world politics has undergone a radical transformation.[1] Having begun largely as a push to critique the long-held dichotomy of emotion and reason, a growing number of international relations scholars now see emotions as an intrinsic part of the social realm and thus also of world politics. Consequently, emotions have been probed for new insights into a wide range of traditional and non-traditional political phenomena. It has now even become common to speak of an "emotional turn" (see Millennium 2010).

Calls to provide a place for emotions in political analysis have been met with little dispute. So compelling is the case for emotions that few would now explicitly challenge the claim that emotions play political roles. But at the same time, new emotions research—proliferating, insightful, and important as it is—has remained a relatively disparate intellectual movement. Both established and junior scholars explore the issues at stake in a diverse and theoretically rich manner, but often do not build on each other as effectively as they could. Emotions matter at so many different levels of analysis that scholars engage them in numerous seemingly unrelated ways, from neuroscientific analyses of brain stimuli to psychoanalytical studies of state leaders and historical investigations into the transformation of collective fear. As a result, key common questions remain unanswered. What is at stake in theorizing political emotions and what is the key contribution of doing so? Is a general theory of emotions in international relations possible, or desirable? What methods are most appropriate to render emotions susceptible to political scrutiny?

The purpose of this chapter is to assess the current state of research on emotions and world politics. We focus, in particular, on how emotions play a key role in collectives and polities. To do so we proceed in two steps.

First, we offer a brief historical survey of how emotions have come to be seen in the field of international relations. We focus, in particular, on the period between 1920 and the 2000s. The interwar period was characterized by a debate between realists and liberals about how to ward off the specter of Nazism. Emotions were an obvious part of dealing with conflict and war, but rarely articulated as such. The postwar move toward a more scientific study of international relations further marginalized the role of emotions, even though emotions were omnipresent and underpinned ensuing Cold War politics. It was only in the 1970s that studies in psychology and foreign policy started to place emotions at the center of scholarly attention. Starting in the 2000s, more and more literature on emotions and world politics emerged, so much so that one can now speak of a major scholarly movement.

Second, engaging this body of knowledge, we identify four key issues that are central to understanding the collective and political role of emotions: 1) the importance of definitions; 2) the position of the body; 3) questions of representation; and 4) the intertwining of emotions and power. We see these realms as basic building blocks, to be scrutinized and expanded, in a collective effort to increase understanding of how emotions not only permeate world politics but also, once taken seriously, uproot many well-entrenched assumptions of international relations scholarship.

We argue that the key challenge consists of theorizing the processes through which individual emotions become collective and political. If emotions are to be relevant to global politics then they have to have some kind of collective dimension. But how exactly individually experienced emotions become political is both highly complex and hotly disputed. States, for instance, have no biological mechanisms and thus cannot experience emotions directly. How, then, can the behavior of states be shaped by emotions?

We further argue that the links between private and collective emotions can best be identified and examined by exploring combined insights from two scholarly tendencies. On one hand are macro theoretical models about the nature and function of political emotions. They are essential and often insightful, but face the problem of understanding how specific emotions, such as fear or empathy, acquire different meanings in different cultural contexts. The ensuing risks of homogenizing emotions are met head on by micro studies, which investigate how specific emotions function in specific circumstances. Often compelling too, these approaches face the challenge of how to offer theoretical insights that go beyond the particular empirical patterns they investigate.

Although we begin now with providing readers with an accessible, one-stop overview of research on emotions and world politics, we do not claim to be comprehensive in this endeavor. Further work needs to be done on central challenges we touch upon only briefly in this chapter, including the gendered and cultural dimensions of emotions or their ethical implications. Questions of method are crucial too, not least because they explain why emotions remain under-studied even though their political role has long been recognized. All too often the call to take emotions seriously has ended up in lament about how difficult it is to study their internal and seemingly elusive nature. While we do not deal with issues of methods directly, the framework we develop provides a theoretical base with which to study precisely how emotions are a fundamental force in everyday world politics.

THE DEVELOPMENT OF EMOTIONS RESEARCH IN THE DISCIPLINE OF INTERNATIONAL RELATIONS: 1920 TO THE 2000s

We now begin with outlining how emotions research has emerged in the discipline of international relations. This outline is, inevitably, a very cursory one. We only identify a few key turning points and gloss over a range of complex and much-debated issues. While accounts vary, it is often assumed that the formal discipline goes back to 1919 and the establishment of the first international relations professorship: the Woodrow Wilson Chair at Aberystwyth University in Wales.

Emotions were central to but largely unrecognized in what is called the first great disciplinary debate. Waged in the interwar period, it had to do with how to ward off the surge of Nazism. Liberals believed that peace and security could be found though international collaboration, international law, and international institutions, most notably the newly founded League of Nations. Realists, by contrast, believed that conflict—and in particular conflict emerging from the rise of Nazi Germany—could not be met with collaboration and institutions. Key, for them, was a focus on the national interest and national security, and on defending them with military means.

Emotions are present in both of these influential approaches to international relations. Trust, for instance, is central to liberal visions of a cooperative international order (Booth and Wheeler 2007). Fear and anger, by contrast, play a key role in political realism (Robin 2004; Ross 2013; Linklater 2014). But these and other emotions have rarely been addressed and theorized directly. In most instances emotions were simply seen as issues or phenomena to which rational decision makers react. The result is a somewhat paradoxical situation where emotions have been implicitly recognized as central but, at the same time, have remained largely neglected in scholarly analyses (Crawford 2000: 116, 118).

Emotions were then further marginalized from the study of international relations during what is called the second great debate. Waged in the 1950s between traditionalists and behaviorists, it led to a situation where the scholarship in international relations was increasingly seen as being modeled on the natural sciences. Emerging from this was research that revolved, in various ways, around a rational actor model. Whether states or economic entities, it was assumed that the key actors in international politics behave rationally and the purpose of scholarship is to develop models that can account for and predict the ensuing dynamics. Numerous commentators today stress that this rational actor paradigm was to become so dominant that emotions were "purged from scholarly explanations" (Mercer 2005: 81–7), that they "virtually dropped from the radar screen of international relations theorists" (Crawford 2000: 117).

Studies in political psychology and foreign policy were among the first international relations approaches to take emotions seriously. Emerging in the 1970s, the respective contributions explored the relationship between emotion and reason in the process of decision making. They opposed the assumption that decisions are taken on the basis of "classical rationality," stressing, instead, that leaders often have no choice but to draw upon ideas and insights that may involve "the emotional rather than the calculating part of the brain" (Hill 2003: 116; see also Jervis, Lebow and Stein 1985). Decision makers, related studies stress, are also shaped by deeply seated emotional predispositions, particularly those that were acquired in the early, formative stages of their life (George and George 1998). Take the historical meeting between Churchill, Roosevelt, and Stalin at the Yalta Conference in February 1945 (see Figure 8.1). Scholars now stress that the politics of the meeting was significantly shaped by both the psychological background of the leaders and the emotional dimensions of their face-to-face interactions (see Costigliola 2012; Holmes 2013: 829–61).

While opening up new ways of understanding emotions, there were also limits to early studies in political psychology. Many approaches, particularly those that dealt with psychology and deterrence, still operated within the rational actor paradigm. Emotions were seen as interferences with or deviations from rationality. They were perceived to create "misperceptions" (Jervis 1976) that undermine responsible political analyses and actions. Numerous scholars explain why reason took on such an exclusive role, even in scholarly endeavors that sought to understand the role of emotions (e.g. Kahler 1998; Mercer 2005). The answers, they believe, have to do with the nature of social science research, which has for decades attempted to subsume emotion to cognition. Even the field of psychology, they stress, was at that time "purely cognitive" (Lebow 2005: 304),

FIGURE 8.1: Reason and emotion in diplomacy and decision making: Churchill, Roosevelt, and Stalin at the Yalta Conference in February 1945, The National Archives photo no. 111-B-4246 (Brady Collection).

paying little attention to questions of affect (Balzacq and Jervis 2004: 565). Such positions leave intact the divide between thinking and feeling which, in a highly problematic way, continues to underpin much of international relations research.

Since the early 2000s more and more research has emerged on emotions and world politics, so much so that by now one could speak about a bourgeoning and increasingly influential body of literature. The respective contributions span a great number of topics and are associated with a range of different theoretical, epistemological, and methodological approaches. We now attempt to examine this body of literature and to identify the key contributions it has made to our understanding of the links between emotions and politics.

THE DEVELOPMENT OF EMOTIONS RESEARCH: BETWEEN COGNITIVE/AFFECTIVE AND LATENT/EMERGENT APPROACHES

Over the past decade numerous scholars have started to address head on the role of emotions in international relations. The need to rethink the dichotomy of emotion and rationality is now well recognized.

There are numerous ways to make sense of this extensive and rapidly growing body of literature. Prevailing classifications revolve around well-accepted psychological categories. They distinguish, for instance, between cognitive and affective, as well as between latent and emergent approaches. Marcus Holmes (2015) has recently applied such a dual axis in a compelling manner. Cognition-oriented scholars consider emotions as a form of knowledge and evaluative thought (Nussbaum 2002: 1–22; Frijda 1986; Hutto 2012: 177). Anger, for instance, implies that something thought to be bad or wrong has happened. Emotions are thus seen as both forms of insight and sources for political decision. Opposing such a cognitive stance, another tradition, going back to William James, sees emotions not primarily as thoughts, judgments, and beliefs, but as non-reflective bodily sensations and moods more appropriately captured with the term "affect" (see, for example, Clore and Huntsinger 2009: 40–4; Massumi 2002; Thrift 2004).

Neuroscientific discoveries have meanwhile validated a more integrated "hybrid" approach, suggesting that emotions arise from a combination of both conscious and unconscious as well as cognitive and bodily perceptions (Jeffery 2011: 144; see also Cunningham, Dunfield and Stillman 2013; LeDoux 1995). This is, in fact, why neuroscience is so important: it provides concrete evidence for the idea that decisions and judgments are fundamentally imbued with emotion. Emotions are thus an intrinsic part of how politics is conducted, perceived, and evaluated.

The distinction between latent and emergent models adds an extra layer of interpretation. Latent models assume emotions are always already present. Fear, for instance, precedes or perhaps even causes political behavior. Emotions are said to precipitate physiological change and cognitive recognition. Emergent models do not necessarily claim the opposite, but, rather, argue for a deeper understanding of the complex links and interrelated nature of cognition, feeling, emotions, and actions. Rather than forming a preexisting background, emotions here are seen as "emergent properties" of an interactive body–mind system (Coan 2010: 278), which itself has been constituted over time through socially and culturally conditioned forms of perception and experience (see also Holmes 2015).

TOWARD AN ALTERNATIVE CONCEPTUALIZATION: BETWEEN MACRO MODELS AND MICRO STUDIES

We opt for an alternative way of making sense of emotions research, one that revolves around a macro/micro distinction. We do so not because such an approach is more accurate than either a cognitive/affective or a latent/emergent classification, but because it offers us an ideal way to synthesize existing emotions research and identify a coherent theoretical path forward. Our conception aims not to preference one theoretical account of emotions over others (such as cognitive versus affective) but to subordinate such debates to what we see as the key challenge facing international relations emotions scholars: understanding the concrete processes through which seemingly individual emotions either become, or are at once, public, social, collective, and political.

At its most basic distinction, macro approaches devise general theories of how emotions matter in world politics, while micro studies focus on how specific emotions gain resonance in particular political circumstances. But we explicitly use the macro/micro distinction in a broader way, as a heuristic tool that highlights connections between several overlapping poles in emotions theorizing: not just those between theoretical models and empirical studies, but also between local and global foci, or between specific emotions and more general affective dispositions. We see these poles as neither fixed nor mutually exclusive. In fact, our whole point is that a combination of them provides a framework to understand and bring out the best from numerous traditions. It allows for unusual but important combinations, as between debates on the phenomenological status of emotions and political inquiries into the role of specific collective emotions.

Let us now consider the macro/micro distinction in more detail. Macro models seek to capture what emotions are and how they function in world politics. While diverse in scope and purpose, macro inquiries are united by one broad agreement: that emotions are more than just individual and private phenomena and, as such, require wider political theorization. Recognizing that emotions are inherently social, macro inquiries maintain that an affective realm underlies all forms of political action, no matter how calculated or strategic such actions appear to be. Respective contributions draw from different disciplines and chart different paths, yet taken together these inquiries examine how emotions help to constitute the social realm in ways that mediate political identities, communities, and ensuing behaviors.

Jonathan Mercer and Neta Crawford are important contributors to these debates. Crawford (2014) theorizes the institutionalization of two particular emotions: fear and empathy; while Mercer offers a model for understanding state-based emotions. Other scholars build on Mercer's earlier work that explores the link between emotions, beliefs, and identity. Brent Sasley, for instance, uses intergroup emotions research to theorize how emotions can converge in a group as large as a state (Sasley 2011).

These and numerous other macro approaches are both crucial and convincing. But they also face conceptual challenges. While they theoretically recognize links between culture and emotions, these models have, by definition, difficulties actually accounting for the content of these links. Expressed in other words, macro models run the risk of homogenizing emotions, of lumping together emotional phenomena that are, in reality, far more complex and diverse. Consider how Andrew Linklater (2014) outlines that anger varies greatly from one cultural and political context to another: how the USA used anger to legitimize the wars in Iraq and Afghanistan is completely different from how, for instance, anger fueled and manifested itself during the Occupy Wall Street movement (see Figure 8.2). Is it desirable—or even possible—to develop models that seek to subsume all of these different emotional phenomena under one conceptual umbrella? Can macro models ever account for how specific emotions acquire different meanings and credence in different contexts?

Micro approaches provide some clues to answering these questions. Micro studies investigate how specific emotions are constituted by and function in particular cultural and political environments. They address, head on, the very challenges associated with macro models, particularly the risk of homogenizing emotions. Micro approaches focus less on establishing the existence of collective emotions and more on analyzing the unique ways and mechanisms through which emotions exist and, in turn, become socially and politically significant. Examples here include studies that examine how emotions associated with humiliation and dishonor constitute communities (Callahan 2004; Fattah and Fierke 2009) or generate antagonistic political practices (Löwenheim and Heimann 2008; Saurette 2006; Tuathail 2003). Others investigate how the emotional dimensions of trauma and memory shape the constitution of modern statehood (Edkins 2003; Fierke 2004; Zehfuss 2007), or how emotions associated with trust, friendship, and honor (or, by contrast, anxiety, suspicion, and anger) influence diplomatic negotiations, alliances, defense policies, and war (Åhäll and Gregory 2015; Eznack 2011; Hall 2011; Lebow

FIGURE 8.2: Anger, culture, and protest: Occupy Wall Street, October 25, 2011, Wikimedia Commons. *This file is licensed under the Creative Commons Attribution 3.0 Unported license.*

2006; Ruzicka and Wheeler 2010; Sasley 2010). Others again study the emotional foundations of ethnic conflict (Petersen 2002), humanitarian intervention (Pupavac 2004), development (Wright 2012), and political economy (Gammon 2008; Widmaier 2010).

Debating the nature, function, and significance of particular emotions is one of the issues at stake in micro studies. Both Mercer (2014) and Crawford (2014) engage empathy but do so from different perspectives. Others, such as McDermott (2014), extend these debates or even question whether or not empathy actually is an emotion. McDermott further critiques that distinct emotions, such as anger, are too often lumped together in broad categories that wrongly assign either positive or negative value to emotional experiences.

Micro studies offer exceptionally rich insights but they too face conceptual challenges. To be convincing, they explore the unique cultural meaning of the emotions they investigate. But how can we extrapolate from this appreciation the broader insight needed for the establishment of theoretical models? Does the attempt to do so inevitably produce a grand narrative that does injustice to the unique context within which emotions emerge? While some have started to address these issues (Fattah and Fierke 2009; Fierke 2013; Bially Mattern 2011), there is still a long way to go until we know exactly what the contextually bound nature of emotions tells us about the prospects of theorizing emotions in world politics. We need more inquires exploring how micro political processes can be understood in a more macro political frame. The ultimate objective here, we suggest, is to avoid either a totalizing grand theory or a form of cultural relativism that eschews larger theoretical propositions.

THE KEY CHALLENGE: HOW DO INDIVIDUAL EMOTIONS BECOME COLLECTIVE AND POLITICAL?

Because of the ability to highlight the interaction between different levels of analysis, a micro/macro framework is ideally suited to address what we believe is the most important challenge in political research on emotions, or at least the one that precedes all others: to theorize the processes that turn individual emotions collective, social, public, and, thus, political. Unless one can show that emotions matter beyond a purely individual and private level, there is no ground to examine their relevance for global politics.

Even though there is broad agreement that emotions are shaped by society and culture and are, as such, more than individual and private, scholars continue to question how to best conceptualize and empirically investigate emotions as shared, collective phenomena. Doing so is seen as critical: understanding and theorizing the role emotions play in shaping and motivating political communities, cuts to the core of why international relations scholars should care about emotions in the first place.

The key, we argue, lies in theorizing the actual processes that render emotions political. Focusing on the specific mechanisms through which emotions are socially embedded and can—in particular circumstances—become collective, enables us to theorize the politics of emotion in a manner that reduces the risk of homogenizing them. Conceived of in this way, through the mechanisms that enable emotions to become meaningful within particular contexts, the culturally and historically specific nature of emotions remains intact, while at the same time enabling understandings of the wider conceptual processes through which emotions play a role in world politics. The ultimate objective of such an approach, which is far beyond the task of a short chapter, would be a model through which emotions—both in terms of specific emotions and in a general sense—can be theorized in a non-essentialist manner (see Lutz 1988: 5). Of course, the middle ground we suggest cannot entirely sidestep the dangers of homogenizing emotions. Any theoretical model risks doing so. But the ensuing consequences can be mitigated by a careful articulation of the processes that link the micro and macro realms.

Thus far, explorations of the links between individual and collective emotions have taken shape, not surprisingly, predominantly at the level of the state (e.g. Löwenheim and Heimann 2008; Eznack 2011). Theorizing the state as an emotional actor, scholars tend to draw links between emotions and the type of factors that bind individuals together. The more people associate with common beliefs or identities, the more they may share emotions, these studies contend, even at the broad level of the state (Mercer 2010; 2014; Sasley 2011). This is how and why, for these and like-minded scholars, a state may experience emotions insofar as the state is essentially a group constituted of individuals who cultivate, share, and identify with each other emotionally.

But not all scholars are convinced by the apparent leap from individual to state emotions. States, some argue, are "ontologically incapable of having feelings" (Digeser 2009: 327). This is not to deny that emotions and affective dispositions play an important role at the level of collectives. Communities are key to how emotions attain meaning and are interpreted (Fierke 2014; see also Ahmed 2004; Lutz 1988). But difficult questions that may enable the theorization of emotions at a level as vast as the state remain largely unanswered. Who is a state and how exactly are its emotions formed and expressed? Whose emotional attachments are representative of the state? What are the emotional links or breaks between states and governments, nations, or various substate groups? And how do we, as Ling (2014) and Crawford (2014) ask, theorize how emotions are embodied in actors and actions that transgress and challenge states, from social movements to transnational institutions?

The task ahead therefore lies in translating a commonsensical position on the importance of collective emotions into a more thorough understanding of how exactly emotions matter at the level of world politics. We now identify four issues that are particularly important for understanding the issues at stake. These are not the only ways in which emotions matter politically, but they offer a starting point from which a more rigorous and reflective theorizing of emotions becomes possible.

CONCEPTUALIZING EMOTION, FEELING, AND AFFECT

Just as complex as emotions is the language used to make sense of them. Most international relations scholars use the term "emotion" loosely, as a broad umbrella term to denote a range of different phenomena. We do so too in this chapter. Yet at the same time we recognize the importance of numerous phenomenological distinctions, such as those between emotions, feeling, and affect.

We now define the main terms used in emotions research. We do so to provide a conceptual road map for readers who are new to this topic. Mostly, however, we show that debates over definitions go to the very core of how to theorize links between private and collective emotions.

Although the terms "emotions" and "feelings" are used interchangeably in everyday language, there is meanwhile an extensive history of distinguishing between them. Neuroscientist Antonio Damasio (2000), for instance, sees feelings as the physiological—or somatic—manifestation of emotional change. When we are afraid of something, our hearts begin to race and our muscles tense. This reaction occurs automatically and almost unconsciously. By contrast, specific emotions, such as fear, only arise after we have become aware of our physical changes; there is an element of information processing to an emotion (see also Scherer 2005: 697–8).

Reflecting on the distinction between emotions and feelings might help us appreciate the connections between body-based micro phenomena and the macro processes through which emotions are communicated to others. While feelings may emerge from within the body, they are at the same time what is at stake in the politics of emotions. Feelings are internal in that they are felt within bodies, yet they are in a sense external as well, insofar as through particular social processes they bridge the divide between and connect individuals and collectives. Central here is that the specific forms feelings take—why we feel in the ways we do—are constituted at least in part through the social and cultural processes through which emotions are shaped in the first place.

The distinction between emotions and affect goes one step further. In some disciplines, such as geography, this distinction is so intensely debated that scholars differentiate between "emotional geography" and "affective geography" (see Thien 2005; Thrift 2004). Emotions are seen as personal and often conscious feelings that have social meaning and political consequences. Related phenomena can in this way be identified and assessed. Affective dynamics, by contrast, are seen to lie beyond representation. They are viewed as much broader phenomena that exist both before and beyond consciousness:

they are a wide range of non-reflective and subconscious bodily sensations, such as mood, intuition, temperament, attachment, disposition, and even memory (in international relations see Ross 2006: 199; Eznack 2011; 2013; Holmes 2015; Sasley 2010).

There is no space here to enter the highly complex and deeply contested exchange between emotions and affect scholars (see Leys 2011). But we would like to note that, for us, the respective distinction is not as clear-cut and as mutually exclusive as some scholars maintain. We emphasize the similarities, rather than the differences, between these two traditions. Affect and emotions can be seen as intrinsically linked, for affective states are subconscious factors that can frame and influence our more conscious emotional evaluations of the social world.

Affect can then provide the conceptual tools to understand how a broad range of psychosocial predispositions produce or mediate political emotions. Recent research by Lucile Eznack (2013) illustrates the issues at stake. Eznack shows how historically cultivated affective dispositions—both positive and negative—can temper or exacerbate hostilities between nation-states and, in doing so, influence the nature of ensuing state behavior. Juxtaposing US anger toward Britain during the 1956 Suez Crisis (see Figure 8.3) with that focused toward the Soviet Union during the 1979–80 Afghanistan intervention, Eznack shows how anger at an ally/friend and an adversary/enemy alters according to the preexisting affective dimensions of their relations.

To use the term "affect" is thus to make a shift from isolating specific micro-based emotions to the more general macro-level recognition that emotion, feeling, and sensation

FIGURE 8.3: Affective predispositions and diplomatic hostilities: British aircraft carriers during the Suez Crisis, 1956, Wikimedia Commons.

combined generate often unconscious and unreflective affective dispositions that connect and transcend individuals (Massumi 2002: 27–8, 217; Thrift 2004: 60).

Definitional disputes can never be settled. Nor can concepts ever capture the far more elusive realities they seek to define. This is why we consciously use the broad term "emotion" in this chapter. But conceptual disputes provide a way into understanding the substantive issues we investigate, particularly the processes through which feelings, emotions, and affect are both individual and collective: affective phenomena are historically and contextually conditioned to act upon both individuals and collectives, in turn implicating particular feelings and emotions that then enact and transform particular socio-political norms and behaviors.

EMOTIONS AND THE BODY

Emotions cannot be understood without theorizing the role of the body. Indeed, emotions are intrinsically linked to bodies. Mercer (2014) speaks of the "no body, no emotions problem." If emotions are tied to our physicality, how exactly can they become collective and acquire political significance? Mercer's answer is seemingly straightforward: that bodies cause emotions but emotions cannot be ontologically reduced to the body. Articulating the implications of such a position is, however, far more difficult. A state, for instance, does not have a physical body. It cannot possibly have emotions. Do politicians and diplomats experience emotions on behalf of the state? Or is it that emotions are attributed to states? Or that they are embodied in larger discursive forces that constitute the state and its meaning?

There is little scholarly agreement on this issue. At one end of the spectrum are positions that stress how emotions are experienced first and foremost in people's bodies. McDermott's work (2014) exemplifies the primacy of the body in emotions theorizing. For her, a focus on physicality is essential, for "emotion must necessarily be grounded in somatic experience in the physical body or it would not exist at all." In this understanding, emotions are seen to arise from a synthesis of bodily experiences, even though the meanings attached to the respective emotions are culturally determined. The body, in other words, is where emotions begin. To divorce the body from accounts of emotion would therefore be to erase the origin and meaning of feelings. In this type of somatic account, the body is so central to emotion that attempts to theorize the collective and political nature of emotions must be approached with a great deal of caution. Take the images from the Iraq War captured by US soldiers who tortured Iraqis in detention in Abu Ghraib prison in 2003. The emotions of the participants as well as the emotions of the viewers are generated by one principal dynamic: the pain and humiliation inflicted upon bodies.

On the other side of the spectrum are scholars who insist that emotions should not—and cannot—be reduced to bodies. L. H. M. Ling (2014) even stresses that emotions have normative and spiritual dimensions that actually "do not require embodiment." Karin Fierke (2014), likewise, recognizes the importance of physiological and neurological studies, but stresses that related insights "should not ultimately be the focus of social and political analysis at the international level." This is the case, she argues, because individual emotions are less significant for understanding global politics than the emotions that surround political phenomena.

These juxtaposing positions represent the tension between body-based micro approaches and more macro-level attempts to theorize international relations. But despite their diverging views, all of these scholars are convinced that emotions matter in world politics. The question is how exactly and to what extent can we understand the issues at stake? Is it possible that emotions can transcend bodies? Do emotions even need to transcend bodies to be politically significant? And, if emotions do play a role in social and political life, how does this shift from individual to collective occur?

We suggest that an appreciation of micro/macro linkages reveals how internal—body-based—emotions become socio-politically significant. Even though we experience emotion emerging from our bodies, feelings are formed and structured within particular social and cultural environments. They are constituted in relation to culturally specific traditions, such as language, habits, and memories. This is to say that specific social and cultural surroundings influence how individuals gain an understanding of what it means to feel (Harré 1986; Lutz 1988: 5). Some scholars even argue that, in this way, emotions are "cultural products," "reproduced in individuals through embodied experience" (Abu-Lughod and Lutz 1990: 12). Emotions always have a history. How we feel in response to particular political events depends on how society suggests we should feel. To experience feelings such as anger, fear, trust, or empathy is dependent on a specific cultural context that renders such emotions meaningful and acceptable.

Insights into the social character of emotion reveal an important recognition: bodies are more than autonomous and atavistic physical entities that operate independently of their environment. Bially Mattern (2011: 66, 76) convincingly demonstrates how individual emotions are always also collective. For her, bodies do not have emotions. Rather, emotions are capabilities that bodies acquire through the contextually bound interplay of biological and social forces. They emerge from a complex combination of conscious feelings, cognition, and subconscious affect. Fierke (2013) nicely illustrates the issues at stake through a study on political self-sacrifice, such as suicide terrorism or civil disobedience. She shows how dying or injured bodies evoke certain emotions, and how these emotions in turn become political by reaching and relating to various audiences. She highlights how this circulation of emotion shapes collective identities. The body, then, is viewed not as an anatomical object or something that is distinct from the mind, but as a more complex mechanism that fuses physical and emotional features with culture and history. Fierke (2014) underscores the cultural dimensions of what may seem "natural" bodily emotions by turning to the issue of intentionality. How individuals interpret others' actions is determined through the complex interplay of processes of communication and abstraction. Whatever the political content of these interactions, emotions "attach" us to each other in ways that either push or pull bodies together (see Ahmed 2004).

In short: neither the body nor the social realm can be privileged over the other. To elevate the body above all would be to neglect that the seemingly internal feelings invoked within bodies—feelings that are traditionally relegated to the micro political realm—are in fact constituted by external, macro-social, and political forces. But to deny the significance of the body would be to neglect not only that the body is the key site of emotional experience but also that it can, through the very socially constituted feelings it embodies, transgress and transform prevailing constellations of emotions, and thus politics. It is therefore imperative that political theorizations position emotions within the human body while, at the same time, recognize that emotions are far from innate or "natural." What people feel physiologically as emotions is the product of social and cultural encounters and of how individuals have been socialized into managing their emotions through and within such encounters.

REPRESENTATION AS A KEY LINK BETWEEN INDIVIDUAL AND COLLECTIVE EMOTIONS

Representation lies at the heart of understanding the processes that link individual and collective emotions. Two reasons stand out (see Bleiker and Hutchison 2008; Hutchison 2014).

First, representations are, in some sense, all we have when it comes to understanding emotions. Even though emotions have social origins and can resonate collectively, emotions are inherently internal. One person can never really know how another person feels. All one can understand is the manner in which emotions are expressed and communicated; whether this is done through touch, gestures, speech, sounds, or images; whether it is from one person to others or in response to events that trigger emotional responses; and whether this event is experienced directly or at a distance through media and other representations. There is always a layer of interpretation, even in neuroscientific studies of brain stimuli.

Second, and more importantly, representation is the process through which individual emotions become collective and political. For some, such as Bryce Huebner (2011: 89, 93), this process is very direct. Huebner argues that social representations are crucial because they work comparably to "representations in an individual mind," thus creating substantial conceptual support for the existence of collective emotions.

There are countless ways in which representations link individual and collective emotions. Consider how televised depictions of a terrorist attack set in place socially embedded emotional processes that shape not only direct survivors, but also a much larger community of people. Representations can occur through images and narratives, by word of mouth, via old and new media sources, and through the countless stories that societies tell about themselves and others (see Figure 8.4). Ross (2014) writes of the "circulation of affect"; of how emotions are consciously and unconsciously diffused in numerous ways, including through their public display. For him, we can only conceive of group-level emotions through the types of meaning that are manifested in the expression of emotions. This is why he urges scholars to investigate how identities are being constituted through narratives, images, and other representations (Ross 2006: 201). These are the processes through which emotions become manifest and defined. They shape identities, attachments, attitudes, behaviors, and communities, and, in doing so, establish the emotional fabric that binds people together (see Abu-Lughod and Lutz 1990: 13–16; Lutz 1988; Scheff 1990). There are already several studies that explicitly or implicitly turn to representation-based research to explore the consequences of how collective emotions are evoked (Fattah and Fierke 2009; Fierke 2002; 2013; Löwenheim and Heimann 2008; Ross 2006; Saurette, 2006; Solomon 2012).

Representations are neither authentic nor passive. There is always a level of interpretation involved, or, to express it differently, there is always a gap between a representation and what is represented therewith. This aesthetic gap is in many ways the source of politics, for it contains and often masks the power to depict the world from a particular perspective (see Bleiker 2009). The literature on enactivism is particularly pertinent here. It shows how we can never represent emotions authentically for we do not have access to another person's mind. But we can understand emotional responses by analyzing behavior and action (Gallagher and Varga 2013). By focusing on perception as an actively lived experience that is part of how we enact and make sense of the social world, this body of literature offers opportunities to understand how emotions transgress

FIGURE 8.4: Representations of terrorism and the circulation of affect: visual depiction of the terrorist attacks of September 11, 2001. Photo by Michael Foran via Wikimedia Commons. *This file is licensed under the Creative Commons Attribution 2.0 Generic license.*

embodiment and take on public and political dimensions (see Caracciolo 2012: 381; Hutto 2012).

IN LIEU OF CONCLUSION: EMOTIONS, POWER, AND INTERNATIONAL RELATIONS

Few realms are more emotional than that of world politics. Politicians intuitively know how to tap into the emotions of their electorates. Fear drives and surrounds war, terrorism, and the construction of strategy and security. Diplomatic negotiations could not be pursued without a basic level of trust. Empathy is central to successful peace-building processes. The list of examples is endless. And although present in many theories, from realism to liberalism, emotions have been mostly taken for granted. They have been seen as phenomena that rational policy makers deal with or react against. It is only over the last decade that emotions have come to be seen as significant, at times critical, forces in world politics. Scholars now increasingly turn to emotions. They do so for different reasons, with different theoretical assumptions and using different methods.

In their very diversity these approaches make a simple but important point: emotions play a significant role in world politics, shaping how individuals and collectives are socialized and interact with each other. But numerous key issues remain unanswered, not least because this new body of literature on emotions remains relatively disparate. Its numerous contributors have not been able to build on each other as effectively as they could, nor have they been able to shape the prevailing debates in international relations scholarship.

This short chapter has sought to assess the current state of research on emotions and world politics. We searched for a middle ground between two seemingly opposing scholarly poles: those advocating macro models of theorizing how emotions matter in world politics, and those pursuing micro studies of how emotions function in particular circumstances. Such a framework is particularly suited to theorize how emotions operate between several parallel levels: individual and collective; local and global; specific and general.

We argued that understanding these criss crossing interactions offers ideal opportunities to address what we believe is the key challenge in emotions research: to understand how individual and body-based emotions become collective and political. We then illustrated the issues at stake through the role of the body, the significance of representation, and the substantive consequences of how emotions are defined.

Once the collective dimensions of emotions are appreciated, an additional topic inevitably becomes central: the links between emotions and power. Surprisingly few scholars in international relations have so far taken on the respective issues. The work of Ling (2014) is an exception. She highlights the gendered and colonial dimensions of anti-emotional international relations research. Others have shown how emotions are part of how we present, constitute, legitimize, and enact political views and politics (see Edkins 2003; Fierke 2013; Steele 2010; Zehfuss 2007). But so far it has been mostly sociologists and anthropologists who have investigated the issues at stake. They suggest that to "talk about emotions is simultaneously to talk about society—about power and politics ... about normality and deviance" (Lutz 1988: 6). Power, then, is central to the constitution of emotional subjectivity; power relations play a key role in determining what can, cannot, should, or even must be said about the self and one's emotions (see also Abu-Lughod and Lutz 1990: 10, 14–15; Rosaldo 1980; Svašek 2005: 8–10). Arlie Hoschchild (1979) writes of "feeling rules," of the normative expectations of how to feel in different social contexts. Such rules determine how individuals should feel in certain circumstances—at, say, the birth of a child, the death of a grandparent, or the loss of a job (see also Barbalet 2001).

These links between power and emotion are, of course, rather different from the way power has customarily been theorized in international relations. It is neither hard nor soft, neither imposed by military force nor coerced through economic pressure or diplomatic initiatives. Emotional power works discursively, diffused through norms, moral values, and other assumptions that stipulate—often inaudibly—how individuals and communities ought to feel and what kind of ensuing behavior is appropriate and legitimate in certain situations.

An appreciation of the links between emotions and power highlights that even if they are individual, emotions are always also collective and political. They frame what is and is not possible in politics. They reveal and conceal, enable and disable. They do so in ways that are inaudible and seemingly apolitical, which is precisely how they become political in the most profound and enduring manner: links between emotions and power shape the contours and content of world politics, all while seemingly erasing the traces of doing so. The task of international relations scholars is to locate, redraw, and expose these traces.

NOTES ON CONTRIBUTORS

Charles Altieri is the Rachael Anderson Stageberg Endowed Chair of English Literature at the University of California, Berkeley. He has written books on several aspects of twentieth-century poetry, literary theory, and modern art. His two most recent books are *Wallace Stevens and the Demands of Modernity* (2013) and *Reckoning with Imagination: Wittgenstein and the Aesthetics of Literary Meaning* (2015).

Roland Bleiker is Professor of International Relations at the University of Queensland, where he coordinates an interdisciplinary research program on Visual Politics. His research focuses on aesthetics, visuality, and emotions in world politics. Recent publications include *Divided Korea: Toward a Culture of Reconciliation* (2005/2008), *Aesthetics and World Politics* (2009/2012), *Visual Global Politics* (2018), and, as coeditor with Emma Hutchison, a forum on "Emotions and World Politics" in *International Theory* (vol. 3, 2014).

Joy Damousi, Professor of History and Australian Research Council Laureate at The University of Melbourne, is Senior Honorary Research Fellow of the ARC Centre of Excellence for the History of Emotions. She has published on various aspects of grief, trauma, and loss during the two world wars. She is author of numerous books, including *Colonial Voices: A Cultural History of English in Australia 1840–1940* (2010) and *Memory and Migration in the Shadow of War* (2015). With Philip Dwyer she is the general editor of a four-volume *World History of Violence* (2018).

Jane W. Davidson is Deputy Director of the ARC Centre of Excellence for the History of Emotions, Associate Dean Research, and Professor of Creative and Performing Arts at The University of Melbourne. Her research interests are in music related to conciliation, expression, and well-being through performance and listening. Recent books include: *My Life as a Playlist* (2014), *Music and Mourning* (ed., 2016), *Hearing Memories: Historical and Psychological Perspectives on Music and Nostalgia* (2018), all with Sandra Garrido. She also directs opera where emotion themes are central, most recently Monteverdi's *Orfeo* (2017) and *Gloria* (2018).

Emma Hutchison is an ARC DECRA Research Fellow in the School of Political Science and International Studies at The University of Queensland. Her work focuses on emotions and trauma in world politics, particularly in relation to security, humanitarianism, and international aid. She has published in numerous academic journals and her book *Affective Communities in World Politics: Collective Emotions After Trauma* (2016) won the British International Studies Association Susan Strange Book Prize.

Mark Jackson is Professor of the History of Medicine, Director of the Wellcome Centre for Cultures and Environments of Health, and Co-Director of the WHO Collaborating Centre on Culture and Health at the University of Exeter. He served as Senior Academic

Adviser (Medical Humanities) to the Wellcome Trust, 2013–16. Recent books include *The Oxford Handbook of the History of Medicine* (ed., 2011), *The Age of Stress: Science and the Search for Stability* (2013), *The History of Medicine: A Beginner's Guide* (2014, shortlisted for the Dingle Prize), *Stress in Post-War Britain, 1945–85* (ed., 2015), and *The Routledge History of Disease* (ed., 2016).

Mary Luckhurst is Associate Director of Research and Professor of Artistic Research and Creative Practice at The University of Melbourne (Faculty of Fine Arts and Music). She is a writer, director, and theater scholar. Her most recent books are *Caryl Churchill* (2015), *Theatre and Ghosts: Modernism, Materiality and Performance* (2014), and *Theatre and Human Rights since 1945* (2015). In 2017 she was the Torch Visiting Professor in the Humanities at Oxford University.

Grace Moore was a Senior Research Fellow at the ARC Centre for Excellence in the History of Emotions, and also held a lectureship at The University of Melbourne. She will shortly take up a post at the University of Otago, New Zealand. Her monograph *Dickens and Empire* was shortlisted for the NSW Premier's Award for Literary Scholarship in 2006. Her most recent book is *The Victorian Novel in Context* (2012). Grace is working on a book-length study of settlers and bushfires, *Arcady in Flames*, while developing a research interest in emotions and the environment. She also publishes on Anthony Trollope and Antipodean ecology.

Anastasia Scrutton is Associate Professor in Philosophy and Religion at the University of Leeds. Her current research is on religious and spiritual interpretations of depression, and divine passibility—the idea that the God of classical theism could have emotions—through the relationship between emotions, intelligence, the will, and the body. Publications include "Why not believe in an evil God? Pragmatic encroachment and some implications for philosophy of religion" (2015), "Two Christian Theologies of Depression" (2016), and "Is depression a sin? A philosophical consideration of Christian voluntarism" (2017).

Peter N. Stearns is Professor of History and Provost Emeritus at George Mason University. Professor Stearns has written on world and emotions history, including two popular textbooks. Other books include *Shame: A Brief History* (2017), *The Industrial Turn in World History* (2016), *Guiding the American University: Challenges and Choices* (2015), *Doing Emotions History* (2013), and *Gender in World History* (2000). Before coming to George Mason University, Professor Stearns taught at The University of Chicago, Rutgers University, and Carnegie Mellon University. He served as Vice-President of the American Historical Association, Teaching Division, from 1995 to 1998. He was also founder and editor of the *Journal of Social History* from 1967 to 2015.

Peta Tait is a scholar, playwright, and Professor at La Trobe University, Melbourne. She is a Fellow of the Australian Academy of the Humanities and has written sixty scholarly articles and chapters. Books include *Fighting Nature: Travelling Menageries, Animal Acts and War Shows* (2016), the coedited *The Routledge Circus Studies Reader* (2016), *Wild and Dangerous Performances* (2012), *Circus Bodies* (2005), and *Performing Emotions* (2002). She is currently researching emotion and affect in theatrical performance for *Emotion* (forthcoming). Her most recent play, *Eleanor and Mary Alice*—about Eleanor Roosevelt and Mary Alice Evatt and human rights, art, and war—was remounted in 2016.

CONTRIBUTORS

Wiebke Thormählen is the Area Leader in History at the Royal College of Music in London. Recently awarded a three-year collaborative research grant from the Arts and Humanities Research Council (*Music, Home and Heritage: Sounding the Domestic in Georgian Britain*) she explores the interaction of the domestic with the public in musical arrangements, in devotional music, and in the relationship between music as domestic social activity and the development of amateur choral societies in Britain. She is co-editor of the *Routledge Companion to Music, Mind and Wellbeing: Historical and Scientific Perspectives* (forthcoming). Her current book project exposes layers of meaning behind different forms of "musical engagements" in early 19th-century London.

Gillian Whitlock is a Professor in the School of Communication and Arts at The University of Queensland, and a Fellow of the Australian Academy of the Humanities Australia. She publishes on life writing, including *Soft Weapons. Autobiography in Transit* (2006), and most recently *Postcolonial Life Narrative: Testimonial Transactions* (2015). She is currently working on *The Testimony of Things*, a monograph on life narrative and forced migration, drawing on the archives of asylum seeker-letters from Nauru.

NOTES

Introduction

1. The *Interpretation of Dreams*, published in 1905, propelled him into the limelight as a leading neurologist.

Chapter 1

1. For a summary of the inquiry, see Lord Southborough 1922.
2. The distinction between commotion and emotion was a commonly accepted formula for differentiating between physically and psychologically injured soldiers (Léri 1918); Léri was a French neurologist, whose responsibilities during the First World War included diagnosing soldiers suffering from neuroses, and whose work was cited in the *Report of the War Office Committee* (1922: 215).
3. The perceived parallels between shell-shocked soldiers and hysterical women, as well as the contrasting therapeutic approaches of Lewis Yealland and W. H. R. Rivers, are discussed in Showalter (1987: 167–94).
4. A wound stripe was worn on the left sleeve and identified a soldier wounded in combat.
5. The history of non-Western theories of emotions has a separate trajectory and historiography and is not explored further here. For useful discussions, see Hsu 2013 and Santangelo 2014.
6. See, for example, Anon. 1872; Snow 1891. For further discussion of contemporary links between emotions, stress, and disease, see Jackson (2014: 56–62).
7. Burke cited Crile, Cannon, and others to reinforce his argument about the need to integrate psychotherapy and medicine.
8. Cannon also explored the role of emotional stress in cases of sudden death (Cannon 1942b).
9. For discussion of the links between Cannon's physiology and politics, see Jackson (2014: 62–75).
10. Helen Flanders Dunbar in particular was influenced by Walter Cannon: "The fundamental work on emotion and adrenals carried on by W. B. Cannon and his co-workers for over twenty years is so well known both in this country and abroad that only brief reference will be made to portions of it" (Dunbar 1946: 164).
11. Alexander's "magic seven" overlapped with Crile's catalog of emotional diseases, as well as with subsequent accounts of stress-related diseases or diseases of adaptation, demonstrating the genealogical links between these domains of clinical inquiry. For explicit reference to these intersections, see Halliday 1950.
12. Postwar allergists also recognized a link between emotion and allergy: see McGovern and Fernandez 1964.
13. For an evaluation of Peshkin's approach, see Stern 1981: 39–47.

14. On child guidance and emotional instability in childhood, see Hendrick 2003; Hayes 2007; and Stewart 2013.
15. Groen cited Alexander and Dunbar in his study of ulcerative colitis. The emotional vulnerability of maladapted or neurotic personalities was also discussed in the most prominent wartime study of stress in combat: Grinker and Spiegel 1945.
16. For explicit reference to behavior as the key indicator of emotional expression, see Gray 1987: 33.
17. On Selye's life and work, see Jackson 2014.
18. For an example of Selye's mechanistic model, see the illustration "Coping with stress," in Selye, "The nature of stress and its relation to cardiovascular disease," in Hans Selye Fonds, P0359/G1,2,0093, Division of Records Management and Archives, University of Montreal.
19. On Wolff and Engel, see Jackson (2014: 158–60, 220, 243). For a discussion of British studies of emotional health and stress, see Hayward 2014a.
20. In a popular advice book written some time later by John Fry, one of the most prominent general practitioners after the Second World War, a chapter was devoted to emotional problems and mental illness: Fry, Moulds, Stube and Gambill (1982: Chapter 15). See also Hayward 2014b.
21. For discussion of these tendencies in British politics, see Toye (2015: 1184–5). See also Halliwell (2013: 107–34) for analysis of the tensions between individual and corporate interests in America.
22. Hall's phrase was borrowed from the work of the Danish author Karin Michaëlis (1912), which narrates the post-divorce struggles of a forty-two-year-old woman through the lens of her diary entries. The American translation of Michaëlis's work was titled "The Critical Age," a term also used by Maranon (1929) in his study of the menopause.
23. For examples of self-help literature for the middle-aged, see Pitkin 1932; Pitkin Jr. 1965; Gillie 1969; and Bleakley 1978.
24. For a similar British publication on yoga and aging, see Dunne 1951.
25. American self-help literature, including Pitkin's work, is discussed in Currell 2007.
26. On the work of the Marriage Guidance Council in the context of debates about increasing state regulation of personal relationships, see Lewis 1990; 1991. The records of the Marriage Guidance Council and Tavistock Institute are in the Wellcome Library, SATCC. The most influential writer on marital tensions in postwar Britain was Henry Dicks, who was an honorary consultant at the Tavistock Clinic—see Dicks 1967.
27. In 1945, there were 15,634 divorces; in 1955, 26,816; in 1965, 37,785; and in 1975, 120,522. Rates of divorce are available from the Office of National Statistics. See also Benson (1997: 94–124).
28. The apotheosis of this satirical style, albeit one with a sober undertone, is perhaps the publication of *The Ladybird Book of the Midlife Crisis* (Hazeley and Morris 2015). See also Joe Ollman's graphic novel *Mid-life* (2011).

Chapter 2

1. "Demon exorcism" is a problematic translation, not least because *yaktovil* differs significantly from Christian exorcism rituals: while in Christianity the demons remain evil, in *yaktovil* they are transformed to relatively benign creatures; while in Christianity they are returned to hell, in *yaktovil* they are simply placed at the margins of the human social world (Kapferer 2006: 157).

Chapter 3

1. While jazz was hugely popular in the Weimar Republic, what was popular here was neither legitimate jazz nor American in origin. See, for example, Robinson 1994.
2. Quoted in Preston-Dunlop (1998), *Rudolf Laban: An Extraordinary Life*, 196.
3. A range of overview studies have summarized these fields and approaches in the twenty-first century: Juslin and Sloboda's (2011) *Oxford Handbook of Music and Emotion* laid out the complex interactions that need to be achieved between philosophical, cultural, historical, anthropological, sociological, psychological, and neuro-biological investigations into music, without however being able to present studies that bring these together. The volume usefully splits the application of findings from their investigation and distinguishes between studies in music making and studies in musical listening.

Chapter 4

1. The significances of intercultural emotion are beyond the scope of this short chapter (for some discussion, see Tait and Shim 2006).

Chapter 5

1. Thus van Gogh noted: "The imagination is certainly a faculty which we must develop, one which alone can lead us to the creation of a more exalting and consoling nature than the single brief glance at reality" (van Gogh 1968). And Gauguin is even more insistent on releasing the energies of the medium: "One does not use colour to draw but always to give musical sensations which flow from itself, from its own nature, from its mysterious and enigmatic interior force" (Gauguin 1896–97).
2. On this point it is useful to consider Hermann Bahr's comment in 1916, which posits what seems to me a terrific contrast between Impressionism and the emerging taste for Expressionist art in Germany: "Impressionism is the falling away of man from spirit. Impressionism is man lowered to the position of gramophone record of the outer world. . . . Half-way in the act of seeing these Impressionists stop, just where the eye, having been challenged should make its reply. . . . Instead of eyes, Impressionists have another sense of ears, but no mouth, for man of the bourgeois period is nothing but an ear, he listens to the world but does not breathe upon it. . . . The Expressionist, on the contrary, tears open the mouth of humanity . . .—once more it seeks to give the spirit's reply" (Hermann Bahr, "Expressionism," in Harrison and Wood 2002: 119–20).
3. No critics capture these demands on consciousness better than Albert Gleizes and Jean Metzinger speaking about Cézanne's ability to merge "profound realism" with "luminous spirituality." They write, "His work, an homogenous block, stirs under our glance; it contracts, withdraws, melts, or illuminates itself and proves beyond all doubt that painting is not, or is no longer—the art of imitating an object by means of lines and colours, but the art of giving to our instinct a plastic consciousness" (Albert Gleizes and Jean Metzinger, "Cubism," in Harrison and Wood 2002: 195).
4. For example, George Braque's "Thoughts on Painting" defines what audiences must consider when painting's "subject is not the object": "One does not imitate the appearance; the appearance is the result. . . . The senses deform, the mind forms. Work to perfect the mind. There is no certainty except in what the mind conceives. . . . Emotion must not be rendered by an emotional trembling. It is not something that is added, or that is imitated.

It is the germ, the work is the flowering" (George Braque, "Thoughts on Painting," in Harrison and Wood 2002: 214–15).
5. Consider, for example, Paul Klee's insistence that the new art place "more value on the powers which do the forming than on the final forms themselves" (Paul Klee, "On Modern Art," in Harrison and Wood 2002: 367).
6. This sharp separation between the domains of nature and of mind or spirit is difficult to imagine now in our egocentric, materialist academic culture. But it is crucial to recognize how the successes of Impressionism could become embarrassments for ambitious younger painters eager to escape compromise with bourgeois life on every possible level.
7. Therefore emotions can usually be easily recognized. The obviousness of Edvard Munch's *The Scream* (1893; National Gallery, Oslo) is part of the point: the painting is driven by what becomes an exclusive intensity of pressure that offers no relief in any action more than holding one's head. Munch refers to the fact that emotions can call upon quite primitive and instinctive features of brain activity: when sensations seem to warrant fear, all our attention gets devoted to flight or preparation for struggle. But other actions can involve considerable complexity and cultural training. Consider how the relation to possible action is realized in Henri Matisse's *Conversation* (1908–12; Hermitage Museum, Saint Petersburg), where all the energy resides in the man and the woman's dignity, achieved by recognizing their incapacity to act on the tension they feel.
8. I speak as if we experienced only one emotion or one set of feelings at a time. But obviously we are complex beings capable of intense affective tension and confusion about which plots we are within or which feelings we can most effectively pursue, or even how feelings are being played against one another. And it is important to recognize that Modernism's insistence on sharp differences between emotions and feelings is not typical of the history of Western art, where typically feelings and emotions reinforce one another.
9. See Roger Frye: "In the imaginative life no such action is necessary and therefore, the whole consciousness may be focused upon the perceptive and the emotional aspects of the experience. In this way we get, in the imaginative life, a different set of values, and a different kind of perception" (From "Essay in Aesthetics," in Harrison and Wood 2002: 76).
10. Consider, for example, how Matisse's *Goldfish* (1912; Pushkin Museum of Fine Arts, Moscow) disciplines that same freedom of colored surfaces in his *Window* so that he can create a magisterially calm parallel between the goldfish, curious and content in their space, and the viewers' ability in their more spacious confinement to make an entire world out of the slow rhythms within a highly limited fragment of the real. Or turn to the rich interplay of blues modulating the movements within the drastically reduced visual field of *Landscape Viewed from a Window* (1912–13; Pushkin Museum of Fine Arts, Moscow). Here the affect is as close as Matisse comes to the Cubist sense of discipline as the means to sumptuousness. Finally notice how desire is staged in *Portrait of Mme Matisse* (1913; Hermitage Museum, Saint Petersburg), not as lust for her sexual being but as responsiveness to what her outfit and posture do for visual intensification.
11. It helps to remember that Guillaume Apollinaire called Fauvism "a kind of introduction to Cubism" (Harrison and Wood 2002: 189) because Picasso, Braque, and the others had the same desire to stage the freeing of creative energy to work out its own dictates and produce modes of feeling capable of freeing painting from its obligations toward objects.
12. For example, that refusal allows audiences to focus on how human creativity makes itself visible without crutches provided by the object world. In Malevich's words, "Objects embody a mass of movements in time. Their forms are various, and consequently their

depictions are various. All these aspects of time in things and their anatomy—the rings of a tree—have become more important than their essence and meaning. . . . Then in our era of Cubism the artist has destroyed objects together with their meaning, essence, and purpose. The new picture has sprung from their fragments. . . . Our world of art has become new, non-objective, pure . . . In the art of Suprematism forms will live, like all living forms of nature. . . . The new realism in painting is very much realism in painting, for it contains no realism of mountains, sky, water" (Kasimir Malevich, "From Cubism to Suprematism in Art, to New Realism in Painting, to Absolute Creation," in Harrison and Wood 2002: 180–1).

13. Actually the fullest possibilities of Surrealism were articulated by Picasso, although he never identified himself as a Surrealist. Had I the space I would offer an extended analysis of his *The Three Dancers* (1925; Tate Gallery, London) because of its demonstration of how the artist's invented figures could determine a center of attention that sharply contrasted a world of mystery that painting could make present to the limited range of our capacities for verbal interpretation. And had I the space I could have taken advantage of T. J. Clark's brilliant book on Picasso's work during the 1920s and 1930s, *Picasso and Truth: From Cubism to Guernica* (Princeton: Princeton University Press, 2013). See especially pp. 123–36 for an eloquent description of *Three Dancers*.

Consider how *Three Dancers* alters the world presented in Matisse's *The Open Window*. For Matisse there was a distinctive inside and outside, mediated by the window but not violated by it. But now Surrealism has intervened. On the literal level of *Three Dancers* there is nothing outside the window but two shades of blue that make cameo appearances in the scene before the window as well. Yet this window without has a significant architectural role in elaborating what can be involved in keeping the work faithful to the energies of fantasy. The promise of an outside to the window in *The Three Dancers* turns out to be instead another projection of the psyche, whose power is the subject of the painting. For, as T. J. Clark points out, the specifics of the imagery engage in a struggle with the spatial force of the painting, as if space represented the realm of rational intelligibility wanting to spread out for dissection the intricate figuration whose immediacy the psyche wants to preserve—for Nietzschean rather than for Freudian reasons.

Each of the three dancers represents a different aspect of what we might call the ontology of dance—dance as the abandon of a maenad, dance as joy, and dance as macabre reminder of what loss of control can entail. And each dancer has to combat two aspects of space—space as formal design and space as that feature which rationalizes what is present in terms of three-dimensional structures. No wonder that the three figures become in many ways adjusted to the overall design features of the window and room. And no wonder the space of the room proves deeply antagonistic to the figures who seek multi-dimensional abandon to all that dance can imply. After all, space is the primary figure Henri Bergson develops for the power of Reason in his influential *Introduction to Metaphysics*. Yet the dancers do not quite succumb. They manage to maintain a powerful tension between the deep interiority of what they represent and the visual space as organized surface. And that tension itself provides a kind of presence for the figures that makes possible a surrender to what is not reconcilable with reason. This abandon has to be played out through all its consequences, including the risk of having it associated with the death's head and the shadowy version of the dancer figure on the left.

So just as painting for the Cubist Picasso sets creativity against the authority of objects, here the figuration embraced by the painting has to embrace the totality of what it constructs. It must include death in the design, and in whatever enables us to put up with

the indifferent blue that may be a kind of death in life that the three dancers resist in their way of insisting on their own space. Then the design can be seen as making present an activity of consciousness that wins the right to fantasy by facing all the otherness provided by Reason's efforts to dominate the scene.
14. Although this image cannot be viewed in this chapter, the reader is encouraged to look for examples of the artist's work on the Internet.
15. For brilliant close readings of Pollock's drip paintings, see Clark 2001 and Varnedoe 1998.
16. Although this image cannot be viewed in this chapter, the reader is encouraged to look for examples of the artist's work on the Internet.
17. "But Rauschenberg had a much more direct effect [than Jasper Johns] on other artists. It was largely to his prancing, careless, and fecund talent that America in the 1960s and 70s owed a basic cultural assumption that a work of art could exist for any length of time, in any material . . ., anywhere . . ., for any purpose . . ., and find any destination it chooses, from the museum to the trashcan" (Hughes 1997: 515). (Characteristically, Robert Hughes stresses all of life being open to art, and not the more important notion basic to Rauschenberg that continues to influence artists—that the materials of ordinary life also define the conditions and obligations that must find their accounting within works of art.)
18. Although this image cannot be viewed in this chapter, the reader is encouraged to look for examples of the artist's work on the Internet.
19. There is a very good elaboration of Deleuze on assemblage in DeLanda 2006.
20. Although this image cannot be viewed in this chapter, the reader is encouraged to look for examples of the artist's work on the Internet.

Chapter 6

1. Examples of this process include the rise of Marxist theory, feminist theory in the 1960s and 1970s, and post-colonial theory in the 1980s and 1990s.
2. The Canadian affect theorist Brian Massumi's work on the ontology of threat demonstrates how literary theory responded to the climate of anxiety in the wake of the attacks (Massumi, 2010). See also https://historiesofemotion.com/2014/11/21/abusing-brian-massumi/ for a discussion of how literary scholars drew parallels between their own emotions and those of historical figures and literary characters.
3. The term "archiving machines" is used by Clough and Halley (2007: 2–3) to characterize the "affective turn" in theory, that they characterize as an expression of new configurations of bodies, technology, and matter that instigate a shift in thought in critical theory—toward, for example, the agency of non-human actors, such as this.
4. "My argument explores how emotions can move through the movement or circulation of objects. Such objects become sticky, or saturated with affect, as sites of personal and social tension. Emotions are after all moving . . ." (Ahmed 2004: 11).
5. The immediate inspiration for Peter Brooks's comments on the necessity for careful and ethical reading is the release of the "Torture Memos" by the United States Department of Justice in the years following 2002, that justifies the use of torture in what Brooks argues is "bad-faith interpretation" (Brooks 2014: 1).
6. See Keen's *Empathy and the Novel* (2007: xviii) for an extended and skeptical discussion of Nussbaum, Pinker, and Hunt as voices from the fields of philosophy, psychology, and history respectively, that represent "the common argument that novel reading results in civic good." For an authoritative analysis of narrative ethics and its engagement with the novel, see Phelan (nd).

7. The Great Books debate refers to controversies over literature and values in the tertiary curriculum, and the apparent threat to the liberal arts curriculum and the Western canon, owing to identity politics and multi-culturalism.
8. Wayne Booth is one of a number of American critics associated with reader response criticism—others include Stanley Fish, Wolfgang Iser, and Michael Riffaterre—that began in the late 1960s and became increasingly influential in the 1970s. They argued that questions of the literary texts and their meanings cannot be disengaged from the role of the reader.
9. Nick Mansfield draws a distinction between "self" and "subject": ". . . the word 'self' does not capture the sense of social and cultural entanglement that is implicit in the word 'subject': the way our immediate daily life is always already caught up in complex political, social and philosophical—that is, shared—concerns" (Mansfield 2000: 3). "Subjectivity," then, "defies our separation into distinct selves" and encourages us to imagine that our interior lives are connected to others, either as objects of need, desire, and interest, or as sharers of some common experience (ibid.). Both Nussbaum and Spivak focus on subjectivity and the capacity of the narrative imagination to cultivate this sense of self in relation to others, despite their very different philosophical engagements.
10. New Criticism was influential in the academy in the postwar period and is associated with the American critics Cleanth Brooks, W. K. Wimsatt, and Monroe Beardsley. It involved a way of reading that focused on the words on the page rather than authorial intention, historical and ideological context, or reader response. These critics argued that to take account of subjective readers' responses was an error, an "affective fallacy."
11. For an overview of recent neuroscience and reading (e.g. the discovery of mirror neurons that indicate a biological foundation for empathy), see Jurecic (2011).
12. For an overview of recent research in psychology and reading, see Keen (2007: Chapter 1).
13. Jane Radway associates middlebrow reading with forums such as book clubs, that offer readers alternatives to academic reading and elite standards of literary value by stressing the affective experience of being "moved" by reading—as we see in the promotion of Dickens's *Great Expectations* on the Oprah Book Club site and in the telecasts that feature Oprah herself as a middlebrow reader.
14. This "sentimentalized pitch" in the promotion of Dickens is disparaged by, for example, Hillary Kelly (2010).
15. "I *feel* I ought to admire the latter [*Jane Eyre*] more than I do, since so many readers like it," remarks the critic J. Hillis Miller in an act of "unruly reading"; "*Jane Eyre* seems to me sentimental wish-fulfilment, in its grand climax of Jane's marriage to a blinded and maimed Rochester, symbolically castrated: 'Reader, I married him'" (Miller 2005: 254, our emphasis). "You never know where reading a given book might lead you" (ibid.), Miller argues, deconstructing an ethical imperative to read empathetically in pursuit of social justice with an affirmation of the unpredictability of every reading and every text, that he characterizes as an erotic event. Virginia Woolf also performs an unruly reading of *Jane Eyre* in her essay *A Room of One's Own*.

Chapter 8

1. This chapter draws upon our previous work, most notably Bleiker and Hutchison (2008: 115–35) and Hutchison and Bleiker (2014: 491–513).

REFERENCES

Abu-Lughod, L. and Lutz, C.A. (1990), "Introduction: Emotion, Discourse, and the Politics of Everyday Life", in L. Abu-Lughod and C.A. Lutz (eds), *Language and the Politics of Emotion*, Cambridge: Cambridge University Press: 1–23.

Åhäll, L. and Gregory, T. (eds) (2015), *Emotions, Politics and War*, New York: Routledge.

Ahmed, S. (2004), *The Cultural Politics of Emotion*, New York: Routledge.

Alberti, F.B. (2010), *Matters of the Heart: History, Medicine and Emotion*, Oxford: Oxford University Press.

Alberti, F.B. (ed.) (2006), *Medicine, Emotion and Disease, 1700–1950*, Basingstoke, UK: Palgrave Macmillan.

Aldred, L. (2000), "Plastic Shamans and Astroturf Sun Dances: New Age Commercialization of Native American Spirituality", *American Indian Quarterly*, 24.3: 329–52.

Alexander, F. (1939), "Psychological Aspects of Medicine", *Psychosomatic Medicine*, 1: 7–18.

Altglas, V. (2014), *From Yoga to Kabbalah: Religious Exoticism and the Logics of Bricolage*, Oxford: Oxford University Press.

Ambos, E. (2011), "The Obsolescence of the Demons? Modernity and Possession in Sri Lanka", in F. Ferrari (ed.), *Health and Religious Rituals in South Asia: Disease, Possession and Healing*, New York: Routledge: 199–212.

American Psychiatric Association (2000), *Diagnostic and Statistical Manual of Mental Disorders* (4th edn, text rev.), Washington, DC: American Psychiatric Association Publishing.

Amoss, P. (1978), *Coast Salish Spirit Dancing*, Seattle: University of Washington Press.

Anon. (1872), "Increase of Heart-Disease", *The Times*, 25 March: 7.

Artaud, A. (1958), *The Theatre and its Double*, New York: Grove Press.

Asmus, E.P. (1985), "The Development of a Multidimensional Instrument for the Measurement of Affective Responses to Music", *Psychology of Music*, 13(1): 19–30.

Astor, D. (1962), "Towards a Study of the Scourge", *Encounter*, August: 60–2.

Australian Music Centre: australianmusiccentre.com.au/artist/davidson-robert.

Bailey, B.L. (1987), "Scientific Truth . . . and Love: The Marriage Education Movement in the United States", *Journal of Social History*, 20(4): 711–32.

Bailey, B.L. (1988), *From Front Porch to Back Seat: Courtship in Twentieth-Century America*, Baltimore: Johns Hopkins University Press.

Bal, P.M. and Veltkamp, M. (2013), "How Does Fiction Reading Influence Empathy? An Experimental Investigation on the Role of Emotional Transportation", PLOS One, 30 January. <http://journals.plos.org/plosone/article?id=10.1371/journal.pone.0055341> [accessed 26 January 2017].

Balzacq, T. and Jervis, R. (2004), "Logics of Mind and International System: A Journey with Robert Jervis", *Review of International Studies*, 30: 564–5.

Baraka, A. (1965), *Dutchman*, London: Samuel French.

Baraka, A. (1967), *A Black Mass*, Sunboy Records.

Barbalet, J.M. (2001), *Emotion, Social Theory, and Social Structure: A Macrosociological Approach*, Cambridge: Cambridge University Press.

Barnes, R. (1982), *The Who: Maximum R&B*. Medford, New Jersey, USA: Plexus Publishing.
Bateson, M.C. (1984), *With a Daughter's Eye: Memoir of Margaret Mead and Gregory Bateson*, New York: W. Morrow.
Beck, U. and Beck-Gernsheim, E. (1995), *The Normal Chaos of Love*, Cambridge: Polity Press.
Beckett, S. (1990), *The Complete Dramatic Works*, London: Faber and Faber.
Benison, S., Barger, A.C., and Wolfe, E.L. (1987), *Walter B. Cannon: The Life and Times of a Young Scientist*, Cambridge, MA: Harvard University Press.
Benison, S., Barger, A.C., and Wolfe, E.L. (1991), "Walter B. Cannon and the Mystery of Shock: A Study of Anglo-American Co-operation in World War I", *Medical History*, 35: 217–49.
Benson, J. (1997), *Prime Time: A History of the Middle Aged in Twentieth-Century Britain*, London: Longman.
Benson, S.P. (1986), *Counter Cultures: Saleswomen, Managers, and Customers in American Department Stores, 1890–1940*, Urbana, IL: University of Illinois Press.
Berggren, K. (1998), *Circle of Shaman: Healing through Ecstasy, Rhythm and Myth*, Rochester, VT: Inner Traditions/Bear & Co.
Berlant, L. (1998), "Poor Eliza", *American Literature*, 70(3), September: 635–68.
Berlant, L. (ed.) (2004), *Compassion: The Culture and Politics of an Emotion*, New York and London: Routledge.
Bernstein, R. (2011), "Children's Books, Dolls, and the Performance of Race; or, The Possibility of Children's Literature", *PMLA*, 126(1): 160–9.
Bially Mattern, J. (2011), "A Practice Theory of Emotion for International Relations", in E. Adler (ed.), *International Practices*, Cambridge: Cambridge University Press: 63–86.
Biess, F. and Gross, D.M. (eds) (2014), *Science and Emotions after 1945: A Transatlantic Perspective*, Chicago: University of Chicago Press.
Bijsterveld, K. (2003), "The Diabolical Symphony of the Mechanical Age", in M. Bull and L. Back (eds), *The Auditory Culture Reader*, Bodmin and King's Lynn, UK: Berg Publishers: 165–89.
Blain, J. (2002), *Nine Worlds of Seid Magic: Ecstasy and Neo-Shamanism in North European Paganism*, London and New York: Routledge.
Blair, E. (2007), *Virginia Woolf and the Nineteenth Century Domestic Novel*, State University of New York Press.
Blamires, H. (1984), *A Short History of English Literature*, New York: Routledge.
Bleakley, E. (1978), *Life Begins at Fifty*, Ilfracombe, UK: Arthur H. Stockwell.
Bleiker, R. (2009), *Aesthetics and World Politics*, New York: Palgrave Macmillan.
Bleiker, R. and Hutchison, E. (2008), "Fear No More: Emotions and World Politics", *Review of International Studies*, 34(S1): 115–35.
Bogacz, T. (1989), "War Neurosis and Cultural Change in England, 1914–22: The Work of the War Office Committee of Enquiry into 'Shell-Shock'", *Journal of Contemporary History*, 24: 227–56.
Bohlmann, P. (2002), "Landscape – Region – Nation – Reich: German Folk Song in the Nexus of National Identity", in C. Applegate and P. Potter (eds), *Music and German National Identity*, Chicago and London: Chicago University Press.
Booth, K. and Wheeler, N.J. (2007), *The Security Dilemma: Fear, Cooperation, and Trust in World Politics*, Basingstoke, UK: Palgrave.
Bourke, J. (1996), *Dismembering the Male: Men's Bodies, Britain and the Great War*, London: Reaktion.
Bourke, J. (2000), "Effeminacy, Ethnicity and the End of Trauma: The Sufferings of 'Shell-Shocked' Men in Great Britain and Ireland, 1914–39", *Journal of Contemporary History*, 35: 57–69.

Bourke, J. (2003), "Fear and Anxiety: Writing about Emotion in Modern History", *History Workshop Journal*, 55: 111–33.

Bourke, J. (2005), *Fear: A Cultural History*, London: Virago Press.

Brady, M. (2013), *Emotional Insight: The Epistemic Role of Emotional Experience*, Oxford: Oxford University Press.

Brauer, J. (2016), "How can Music be Torturous?: Music in Nazi Concentration and Extermination Camps", *Music and Politics*, 10(1): 1–34.

Brecht, B. (1987), *Brecht on Theatre*, trans. J. Willett, New York: Hill and Wang.

Brooks, G. (2005), *March*, Sydney: Harper Perennial.

Brooks, P. (2014), "Introduction" in P. Brooks (ed.) with H. Jewett, *The Humanities and Public Life*, New York: Fordham University Press: 1–14.

Brooks, P. (ed.) with H. Jewett (2014), *The Humanities and Public Life*, New York: Fordham University Press.

Brown, B. (2004), *Women and Shame: Reaching Out, Speaking Truths and Building Connection*, Houston: 3C Press.

Brown, B. (2012), Listening to Shame, TED video, March. <https://www.ted.com/talks/brene_brown_listening_to_shame?language=en> [accessed 27 January 2016].

Burke, N.H.M. (1926), "Some Aspects of the Inter-Relation between Bodily and Mental Disease", *British Journal of Medical Psychology*, 6: 110–20.

Cage, J. (2011), *Silence: Lectures and Writings*, Middletown, CT: Wesleyan University Press.

Callahan, W.A. (2004), "National Insecurities: Humiliation, Salvation and Chinese Nationalism", *Alternatives: Global, Local, Political*, 29(2): 199–218.

Campbell, C. (1987), *The Romantic Ethic and the Spirit of Modern Consumerism*, Oxford: Basil Blackwell.

Campbell, E. (2010), *Boulez, Music and Philosophy*, Cambridge: Cambridge University Press.

Cannon, W.B. (1914), "The Interrelations of Emotions as Suggested by Recent Physiological Researches", *American Journal of Psychology*, 25: 256–82.

Cannon, W.B. (1922a), "Some Conditions Controlling Internal Secretion", *Journal of the American Medical Association*, 79: 92–5.

Cannon, W.B. (1922b), "New Evidence for Sympathetic Control of Some Internal Secretions", *American Journal of Psychiatry*, 79: 15–30.

Cannon, W.B. (1927), "The James-Lange Theory of Emotions: A Critical Examination and an Alternative Theory", *American Journal of Psychology*, 39: 106–24.

Cannon, W.B. (1928), "The Mechanism of Emotional Disturbance of Bodily Functions", *New England Journal of Medicine*, 198: 877–84.

Cannon, W.B. (1929), "Organization for Physiological Homeostasis", *Physiological Reviews*, 9: 399–431.

Cannon, W.B. (1933), "Biocracy: Does the Human Body Contain the Secret of Economic Stabilization?", *The Technology Review*, 35: 203–27.

Cannon, W.B. (1935), "Stresses and Strains of Homeostasis", *American Journal of the Medical Sciences*, 189: 1–14.

Cannon, W.B. (1936), "The Rôle of Emotion in Disease", *Annals of Internal Medicine*, 9: 1453–65.

Cannon, W.B. (1937), *Digestion and Health*, London: Martin Secker and Warburg.

Cannon, W.B. (1939), *Bodily Changes in Pain, Hunger, Fear and Rage*, 2nd edn, New York: D. Appleton-Century Co.

Cannon, W.B. (1941), "The Body Physiologic and the Body Politic", *Science*, 93: 1–10.

Cannon, W.B. (1942a), *The Body as a Guide to Politics*, London: Watts and Co.

Cannon, W.B. (1942b), "'Voodoo' Death", *American Anthropologist*, 44: 169–81.
Cannon, W.B. [1932] (1939), *The Wisdom of the Body*, New York: W. W. Norton and Company.
Caracciolo, M. (2012), "Narrative, Meaning, Interpretation: An Enactivist Approach", *Phenomenology and the Cognitive Sciences*, 11: 367–84.
Carey, P. (1997), *Jack Maggs*, Brisbane: University of Queensland Press.
Carnegie, D. (1998), *How to Win Friends and Influence People*, New York: Pocket Books.
Carnicke, S. (1998/2009), *Stanislavsky in Focus*, London: Routledge.
Castaneda, C. (1968), *The Teaching of Don Juan*, Berkeley, CA: University of California Press.
Chaudhuri, U. (1986), *No Man's Stage: A Semiotic Study of Jean Genet's Major Plays*, Ann Arbor: UMI Research Press.
Chauncey, G. (1994), *Gay New York: Gender, Urban Culture, and the Making of the Gay Male World, 1890–1940*, New York: Basic Books.
Chauncey, G. (2004), *Why Marriage? The History Shaping Today's Debate Over Gay Equality*, New York: Basic Books.
Chekhov, A. (1977/1991), *Five Plays*, R. Hingley (trans.), Oxford: Oxford University Press.
Chettiar, T. (2016), "'More than a Contract': The Emergence of a State-Supported Marriage Welfare Service and the Politics of Emotional Life in Post–1945 Britain", *Journal of British Studies*, 55: 566–91.
Christensen, T. (2002), *The Cambridge History of Western Music Theory*, Cambridge: Cambridge University Press.
Churchill, C. (2000), *Far Away*, London: Nick Hern.
Churchill, C. (2012), *Love and Information*, London: Nick Hern.
Clark, T.J. (2001), *Farewell to an Idea*, New Haven, CT: Yale University Press.
Clark, T.J. (2013) *Picasso and Truth: From Cubism to Guernica*, Princeton, NJ: Princeton University Press.
Clarke, E. and Cook, N. (eds) (2004), *Empirical Musicology: Aims, Methods, Prospects*, Oxford: Oxford University Press.
Clift, S.M. and Hancox, G. (2001), "The Perceived Benefits of Singing: Findings from Preliminary Surveys of a University College Choral Society", *Journal of the Royal Society for the Promotion of Health*, 121: 248–56.
Climenhaga, R. (ed.) (2012), *The Pina Bausch Sourcebook: The Making of Tanztheater*, Oxford: Routledge.
Clore, G.L. and Huntsinger, J.R. (2009), "How the Object of Affect Guides its Impact", *Emotion Review*, 1(1): 39–54.
Clough, P.T. and Halley, J. (2007), *The Affective Turn: Theorizing the Social*, Durham and London: Duke University Press.
Coan, J.A. (2010), "Emergent Ghosts of the Emotion Machine", *Emotion Review*, 2(3): 274–85.
Cody, G. and Sprinchorn, E. (eds) (2007), *The Columbia Encyclopedia of Modern Drama*, Vols 1 and 2, New York: Columbia University Press.
Cohen, D. (2013), *Family Secrets: Shame and Privacy in Modern Britain*, New York: Oxford University Press.
Cohen, P. (2012), *In Our Prime: The Invention of Middle Age*, New York: Scribner.
Comstock, G.W. and Partridge, K.B. (1972), "Church Attendance and Health", *Journal of Clinical Epidemiology*, 25.12: 665–72. DOI <http://dx.doi.org/10.1016/0021-9681(72)90002-1>.
Coontz, S. (2006), *Marriage, a History: How Love Conquered Marriage*, New York: Penguin Books.
Copeland, R. and Cohen, M. (eds) (1983), *What is Dance?*, Oxford: Oxford University Press.

Costigliola, F. (2012), *Roosevelt's Lost Alliances: How Personal Politics Helped Start the Cold War*, Princeton, NJ: Princeton University Press.
Crawford, N.C. (2000), "The Passion of World Politics: Propositions on Emotions and Emotional Relationships", *International Security*, 24(4): 116–36.
Crawford, N.C. (2014), "Institutionalizing Passion in World Politics: Fear and Empathy", *International Theory*, 6(3): 535–57.
Crease, R.P. (2003), "Jazz and Dance" in M. Cooke and D. Horn (eds), *The Cambridge Companion to Jazz*, Cambridge: Cambridge University Press: 69–80.
Crile, G.W. [1915] (2006), *The Origin and Nature of the Emotions*, Charleston, SC: BiblioBazaar.
Cross, I. and Morley, I. (2009), "Communicative Musicality: Exploring the Basis of Human Companionship", in S. Malloch and C. Trevarthen (eds), *Communicative Musicality: Exploring the Basis of Human Companionship*, Oxford: Oxford University Press: 61–81.
Csikszentmihalyi, M. (1990). *Flow: The Psychology of Optimal Experience*, New York, NY: Harper Collins.
Cunningham, W.A., Dunfield, K.A., and Stillman, P.E. (2013), "Emotional States from Affective Dynamics", *Emotion Review*, 5(4): 344–55.
Currell, S. (2007), "Depression and Recovery: Self-help and America in the 1930s", in D. Bell and J. Hollows (eds), *Historicizing Lifestyle: Mediating Taste, Consumption and Identity from the 1900s to 1970s*, Surrey, UK: Ashgate Publishing: 131–44.
Curthoys, A. and Damousi, J. (eds) (2004). *What Did You Do in the Cold War, Daddy? Personal Stories from a Troubled Time*, Sydney: New South Publishing.
Cusick, S.G. (2015), "Music as Torture, Music as Weapon", in M. Bull and L. Back (eds), *The Auditory Culture Reader*, 2nd edn, London and New York: Bloomsbury Publishing: 379–93.
"Cyberbullying: What it is and how to get help", *Australian Human Rights Commission*. <https://www.humanrights.gov.au/cyberbullying-what-it-and-how-get-help-violence-harassment-and-bullying-fact-sheet>.
Daly, A. (1995), *Done into Dance: Isadora Duncan in America*, Bloomington, IN: Indiana University Press.
Damasio, A. (1994), *Descartes' Error: Emotion, Reason and the Human Brain*, London: Putnam Publishing.
Damasio, A. (2000), *The Feeling of What Happens: Body and Emotion in the Making of Consciousness*, London: Vintage.
Damousi, J. (2005), *Freud in the Antipodes*, Sydney: The University of New South Wales Press.
Damousi, J. (2014), "Mourning Practices" in J. Winter (ed.), *The Cambridge History of The First World War, Volume III: Civil Society* (pp. 358–9), Cambridge: Cambridge University Press.
Davidson, J.W. and Garrido, S. (2014), *My Life as a Playlist*, Perth: University of Western Australia Publishing.
Dawkins, R. (2006), *The God Delusion*, Boston, MA: Houghton Mifflin.
De Silva, P. (1994), *Buddhist and Freudian Psychology*, Singapore: Singapore University Press.
de Swaan, A. (1981), "The Politics of Agoraphobia", *Theory and Society* 10(3): 359–85.
Decroupet, P. and Ungeheuer, E. (1998), "Through the Sensory Looking-Glass: The Aesthetic and Serial Foundations of *Gesang der Jünglinge*", *Perspectives of New Music*, 36(1): 97–142.
Dein, S. (nd), Religion and Mental Health: Current Findings, Royal College of Psychiatrists. <https://www.rcpsych.ac.uk/pdf/Simon%20Dein%20Religion%20and%20Mental%20Health.%20Current%20Findings.pdf> [accessed September 18, 2015].
DeLanda, M. (2006), *A New Philosophy of Society: Assemblage Theory and Social Complexity*, London: Continuum.

Delumeau, J. (1990), *Sin and Fear: The Emergence of the Western Guilt Culture, 13th–18th Centuries*, London: Palgrave Macmillan.
Deveare Smith, A. (1992), *Twilight: Los Angeles*, New York: Dramatists Play Service.
Deveare Smith, A. (1997), *Fires in the Mirror*, New York: Dramatists Play Service.
Dicks, H. (1967), *Marital Tensions: Clinical Studies towards a Psychological Theory of Interaction*, London: Routledge and Kegan Paul.
Digeser, P. (2009), "Friendship Between States", *British Journal of Political Science*, 39(2): 323–44.
Dixon, T. (2003), *From Passions to Emotions: The Creation of a Secular Psychological Category*, Cambridge: Cambridge University Press.
Dixon, T. (2006), *From Passions to Emotions: The Creation of a Secular Psychological Category*, Cambridge: Cambridge University Press.
Dixon, T. (2012), "'Emotion': The History of a Keyword in Crisis", *Emotion Review*, 4: 338–44.
Dragastin, S. (1968), "The Religious Factor in the Structure of Psychological Well-being", PhD Dissertation, University of Chicago.
Draper, G. (1930), *Disease and the Man*, London: Kegan Paul, Trench, Trubner and Co.
Dror, O.E. (2005), "Dangerous Liaisons: Science, Amusement and the Civilizing Process", in P. Gouk and H. Hills (eds), *Representing Emotions: New Connections in the Histories of Art, Music and Medicine*, Aldershot and Burlington, VT: Ashgate: 223–34.
Dror, O.E. (1999), "The Scientific Image of Emotion: Experience and Technologies of Inscription", *Configurations*, 7: 355–401.
Dror, O.E. (2001), "Techniques of the Brain and the Paradox of Emotions, 1880–1930", *Science in Context*, 14: 643–60.
Dror, O.E. Hitzer, B., Laukötter, A., and León-Sanz, P. (2016), "An Introduction to *History of Science and the Emotions*", *Osiris*, 31: 1–18.
Dümling, A. and Girth, P. (eds) (1988), *Entartete Musik. Zur Düsseldorfer Ausstellung von 1938. Eine kommentierte Rekonstruktion*, Düsseldorf: Kleinherne.
Dunbar, H.F. (1946), *Emotions and Bodily Changes: A Survey of Literature on Psychosomatic Interrelationships, 1910–1945*, New York: Columbia University Press.
Dunbar, H.F. (1947), *Mind and Body: Psychosomatic Medicine*, New York: Random House.
Dunbar, R.I.M., Kaskatis, K., MacDonald, I., and Barra, V. (2012), "Performance of Music Elevates Pain Threshold and Positive Affect: Implications for the Evolutionary Function of Music", *Evolutionary Psychology*, 10(4): 688–702.
Duncan, P. (2017), *David Bowie: The Man Who Fell to Earth*. Cologne, Germany: Taschen.
Dunne, D. (1951), *Yoga for Everyman: How to Have Long Life and Happiness*, London: Gerlad Duckworth.
Edkins, J. (2003), *Trauma and the Memory of Politics*, Cambridge: Cambridge University Press.
Eerola, T. and Vuoskoski, J.K. (2013), "A Review of Music and Emotion Studies: Approaches, Emotion Models, and Stimuli", *Music Perception: An Interdisciplinary Journal*, 30(3): 307–40.
Eliade, M. (1964) [1951], *Shamanism: Archaic Techniques of Ecstasy*, New York: Pantheon.
Elias, N. (1982), *The Civilizing Process*, New York: Pantheon Books.
Elias, N. and Dunning, E. (1986), *Quest for Excitement: Sport and Leisure in the Civilizing Process*, New York: Basil Blackwell.
Erichsen, J.E. (1867), *On Railway and Other Injuries of the Nervous System*, Philadelphia: Henry C. Lea.
Erikson, E.H. (1994), *Identity and the Life Cycle*, New York: W. W. Norton and Company.

Esslin, M. (1968), *The Theatre of the Absurd*, Harmondsworth, UK: Penguin.
Evan Bonds, M. (1991), *Wordless Rhetoric: Musical Form and the Metaphor of the Oration*, Cambridge, MA: Harvard University Press.
Eyerman, R. and Jamison, A. (1998), *Music and Social Movements: Mobilizing Traditions in the Twentieth Century*, Cambridge: Cambridge University Press.
Eysenck, H.J. (1965), *Smoking, Health, and Personality*, London: Weidenfeld and Nicolson.
Eysenck, H.J. (1991), *Smoking, Personality and Stress: Psychosocial Factors in the Prevention of Cancer and Coronary Heart Disease*, New York: Springer-Verlag.
Eysenck, H.J. (1994), "Cancer, Personality and Stress: Prediction and Prevention", *Advances in Behaviour Research and Therapy*, 16: 167–215.
Eznack, L. (2011), "Crises as Signals of Strength: The Significance of Affect in Close Allies' Relationships", *Security Studies*, 20(2): 238–65.
Eznack, L. (2013), "The Mood Was Grave: Affective Dispositions and States' Anger-Related Behaviour", *Contemporary Security Policy*, 34(3): 552–80.
Farr, C.K. and Harker, J. (eds) (2008), *The Oprah Affect: Critical Essays on Oprah's Book Club*, Albany, NY: State University of New York Press.
Fass, P.S. (1999), *Kidnapped: Child Abduction in America*, Cambridge, MA: Harvard University Press.
Fattah, K. and Fierke, K.M. (2009), "A Clash of Emotions: The Politics of Humiliation and Political Violence in the Middle East", *European Journal of International Relations*, 15(1): 67–93.
Felski, R. (2008), *Uses of Literature*, Malden, MA: Blackwell Publishing.
Felski, R. (2015a), "Doing the Humanities (with Bruno Latour)", Unpublished conference paper, "Recomposing the Humanities with Bruno Latour", University of Virginia, September 18.
Felski, R. (2015b), *The Limits of Critique*, Chicago: University of Chicago Press.
Fierke, K.M. (2002), "The Liberation of Kosovo: Emotion and the Ritual Reenactment of War", *Focaal: European Journal of Anthropology*, 39: 93–113.
Fierke, K.M. (2004), "Whereof We Can Speak, Thereof We Must Not Be Silent: Trauma, Political Solipsism and War", *Review of International Studies*, 30(4): 471–91.
Fierke, K.M. (2013), *Political Self-Sacrifice: Agency, Body and Emotion in International Relations*, Cambridge: Cambridge University Press.
Fierke, K.M. (2014), "Emotion and Intentionality", *International Theory*, 6(3): 563–7.
Freeman, J. (1950), *Hay-Fever: A Key to the Allergic Disorders*, London: William Heinemann.
Freud, S. (1907), *Obsessive Acts, Religious Practices*. Reprinted (1953–1974) in the *Standard Edition of the Complete Psychological Works of Sigmund Freud*, Vol. 7, J. Strachey (ed.), London: Hogarth Press.
Frey, W.H. and Langseth, M. (1985), *Crying: The Mystery of Tears*, Minneapolis, MN: Winston Press.
Frijda, N.H. (1986), *The Emotions*, Cambridge: Cambridge University Press.
Frith, S., Straw, W., and Street, J. (2001), *The Cambridge Companion to Pop and Rock*, Cambridge: Cambridge University Press.
Fry, J., Moulds, A., Stube, G., and Gambill, E. (1982), *The Family Good Health Guide: Common Sense on Common Health Problems*, Lancaster, UK: MTP Press.
Fugard, A., Kani, J., and Ntshona, W. (1975), *The Island*, London: Samuel French.
Fulcher, J.F. (ed.) (2011), *The Oxford Handbook of the New Cultural History of Music*, Oxford and New York: Oxford University Press.
Furedi, F. (2015), *The Power of Reading: From Socrates to Twitter*, London: Bloomsbury.
Gaillot, M., Nancy, J.L., and Maffesoli, M. (1998), *Multiple Meaning: Techno, an Artistic and Political Laboratory of the Present*, Paris: Editions Dis Voir.

Gallagher, S. and Varga, S. (2013), "Social Constraints on the Direct Perception of Emotion and Intentions", *Topoi: An International Review of Philosophy*, 33: 185–99.

Gammon, E. (2008), "Affect and the Rise of the Self-Regulatory Market", *Millennium: Journal of International Studies*, 37(2): 251–78.

Garber, M. (2004), "Compassion" in L. Berlant (ed.), *Compassion: The Culture and Politics of an Emotion*, New York and London: Routledge: 15–28.

Garner, S.B. (1994), *Bodied Spaces: Phenomenology and Performance in Contemporary Drama*, Ithaca, NY: Cornell University Press.

George, A.L. and George, J.L. (1998), *Presidential Personality and Performance*, Boulder, CO: Westview.

Gilliam, B. (ed.) (1994), *Music and Performance during the Weimar Republic*, Cambridge: Cambridge University Press.

Gillie, A. (1969), *Do Something about that Middle Age*, London: Wingate-Baker.

Glass, J., Simon, R., and Anderson, M. (2016), "Social Policies, Parenthood, and Happiness in 22 Countries", briefing paper prepared for the Council on Contemporary Families, June 16. <https://contemporaryfamilies.org/brief-parenting-happiness/> [accessed 4 August 2016].

Goldman, J. (2011), *The Musical Language of Pierre Boulez: Writings and Compositions*, Cambridge: Cambridge University Press.

Goleman, D. (1995), *Emotional Intelligence: Why it Can Matter More Than IQ*, New York: Bantam Books.

Gordon, M. (2000), "Salvaging Strasberg at the Fin de Siècle", in D. Krasner (ed.), *Method Acting Reconsidered*, New York: St Martin's Press: 43–60.

Gouk, P. and Hills, H. (eds) (2005), *Representing Emotions: New Connections in the Histories of Art, Music and Medicine*, Aldershot, UK: Ashgate.

Grant, M.J. and Papaeti, A. (2013), *Torture: Journal on Rehabilitation of Torture Victims and Prevention of Torture*, Thematic Issue on Music in Detention, 23(2).

Graver, L., and Federman, R. (1979), *Samuel Beckett: The Critical Heritage*, London: Routledge and Kegan Paul.

Gray, J.A. (1987), *The Psychology of Fear and Stress*, Cambridge: Cambridge University Press.

Grinker, R.R. and Spiegel, J.P. (1945), *Men Under Stress*, Philadelphia: Blakiston.

Griswold, R.L. (1993), *Fatherhood in America: A History*, New York: BasicBooks.

Groen, J. (1947), "Psychogenesis and Psychotherapy of Ulcerative Colitis", *Psychosomatic Medicine*, 9: 151–74.

Gross, D.M. (2006), *The Secret History of Emotion: From Aristotle's Rhetoric to Modern Brain Science*, Chicago: University of Chicago Press.

Gullette, M.M. (2004), *Aged by Culture*, Chicago: University of Chicago Press.

Hall, G.S. (1921), "The Dangerous Age", *Pedagogical Seminary*, 28: 275–94.

Hall, S. (1993), "Cultural Identity and Diaspora" in P. Williams and L. Chrismas (eds), *Colonial Discourse and Postcolonial Theory: A Reader*, Oxford and New York: Routledge, 2013.

Hall, T.H. (2011), "We Will Not Swallow This Bitter Fruit: Theorizing the Diplomacy of Anger", *Security Studies*, 20(4): 521–55.

Hallam, S., Cross, I., and Thaut, M. (2011), *Oxford Handbook of Music Psychology*, Oxford: Oxford University Press.

Halliday, J.L. (1950), "Significance of the Discovery of the Effects of Cortisone", *Lancet*, 256: 365–6.

Halliday, J.L. (1948), *Psychosocial Medicine: A Study of the Sick Society*, London.

Halliwell, E. (nd), Mindfulness Report. <http://www.livingmindfully.co.uk/downloads/Mindfulness_Report.pdf> [accessed 10 October 2015].

Halliwell, M. (2013), *Therapeutic Revolutions: Medicine, Psychiatry, and American Culture, 1945–1970*, New Brunswick, NJ: Rutgers University Press.

Handke, P. (1997), *Plays 1*, London: Methuen.

Hanlon, P. and Lyon, A. (2011), "Making the Case for a 'Fifth Wave' in Public Health", *Public Health*, 125: 30–6.

Harner, M. (1980), *The Way of the Shaman: A Guide to Power and Healing*, San Francisco: Harper & Row.

Harré, R. (ed.) (1986), *The Social Construction of Emotions*, Oxford: Basil Blackwell.

Harris, J. (2004), *Britpop!: Cool Britannia and the Spectacular Demise of English Rock*, Boston, MA: Da Capo Publishing.

Harrison, C. and Wood, P. (eds) (2002), *Art in Theory 1900–2000: An Anthology of Changing Ideas*, 2nd edn, Hoboken, NJ: Wiley-Blackwell.

Harvey, G. (2013), *Food, Sex and Strangers: Understanding Religion as Everyday Life*, New York: Routledge.

Harvey, G. (2015), "Food, Sex and Spirituality", in C. Coates and M.M. Emerich (eds), *Practical Spiritualities in a Media Age*, London: Bloomsbury, 189–204.

Hayes, S. (2007), "Rabbits and Rebels: The Medicalisation of Maladjusted Children in Mid-Twentieth-Century Britain", in M. Jackson (ed.), *Health and the Modern Home*, New York: Routledge: 128–52.

Hayward, R. (2014a), "Sadness in Camberwell: Imagining Stress and Constructing History in Postwar Britain", in D. Cantor and E. Ramsden (eds), *Stress, Shock, and Adaptation in the Twentieth Century*, Rochester, NY: University of Rochester Press: 320–42.

Hayward, R. (2014b), *The Transformation of the Psyche in British Primary Care 1880–1970*, London: Bloomsbury.

Hazeley, J.A. and Morris, J.P. (2015), *The Ladybird Book of the Midlife Crisis*, Loughborough, UK: Ladybird Books.

Heath, K. (2009), *Aging by the Book: The Emergence of Midlife in Victorian Britain*, Albany, NY: State University of New York Press.

Hendrick, H. (2003), "Children's Emotional Well-Being and Mental Health in Early Post-Second World War Britain: The Case of Unrestricted Hospital Visiting", in M. Gijswijt-Hofstra and H. Marland (eds), *Cultures of Child Health in Britain and the Netherlands in the Twentieth Century*, Amsterdam: Rodopi: 213–42.

Heriot-Maitland, C., Knight, M., and Peters, E. (2012), "A Qualitative Comparison of Psychotic Like Phenomena in Clinical and Non-Clinical Populations", *British Journal of Clinical Psychology*, 51: 37–53.

Hill, C. (2003), *The Changing Politics of Foreign Policy*, Basingstoke, UK: Palgrave.

Hobhouse, L.T. (1915), *The World in Conflict*, London: T. Fisher Unwin.

Hochschild, A.R. (2012), *The Managed Heart: Commercialization of Human Feeling*, Berkeley, CA: University of California Press.

Hodge, A. (2012) [2000], *Twentieth-Century Actor Training*, London: Routledge.

Holledge, J. and Tompkins, J. (2000), *Women's Intercultural Performance*, London: Routledge.

Holmes, M. (2013), "The Force of Face-to-Face Diplomacy: Mirror Neurons and the Problem of Intentions", *International Organization*, 67(4), 829–61.

Holmes, M. (2015), "Believing This and Alieving That: Theorizing Affect and Intuitions in International Politics", *International Studies Quarterly*, 59(4): 706–20.

Horwitz, A.V. (2013), *Anxiety: A Short History*, Baltimore, MD: Johns Hopkins University Press.

Hoschchild, A. (1979), "Emotion Work, Feeling Rules and Social Structure", *American Journal of Sociology*, 85(3): 551–75.
Hsu, E. (2013), "'Holism' and the Medicalization of Emotion: The Case of Anger in Chinese Medicine", in P. Horden and E. Hsu (eds), *The Body in Balance: Humoral Medicines in Practice*, New York: Bergahn: 197–217.
Huebner, B. (2011), "Genuine collective emotions", *European Journal for Philosophy of Science*, 1(1): 89–118.
Hughes, R. (1997), *American Visions: The Epic History of Art in America*, New York: Alfred A. Knopf.
Hunt, L. (2007), *Inventing Human Rights. A History*, New York and London: W. W. Norton and Company.
Hutcheon, L. (2006), *A Theory of Adaptation*, New York and London: Routledge.
Hutchison, E. (2014), "A Global Politics of Pity? Disaster Imagery and the Emotional Construction of Solidarity after the 2004 Asian Tsunami", *International Political Sociology*, 8(1): 1–19.
Hutchison, E. and Bleiker, R. (2014), "Theorizing Emotions in World Politics", *International Theory*, 6(3): 491–514.
Hutto, D.D. (2012), "Truly Enactive Emotion", *Emotion Review*, 4(2): 176–81.
Hutton, R. (2001), *Shamans: Siberian Spirituality and the Western Imagination*, New York: Hambleton and London.
Hyam, H. (2007), *Fred and Ginger: The Astaire-Rogers Partnership 1934–1938*, Brighton: Pen Press Publications.
Ibsen, H. (1982), *Plays: Two*, M. Meyer (trans.), London: Eyre Methuen.
Idom, M. (2013), *New Music at Darmstadt: Nono, Stockhausen, Cage, and Boulez*, Cambridge: Cambridge University Press.
Illouz, E. (2003), *Oprah Winfrey and the Glamour of Misery: An Essay on Popular Culture*, New York: Columbia University Press.
Illouz, E. (2007), *Cold Intimacies: The Making of Emotional Capitalism*, Cambridge: Polity.
Jackson, L., Hayward, M., and Cooke, A. (2010), "Developing Positive Relationships with Voices: A Preliminary Grounded Theory", *International Journal of Social Psychiatry*, 57(5): 487–95.
Jackson, M. (2006), *Allergy: The History of a Modern Malady*, London: Reaktion.
Jackson, M. (2014), *The Age of Stress: Science and the Search for Stability*, Oxford: Oxford University Press.
Jackson, M. (2015), "Men and Women Under Stress: Neuropsychiatric Models of Resilience during and after the Second World War", in M. Jackson (ed.), *Stress in Post-war Britain, 1945–85*, London: Pickering and Chatto: 111–29, 219–26.
Jackson, S.W. (2001), "The Wounded Healer", *Bulletin of the History of Medicine*, 75(1): 1–36.
Jacobson, L. (2004), *Raising Consumers: Children and the American Mass Market in the Early Twentieth Century*, New York: Columbia University Press.
Jain, A.R. (2012), "The Malleability of Yoga: A Response to Christian and Hindu Opponents of the Popularization of Yoga", *Journal of Hindu-Christian Studies*, 25, 1–18. <http://digitalcommons.butler.edu/jhcs/vol25/iss1/4/> [accessed 5 February 2017].
James, W. (1902), *The Varieties of Religious Experience: A Study in Human Nature*, London: Longmans, Green and Co.
James, W. (1929), *The Varieties of Religious Experience*, New York: University Virginia.
Jaques, E. (1965), "Death and the Mid-Life Crisis", *International Journal of Psycho-Analysis*, 46: 502–14.

Jaques, E. (1970), *Work, Creativity, and Social Justice*, London: Heinemann.
Jaques, E. (2002), *The Life and Behavior of Living Organisms: A General Theory*, Westport, CT: Praeger.
Jeffery, R. (2011), "Reason, Emotion and the Problem of World Poverty: Moral Sentiment Theory and International Ethics", *International Theory*, 3(1): 143–78.
Jervis, R. (1976), *Perception and Misperception in International Politics*, Princeton, NJ: Princeton University Press.
Jervis, R., Lebow, R.N., and Stein, J.G. (1985), *Psychology and Deterrence*, Baltimore, MD: John Hopkins University Press.
Johnson, B. (2003), "Jazz as Cultural Practice", in M. Cooke and D. Horn (eds), *The Cambridge Companion to Jazz*, Cambridge: Cambridge University Press: 96–113.
Jones, E. and Wessely, S. (2005), *Shell Shock to PTSD: Military Psychiatry from 1900 to the Gulf War*, Hove and New York: Psychology Press.
Jones, L. (2006), *Mister Pip*, Melbourne: Text Publishing.
Jung, C. (1978), *Psychology and Religion: Religion East and West*, in H. Read, M. Fordham, G. Adler and W. McGuire (eds); R.F.C. Hull (trans.), *The Collected Works of C. G. Jung*, vol. 11 of 21, Princeton, NJ: Princeton University Press (1953–79).
Jung, C.G. (1940), *The Integration of the Personality*, London: Kegan Paul, Trench, Trubner and Co.
Jung, Carl G. (1945), *Modern Man in Search of a Soul*, London: Kegan Paul, Trench, Trubner and Co.
Jurecic, A. (2011), "Empathy and the Critic", *College English*, 74(1), September: 10–27.
Juslin, P.N. and Laukka, P. (2004), "Expression, Perception, and Induction of Musical Emotions: A Review and a Questionnaire Study of Everyday Listening", *Journal of New Music Research*, 33(3): 217–38.
Juslin, P.N. and Sloboda, J. (2011), *Handbook of Music and Emotion: Theory, Research, Applications*, Oxford: Oxford University Press.
Kahler, M. (1998), "Rationality in International Relations", *International Organization*, 52(4): 919–41.
Kandinsky, W. (1977), *Concerning the Spiritual in Art*, Trans. M.T.H. Sadler, USA: Dover.
Kane, S. (2001), *Complete Plays*, London: Methuen.
Kant, M. (2007), "European Ballet in the Age of Ideologies", in M. Kant (ed.), *Cambridge Companion to Ballet*, Cambridge: Cambridge University Press, 272–90.
Kapferer, B. (2006), "Sorcery and the Beautiful: A Discourse on the Aesthetics of Ritual", in B. Kapferer and A. Hobart (eds), *Aesthetics in Performance: Formations of Symbolic Construction and Experience*, Oxford and New York: Berghahn Books.
Karina, L. and Kant, M. (2003), *Hitler's Dancers: German Modern Dance and the Third Reich*, New York: Berghan Books.
Kasson, J.F. (1990), *Rudeness and Civility: Manners in Nineteenth-Century Urban America*, New York: Hill and Wang.
Katz, R., Biesele, M., and St Denis, V. (1997), *Healing Makes our Hearts Happy: Spirituality and Cultural Transformation among the Kalahari*, Hong Kong: Inter Traditions International.
Keen, S. (2006), "A Theory of Narrative Empathy", *Narrative*, 14(3), October: 207–36.
Keen, S. (2007), *Empathy and the Novel*, Oxford: Oxford University Press.
Keil, W. (2003), "Die Verwirklichung des romantischen Klangideals im Theremin" ("The Realization of the Romantic Ideal of Sound by the Theremin"), *Alte Musik und "Neue" Medien. Series: Diskordanzen*, 14, Hildesheim: Georg Olms Verlag: 9–27.

Kelly, H. (2010), "Bad Expectations", *New Republic*, 14, December. <https://newrepublic.com/article/79875/bad-expectations-oprah-winfrey-book-club-dickens> [accessed 26 January 2017].

Kelly, T.F. (2000), *First Nights. Five Musical Premieres*, New Haven, CT and London: Yale University Press.

Kennaway, J. (2012), *Bad Vibrations: The History of the Idea of Music as Cause of Disease*, Farnham and Burlington, VT: Ashgate.

Kidd, D.C. and Castano, E. (2013), "Reading Literary Fiction Improves Theory of Mind", *Science*, 3 October. <http://science.sciencemag.org/content/early/2013/10/02/science.1239918.abstract?sid=f192d0cc-1443-4bf1-a043-61410da39519> [accessed 26 January 2017].

Kirschner, S. and Tomasello, M. (2010), "Joint Music-Making Promotes Prosocial Behavior in 4-year-old Children", *Evolution and Human Behavior*, 31(5): 354–64.

Klein, N. (2017). <http://www.naomiklein.org/reviews/bono-ization-activism>.

Koenig, H., King, D., and Carson, V. (2012), *Handbook of Religion and Health*, Oxford: Oxford University Press.

Krasner, D. (2011), *A History of Modern Drama*, Vol. 1, Chichester, UK: Wiley-Blackwell.

Krippner, S. (2007), "Os Primeiros Curadores da Humanidade: Abordagens Psicológicas e Psiquiátricas Sobre os Xamãs e o Xamanismo", *Revista de Psiquiatria Clínica*, 34(1). <http://www.scielo.br/scielo.php?script=sci_arttext&pid=S0101-60832007000700004&lng=pt&nrm=iso&tlng=pt> [accessed 11 October 2015].

Lamb, S. (2005), "Forgiveness Therapy: The Context and Conflict", *Journal of Theoretical and Philosophical Psychology*, 25(1): 61–80. <http://www.zku.amu.edu.pl/kuba/angelski/Forgiveness_Therapy.pdf> [accessed 5 February 2017].

Lang, M. (2009), *The Woodstock Experience*, London: Genesis Publications.

Lang, M., Shaw, D.J., Reddish, P., Wallot, S., Mitkidis, P., and Xygalatas, D. (2016), "Lost in the Rhythm: Effects of Rhythm on Subsequent Interpersonal Coordination", *Cognitive Science* 40(7): 1797–1814.

Lange, C.G. (1912), "The Mechanism of the Emotions", in B. Rand (ed.), *The Classical Psychologists*, Boston: Houghton Mifflin: 672–84.

Lange, C.G. and James, W. (1922), *The Emotions*, Baltimore, MD: Williams & Wilkins.

Langhamer, C. (2013), *The English in Love: The Intimate Story of an Emotional Revolution*, Oxford: Oxford University Press.

Lasch, C. (1977), *Heaven in a Heartless World: The Family Besieged*, New York: Basic Books.

Lazarus, R.S. (1961), *Adjustment and Personality*, New York: McGraw-Hill.

Lazarus, R.S. (1966), *Psychological Stress and the Coping Process*, New York: McGraw-Hill.

Lazarus, R.S. and Folkman, S. (1984), *Stress, Appraisal and Coping*, New York: Springer.

Lazarus, R.S., Speisman, J.C., and Mordkoff, A.M. (1963), "The Relationship between Autonomic Indicators of Psychological Stress: Heart Rate and Skin Conductance", *Psychosomatic Medicine*, 25: 19–30.

Lazarus, R.S., Speisman, J.C., Mordkoff, A.M., and Davison, L.A. (1962), "A Laboratory Study of Psychological Stress Produced by a Motion Picture Film", *Psychological Monographs: General and Applied*, 76: 1–35.

Lebow, R.N. (2005), "Reason, Emotion and Cooperation", *International Politics*, 42(3): 283–313.

Lebow, R.N. (2006), "Fear, Interest and Honor: Outlines of a Theory of International Relations", *International Affairs*, 82(3): 431–48.

LeDoux, J.E. (1995), "Emotion: Clues From the Brain", *Annual Review of Psychology*, 46: 209–35.

Leese, P. (2002), *Shell Shock: Traumatic Neurosis and the British Soldiers of the First World War*, Basingstoke, UK: Palgrave Macmillan.
Lehmann, H-T. (2006), *Postdramatic Theatre*, K. Jürs-Munby (trans.), London: Routledge.
Léri, A. (1918), *Commotions et Émotions de Guerre*, Paris: Masson (English translation, 1919, London: University of London Press).
Lerner, P. (2003), *Hysterical Men: War, Psychiatry and the Politics of Trauma in Germany, 1890–1930*, Ithaca, NY: Cornell University Press.
Levi, E. (1994), *Music in the Third Reich*, London: St. Martin's Press.
Lewis, J. (1990), "Public Institution and Private Relationship: Marriage and Marriage Guidance, 1920–1968", *Twentieth Century British History*, 1: 233–63.
Lewis, J. (1991), *Whom God Hath Joined Together: The Work of Marriage Guidance*, London: Routledge.
Lewis, M. (2000), "Self-Conscious Emotions: Embarrassment, Pride, Shame, and Guilt", in Michael Lewis and Jeannette M. Haviland-Jones (eds), *Handbook of Emotions*, New York: The Guilford Press: 623–36.
Leys, R. (2011), "The Turn to Affect: A Critique", *Critical Inquiry*, 37(3): 434–72.
Ling, L.H.M. (2014), "Decolonizing the International: Towards Multiple Emotional Worlds", *International Theory*, 6(3): 579–83.
Loewenthal, K. (2007), *Religion, Culture and Mental Health*, Cambridge: Cambridge University Press.
Löwenheim, O. and Heimann, G. (2008), "Revenge in International Politics", *Security Studies*, 17(4): 685–724.
Luckhurst, M. (2015), *Caryl Churchill*, London: Routledge.
Luckhurst, M. and Morin, E. (2015), *Theatre and Human Rights since 1945: Things Unspeakable*, London: Palgrave.
Lupton, D. (1998), *The Emotional Self*, London: Sage.
Lutz, C.A. (1988), *Unnatural Emotions: Everyday Sentiments on a Micronesian Atoll and their Challenge to Western Theory*, Chicago: University of Chicago Press.
Lynch, D.S. (2014), *Loving Literature: A Cultural History*, Chicago: University of Chicago Press.
Lynd, H.M. and Lynd, R.S. (1937), *Middletown in Transition: A Study in Cultural Conflicts*, New York: Harcourt, Brace.
Lyon, A. (2003), *The Fifth Wave*, Edinburgh: Scottish Council Foundation.
Lystra, K. (1989), *Searching the Heart: Women, Men, and Romantic Love in Nineteenth-Century America*, New York: Oxford University Press.
Mace, D.R. (1948), *Marriage Crisis*, London: Delisle.
Malague, R. (2012), *An Actress Prepares: Women and "the Method"*, Abingdon, UK: Routledge.
Maletic, V. (1987), *Body – Space – Expression: The Development of Rudolf Laban's Movement and Dance Concepts*, Berlin: Mouton de Gruyter.
Malleson, J. (1953), "An Endocrine Factor in Certain Affective Disorders", *Lancet*, 265: 158–64.
Mansfield, N. (2000), *Subjectivity. Theories of the Self from Freud to Haraway*, Sydney: Allen & Unwin.
Maranon, G. (1929), *The Climacteric (The Critical Age)*, London: Henry Kimpton.
Martin, C. (2014), *Capitalizing Religion: Ideology and the Opiate of the Bourgeoisie*, London: Bloomsbury.
Martin, D. and Wrightsman, L.S. Jr. (1965), "The Relationship between Religious Behavior and Concern about Death", *Journal of Social Psychology*, 65, 317–23.

Martin, E. (2004), "Talking Back to Neuroreductionism", in H. Thomas and J. Ahmed (eds), *Cultural Bodies: Ethnography and Theory*, Oxford: Blackwell: 190–211.

Maslow, A. (1964), *Religions, Values, and Peak Experiences*, Columbus, OH: Ohio State University Press.

Maslow, A. (1968), *Toward a Psychology of Being*, New York: Van Nostrand Reinhold.

Massumi, B. (2002), *Parables for the Virtual: Movement, Affect, Sensation*, Durham, NC: Duke University Press.

Massumi, B. (2010), "The Future Birth of the Affective Fact: The Political Ontology of Threat" in M. Greg and G.J. Seigworth (eds), *The Affect Theory Reader*, Durham and London: Duke University Press.

Mathew, N. and Walton, B. (eds) (2013), *The Invention of Beethoven and Rossini: Historiography, Criticism, Analysis*, Cambridge: Cambridge University Press.

Matt, S.J. and Stearns, P.N. (eds) (2013), *Doing Emotions History*, Champaign, IL: University of Illinois Press.

Matt, S.J. (2011), *Homesickness: An American History*, New York: Oxford University Press.

May, R. (1953), *Man's Search for Himself*, New York: W. W. Norton and Company.

McCall, T. (2007), "38 Health Benefits of Yoga", *Yoga Journal*, 28 August. <http://www.yogajournal.com/article/health/count-yoga-38-ways-yoga-keeps-fit/> [accessed 7 October 2015].

McCarthy-Jones, S. and Davidson, L. (2013), "When Soft Voices Die: Auditory Verbal Hallucinations and a Four Letter Word (Love)", *Mental Health, Religion and Culture*, 16(4): 367–83.

McDermott, R. (2014), "The Body Doesn't Lie: A Somatic Approach to the Study of Emotions in World Politics", *International Theory*, 6(3): 557–62.

McDonald, R. (2015), *The Values of Literary Studies*, Cambridge: Cambridge University Press.

McGovern, J.P. and Fernandez, A.A. (1964), "On the Role of Emotional Factors in Allergy", *Journal of Asthma Research*, 1: 213–18.

McGuire, C.E. (2009), *Music and Victorian Philanthropy: The Tonic Sol-fa Movement*, Cambridge: Cambridge University Press.

McKinley, J. (1999), "Get that Man some Prozac; If the Dramatic Tension is all in His Head", *The New York Times*, 28 February. <http://www.nytimes.com/1999/02/28/weekinreview/ideas-trends-get-that-man-some-prozac-if-the-dramatic-tension-is-all-in-his-head.html> [accessed 17 September 2015].

McLaughlin, N. (1996), "Nazism, Nationalism, and the Sociology of Emotions: Escape from Freedom Revisited", *Sociological Theory*, 14, (3) 241–61.

McMahon, D.M. (2007), *Happiness: A History*, New York: Atlantic Monthly Press.

Meisner, S. and Longwell, D. (1987), *Sanford Meisner on Acting*, New York: Vintage Books.

Mendl, R.W.S. (1927), *The Appeal of Jazz*, London: P. Allen & Co.

Mercer, J. (2005), "Rationality and Psychology in International Politics", *International Organization*, 59(1): 77–106.

Mercer, J. (2010), "Emotional Beliefs", *International Organization*, 64(1): 1–31.

Mercer, J. (2014), "Feeling like a State: Social Emotion and Identity", *International Theory*, 6(3): 515–35.

Mercier, C. (1890), *Sanity and Insanity*, London: Walter Scott.

Merker, B.H., Madison, G.S., and Eckerdal, P. (2009), "On the Role and Origin of Isochrony in Human Rhythmic Entrainment", *Cortex*, 45(1): 4–17.

Merridale, C. (2000), "The Collective Mind: Trauma and Shell-Shock in Twentieth-Century Russia", *Journal of Contemporary History*, 35: 39–55.

Meyer, L.B. (1956), *Emotion and Meaning in Music*, Chicago: The University of Chicago Press.

Michaëlis, K. (1912), *The Dangerous Age*, New York.

Milbank, J. and Pabst, A. (2016), *The Politics of Virtue: Post-Liberalism and the Human Future*, Lanham, MD: Rowman and Littlefield.

Millennium (2010), Forum Section on "The Emotional Turn", *Millennium: Journal of International Studies*, 39(1): 89–144.

Miller, A. (1989), *Plays*, London: Methuen Drama.

Miller, A. (2000/1949), *Death of a Salesman: Certain Private Conversations in Two Acts and a Requiem*, London: Penguin Classics.

Miller, J.H. (2005), "How to Read Literature" in J. Wolfreys (ed.), *The J. Hillis Miller Reader*, Edinburgh: Edinburgh University Press: 251–8.

Miller, L.E. (2001), "Cage, Cunningham, and Collaborators: The Odyssey of *Variations V*", *The Musical Quarterly*, 85(3): 545–67.

Mintz, S. (2004), *Huck's Raft: A History of American Childhood*, Cambridge, MA: Belknap Press of Harvard University Press.

Mintz, S. (2015), *The Prime of Life: A History of Modern Adulthood*, Cambridge, MA: Harvard University Press.

Moberg, D.O. (1956), "Religious Activities and Personal Adjustment in Old Age", *Journal of Social Psychology*, 43: 261–7.

Modell, J. (1989), *Into One's Own: From Youth to Adulthood in the United States, 1920–1975*, Berkeley, CA: University of California Press.

"Modern Day Presidential: Donald Trump defends use of social media in Twitter Storm", *The Telegraph*, 2 July 2017.

Moi, T. (2006), *Henrik Ibsen and the Birth of Modernism*, Oxford: Oxford University Press.

Morrison, T. (2012), *Desdemona*, London: Oberon Press.

Morrison, T. (2004), *Beloved*, New York: Vintage International.

Moss, G.L. (2000), "Shell-Shock as a Social Disease", *Journal of Contemporary History*, 35: 101–8.

Mumford, M. (2009), *Bertolt Brecht*, London: Routledge (e-book).

Murcia, C.Q. and Kreutz, G. (2012), "Dance and Health: Exploring Interactions and Implications", *Music, Health, and Wellbeing*, Oxford: Oxford University Press: 125–35.

Murray, M. and Lamont, A. (2012), "Community Music and Social/Health Psychology: Linking Theoretical and Practical Concerns", in R. MacDonald, G. Kreutz and L. Mitchell (eds), *Music, Health, & Wellbeing*, Oxford: Oxford University Press: 76–86.

Myers, C.S. (1915–16), "A Contribution to the Study of Shell Shock", *Lancet*, 13 February 1915: 316–20; *Lancet*, 8 January 1916: 65–9; *Lancet*, 18 March 1916: 608–13.

Myers, W. (2015), "11 Unexpected Health Benefits of Yoga", Everyday Health. <http://www.everydayhealth.com/fitness-pictures/10-surprising-health-perks-of-yoga.aspx#02> [accessed 7 October 2015].

Nafisi, A. (2003), *Reading Lolita in Tehran. A Memoir in Books*, Sydney: Hodder.

Neisser, U. (1967), *Cognitive Psychology*, New York: Meredith Publishing Company.

NHS (2015), Reiki/spiritual healer, NHS Jobs. <https://www.jobs.nhs.uk/xi/vacancy/3dd4cf54 4c0502eb362f8492aea7dd7b/?vac_ref=913927029#.VhQxUcnFdZI.facebook> [accessed 7 October 2015].

Noble, T. and McGrath, H. (2008), "The Positive Educational Practices Framework: A Tool for Facilitating the Work of Educational Psychologists in Promoting Pupil Wellbeing," *Educational and Child Psychology*, 25(2), 119–34.

North, A.C. and Hargreaves D.J. (eds) (2008), *The Social and Applied Psychology of Music*, Oxford: Oxford University Press.

Norton Taylor, R. (1999), *The Colour of Justice*, London: Oberon Books.

Nussbaum, M. (1997), *Cultivating Humanity: A Classical Defense of Reform in Liberal Education*, Cambridge, MA: Harvard University Press.

Nussbaum, M. (2002), *Upheavals of Thought: The Intelligence of Emotions*, Cambridge: Cambridge University Press.

Nwalutu, M.O. (2012), "Healing Bereavement through Rituals: A Review of the WeppaWanno Widowhood Purification Practices", *Sociology Mind*, 2(3): 313–24.

O'Gorman, F. (2015), *Worrying: A Literary and Cultural History*, London: Bloomsbury.

Office of National Statistics, divorce statistics. <http://www.ons.gov.uk/peoplepopulationandcommunity/birthsdeathsandmarriages/divorce/bulletins/divorcesinenglandandwales/2014-02-06> [accessed 21 July 2016].

Ollman, J. (2011), *Mid-life*, Montréal: Drawn and Quarterly.

Oppenheim, J. (1991), *Shattered Nerves*, Oxford: Oxford University Press.

O'Shaughnessy, N. (2003), *Selling Hitler: Propaganda and the Nazi Brand*, C. Hurst & Co. <http://www.slate.com/articles/news_and_politics/fascism/2017/03/how_nazi_propaganda_encouraged_the_masses_to_co_produce_a_false_reality.html>.

Oxenhandler, N. (1988), "The Changing Concept of Literary Emotion: A Selective History", *New Literary History,* 20(1), Critical Reconsiderations (Autumn): 105–21

Palmer, A. (2004), *Fictional Minds*, Lincoln, NE and London: University of Nebraska Press.

Pargament, K., Koenig, H., and Perez, L. (2000), "The Many Methods of Religious Coping. Development and Initial Validation of the RCOPE", *Journal of Clinical Psychology*, 56(4): 519–43.

Pargament, K.I. (2010), "Religion and Coping: The Current State of Knowledge", in S. Folkman (ed.), *Oxford Handbook of Stress and Coping*, Oxford: Oxford University Press: 269–88.

Parker, S. (2015), *Bertolt Brecht: A Literary Life*, London: Bloomsbury.

Peshkin, M. Murray (1959), "Intractable Asthma of Childhood: Rehabilitation at the Institutional Level with a Follow-Up of 150 Cases", *International Archives of Allergy*, 15: 91–112.

Petersen, R.D. (2002), *Understanding Ethnic Violence: Fear, Hatred and Resentment in Twentieth-Century Eastern Europe*, Cambridge: Cambridge University Press.

Pew, C. (1999), "From Weimar Movement Choir to Nazi Community Dance: The Rise and Fall of Rudolf Laban's *Festkultur*", *Dance Research,* 19(2): 73–96.

Phelan, J. (nd), "Narrative Ethics" in *The Living Handbook of Narratology*. <http://www.lhn.uni-hamburg.de/article/narrative-ethics> [accessed 25 March 2016].

Phelan, N. and Volin, M. (1965), *Yoga Over Forty*, New York: Harper and Row: 69–75.

Phelan, P. (2009), "Renewing the Ado: Blau and Beckett", *Modern Language Quarterly* 70(1): 11–18.

Pinker, S. (2011), *The Better Angels of Our Nature: Why Violence Has Declined*, New York: Viking-Penguin.

Pinkerton, P. and Weaver, C.M. (1970), "Childhood Asthma", in O.W. Hill (ed.), *Modern Trends in Psychosomatic Medicine 2,* London: Butterworths: 81–104.

Pitkin Jr., W. (1965), *Life Begins at Fifty*, New York: Simon and Schuster.

Pitkin, W.B. (1932), *Life Begins at Forty*, New York: McGraw-Hill.

Plamper, J. (2015), *The History of Emotions: An Introduction*, trans. Keith Tribe, Oxford: Oxford University Press.

Platvoet, J. (2001), "Chasing off God: Spirit Possession in a Sharing Society" in G. Harvey and M. Ralls MacLeod (eds), *Indigenous Religious Musics*, Aldershot, UK: Ashgate: 122–35.

Playne, C.E. (1925), *The Neuroses of the Nations*, London: George Allen and Unwin.

Playne, C.E. (1928), *The Pre-war Mind in Britain*, London: George Allen and Unwin.

Popenoe, P. (1943), *Marriage, Before and After*, New York: W. Funk, inc., HathiTrust.

Potegal, M. and Novaco, R.W. (2010), "A Brief History of Anger", in M. Potegal, G. Stemmler and C. Spielberger (eds), *International Handbook of Anger*, New York: Springer-Verlag: 9–24.

Potter, D. (1954), *People of Plenty: Economic Abundance and the American Character*, Chicago: University of Chicago Press.

Potter, K. and Gann, K. (2016), *The Ashgate Research Companion to Minimalist and Postminimalist Music*, London: Routledge.

Potter, P. (1998), *Most German of the Arts: Musicology and Society from the Weimar Republic to the End of Hitler's Reich*, New Haven, CT: Yale University Press.

Preston-Dunlop, V. (1998), *Rudolf Laban: An Extraordinary Life*, London: Dance Books Ltd.

Prinz, J. (2003), "Emotions Embodied", in R.C. Solomon (ed.), *Thinking about Feeling: Contemporary Philosophers on Emotions*, New York: Oxford University Press: 44–60.

Pupavac, V. (2004), "War on the Couch: The Emotionality of the New International Security Paradigm", *European Journal of Social Theory*, 7(2): 149–70.

Putnam, R.D. (2001), *Bowling Alone: The Collapse and Revival of American Community*, New York: Touchstone Books by Simon and Schuster.

Ratcliffe, M., Broome, M., Smith, B., and Bowden, H. (2014), "A Bad Case of the Flu? The Comparative Phenomenology of Depression and Somatic Illness", in M. Ratcliffe and A. Stephan, *Depression, Emotion and the Self: Philosophical and Interdisciplinary Perspectives*, Exeter, UK: Imprint Academic Ltd: 163–82.

Rauschenberg, R. (1996), "Untitled Statement (1959)", in K. Stiles and P. Selz (eds), *Theories and Documents of Contemporary Art*, Berkeley, CA: University of California Press.

Reddy, W.M. (2001), *The Navigation of Feeling: A Framework for the History of Emotions*, Cambridge: Cambridge University Press.

Reich, W. (1933/1970), *The Mass Psychology of Fascism*, New York: Farrar, Straus & Giroux Inc.

Report of the War Office Committee of Enquiry into 'Shell-Shock' (1922), London, Cmd. 1734: 3.

Revill, D. (1992), *The Roaring Silence: John Cage: A Life*, New York: Arcade Publishing.

Reznikoff, M. (1955), "Psychological Factors in Breast Cancer: A Preliminary Study of Some Personality Trends in Patients with Cancer of the Breast", *Psychosomatic Medicine*, 17: 96–108.

Rhys, J. [1966] (1980), *Wide Sargasso Sea*, Harmondsworth: Penguin Books.

Richardson, A. (ed.) (2013), *After Darwin: Animals, Emotions, and the Mind*, Amsterdam: Rodopi.

Robin, C. (2004), *Fear: The History of a Political Idea*, Oxford: Oxford University Press.

Robinson, J.B. (1994), "Jazz Reception in Weimar Germany", in B. Gilliam (ed.), *Music and Performance During the Weimar Republic*, Cambridge: Cambridge University Press.

Rosaldo, M. (1980), *Knowledge and Passion: Ilongot Notions of Self and Social Life*, Cambridge: Cambridge University Press.

Rosenberg, T. (2013), "The Soundtrack of Revolution Memory, Affect and the Power of Protest Song", *Journal of Current Cultural Research*, 5: 175–88.

Rosenblatt, P.C. (1983), *Bitter, Bitter Tears: Nineteenth-Century Diarists and Twentieth-Century Grief Theories*, Minneapolis: University of Minnesota Press.

Rosenwein, B. (2006), *Emotional Communities in the Early Middle Ages*, Cornell: Cornell University Press.
Rosenzweig, L.W. (1999), *Another Self: Middle-Class American Women and Their Friends in the Twentieth Century*, New York: New York University Press.
Ross, A.A.G. (2013), "Realism, Emotion, and Dynamic Allegiances in Global Politics", *International Theory*, 5(2): 273–99.
Ross, A.A.G. (2006), "Coming in From the Cold: Emotions and Constructivism", *European Journal of International Relations*, 12(2): 197–222.
Ross, A.A.G. (2014), *Mixed Emotions: Beyond Hatred in International Conflict*, Chicago: Chicago University Press.
Roth, M. (1964), "Psychiatric Aspects of Middle Age", in Report of a Symposium on the Hazards of Middle Age, *Journal of the Royal College of Practitioners*, Supplement No. 1 to Volume 7, January: 27–43.
Rotundo, E.A. (1993), *American Manhood: Transformations in Masculinity from the Revolution to the Modern Era*, New York: BasicBooks.
Russolo, L. (1913), *The Art of Noise: Futurist Manifesto*, Trans. Robert Filiou, New York: Something Else Press, 1967.
Ruzicka, J. and Wheeler, N.J. (2010), "The Puzzle of Trusting Relationships in the Nuclear Non-Proliferation Treaty", *International Affairs*, 86(1): 69–85.
Salovey, P. (ed.) (1991), *The Psychology of Jealousy and Envy*, New York: Guilford Press.
Samuel, G. (2008), *Origins of Yoga and Tantra: Indic Religions to the Thirteenth Century*, Cambridge: Cambridge University Press.
Samuel, G. (2014), "Between Buddhism and Science, Between Mind and Body", *Religions*, 5: 560–79, DOI: 10.3390/rel5030560.
Sanders, J. (2006), *Adaptation and Appropriation*, London and New York: Routledge.
Sandner, D.F. (1996), "Native North American Healers", in B.W. Scotton, A.B. Chinen and J.R. Battista (eds), *Textbook of Transpersonal Psychiatry and Psychology*, New York: BasicBooks: 145–54.
Santangelo, P. (2014), "The Perception of Pain in Late Imperial China", in R. Boddice (ed.), *Pain and Emotion in Modern History*, Basingstoke, UK: Palgrave Macmillan: 36–52.
Sarot, M. (1992), *God, Passibility and Corporeality*, Kampen, The Netherlands: Kok Pharos Publishing House.
Sasley, B. (2010), "Affective Attachments and Foreign Policy: Israel and the 1993 Oslo Accords", *European Journal of International Relations*, 16(4): 687–709.
Sasley, B. (2011), "Theorizing States' Emotions", *International Studies Review*, 13(3): 453–76.
Saurette, P. (2006), "You Dissin Me? Humiliation and Post 9/11 Global Politics", *Review of International Studies*, 32(3): 495–522.
Scarry, E. (2014), "Poetry, Injury, and the Ethics of Reading" in P. Brooks (ed.) with H. Jewett, *The Humanities and Public Life*, New York: Fordham University Press: 41–8.
Scheer, M. (2012), "Are Emotions a Kind of Practice (and Is That What Makes Them Have a History)? A Bourdieuian Approach to Understanding Emotion", *History and Theory* (51): 193–220.
Scheff, T.J. (1990), *Microsociology: Discourse, Emotion and Social Structure*, Chicago: Chicago University Press.
Schenker, H. (1925–30), *Das Meisterwerk in der Musik*, Munich, Wien: Drei Masken Verlag.
Scherer, K.R. (2005), "What are Emotions? And How Can They Be Measured?", *Social Science Information*, 44(4): 695–729.

Schlink, B. (1997), *The Reader*, trans. C.B. Janeway, London: Phoenix.

Schmidt, B. and Huskinson, L. (eds) (2010), *Spirit Possession and Trance: New Interdisciplinary Perspectives*, London: Continuum.

Schwartz, J. (1999), *Cassandra's Daughter: A History of Psychoanalysis*, London: Penguin.

Scrutton, A.P. (2011), *Thinking through Feeling: God, Emotion and Passibility*, New York: Continuum.

Scrutton, A.P. (2015a), "Two Christian Theologies of Depression", *Philosophy, Psychiatry and Psychology*, 22(4): 275–89. DOI: 10.1353/ppp.2015.0046.

Scrutton, A.P. (2015b), "Why Not Believe in an Evil God? Pragmatic Encroachment and Some Implications for Philosophy of Religion", *Religious Studies*, DOI: 10.1017/S0034412515000360.

Scrutton, A.P. (2016), "Can Jinn be a Tonic? The Therapeutic Value of Spirit-Related Beliefs, Practices and Experiences", *Filosofia Unisinos*, 17(2): 171–84.

Seccombe, W. (1993), *Weathering the Storm: Working-Class Families from the Industrial Revolution to the Fertility Decline*, London and New York: Verso.

Seligman, M.E.P. (2002), *Authentic Happiness: Using the New Positive Psychology to Realize your Potential for Lasting Fufillment*, New York, NY: Free Press.

Seligman, M.E.P. (2011), *Flourish: A Visionary New Understanding of Happiness and Wellbeing*, New York, NY: Free Press.

Selye, H. (nd), "The nature of stress and its relation to cardiovascular disease", in H.S. Fonds, P0359/G1,2,0093, Division of Records Management and Archives, University of Montreal.

Selye, H. (1974), *Stress without Distress*, New York: Harper & Row.

Senelick, L. (1997), *The Chekhov Theatre: A Century of the Plays in Performance*, London: Routledge.

Shephard, B. (2002), *A War of Nerves: Soldiers and Psychiatrists 1914–1994*, London: Pimlico.

Shields, S.A. and Koster, B.A. (1989), "Emotional Stereotyping of Parents in Child Rearing Manuals, 1915–1980", *Social Psychology Quarterly*, 52(1): 44–55.

Showalter, E. (1987), *The Female Malady: Women, Madness, and English Culture, 1830–1980*, London: Virago.

Singer, B. (1995), "Modernity, Hyperstimulus, and the Rise of Popular Sensationalism", in L. Charney and V.R. Schwartz (eds), *Cinema and the Invention of Modern Life*, pp. 72–99, Berkeley, California: University of California Press.

Singh, A.N. (1999), "Shamans, Healing and Mental Health", *Journal of Child and Family Studies*, 8(2): 131–4.

Sloan R.P. (2006), *Blind Faith: The Unholy Alliance of Religion and Medicine*, New York: St Martin's Press.

Sloan, R.P., Bagiella, E., and Powell, T. (1999), "Religion, Spirituality and Medicine", *Lancet*, 353: 664–7.

Sloboda, J.A. (ed.) (1988), *Generative Processes in Music: the Psychology of Performance, Improvisation and Composition*, Oxford, UK: Clarendon Press.

Small, H. (2013), *The Value of the Humanities*, Oxford: Oxford University Press.

Smith-Rosenberg, C. (1975), "The Female World of Love and Ritual: Relations Between Women in Nineteenth-Century America", *Signs*, 1(1): 1–29.

Smith, F. (2011), "Possession in Theory and Practice: Historical and Contemporary Models" in F. Ferrari (ed.), *Health and Religious Rituals in South Asia: Disease, Possession and Healing*, Oxford: Routledge: 3–17.

Smith, G.E. and Pear, T.H. (1917), *Shell-Shock and its Lessons*, London: Longmans Green: 5–12.

Snow, H. (1891), *The Proclivity of Women to Cancerous Diseases and to Certain Benign Tumours*, London: J. & A. Churchill.
Solomon, A. (2008), "Notes on an Exorcism", The Moth, 29 October. <http://themoth.org/posts/stories/notes-on-an-exorcism> [accessed 1 October 2015].
Solomon, R. (2001), *True to Our Feelings: What Our Emotions Are Really Telling Us*, Oxford: Oxford University Press.
Solomon, T. (2012), "'I wasn't angry because I couldn't believe it was happening': Affect and Discourse in Response to 9/11", *Review of International Studies*, 38(4): 907–28.
Southborough, Lord G.C.B. (1922), "Shell-Shock", *The Living Age*, 14 October: 69–73.
Spivak, G. (1985), "Three Women's Texts and a Critique of Imperialism", *Critical Inquiry*, 12(1), Autumn: 235–61.
Spivak, G. (2004), "Righting Wrongs", *South Atlantic Quarterly*, 103(2–3), Spring/Summer 2004: 523–81.
Stanislavski, K. (2010), *An Actor's Work*, J. Benedetti (trans.), London: Routledge.
Stearns, C.Z. and Stearns, P.N. (1986), *Anger: The Struggle for Emotional Control in America's History*, Chicago: University of Chicago Press.
Stearns, P.N. (1989), *Jealousy: The Evolution of an Emotion in American History*, New York: New York University Press.
Stearns, P.N. (1994), *American Cool: Constructing a Twentieth-Century Emotional Style*, New York: New York University Press.
Stearns, P.N. (2003), *Anxious Parents: A History of Modern Childrearing in America*, New York: New York University Press.
Stearns, P.N. (2006), *American Fear: The Causes and Consequences of High Anxiety*, New York: Routledge.
Stearns, P.N. (2007), *Revolutions in Sorrow: The American Experience of Death in Global Perspective*, Boulder, CO: Paradigm Publishers.
Stearns, P.N. (2010), "Defining Happy Childhoods: Assessing a Recent Change", *Journal of the History of Childhood and Youth*, 3(2): 165–86.
Stearns, P.N. (forthcoming), *Shame: A Brief History*, Urbana, IL: University of Illinois Press.
Stearns, P.N. and Stearns, C.Z. (1985), "Emotionology: Clarifying the History of Emotions and Emotional Standards", *American Historical Review*, 90: 814–36.
Stearns, P.N. and Stearns, C. (2015), "American Schools and the Uses of Shame: An Ambiguous History", *History of Education*, 46(1): 58–75.
Steele, B.J. (2010), *Defacing Power: The Aesthetics of Insecurity in Global Politics*, Ann Arbor, MI: University of Michigan Press.
Stern, A. (1981), *Asthma and Emotion*, New York: Gardner Press.
Stewart, J. (2013), *Child Guidance in Britain, 1918–1955: The Dangerous Age of Childhood*, London: Pickering and Chatto.
Stopes, M.C. (1928), *Enduring Passion*, London: Putnam.
Stopes, M.C. (1936), *Change of Life in Men and Women*, London: Putnam.
Strange, J-M. (2015), *Fatherhood and the British Working Class, 1865–1914*, New York: Cambridge University Press.
Susman, W. (1984), "'Personality' and the Making of Twentieth-Century Culture", in Warren Susman (ed.), *Culture as History: The Transformation of American Society in the Twentieth Century*, New York: Pantheon Books.
Svanberg, J. (2003), *Schamantropologi i Gränslandet Mellan Forskning och Praktik: En Studie av Förhållandet Mellan Schamanismforskning och Neoschamanism*, Åbo, Finland: Åbo Akademis Förlag/Åbo Akademi University Press.

Svašek, M. (2005), "Introduction: Emotions in Anthropology", in Kay Milton and Maruška Svašek (eds), *Mixed Emotions: Anthropological Studies of Feeling*, Oxford and New York: Berg: 1–24.
Swindall, L.R. (2015), *Paul Robeson: A Life of Activism and Art*, Maryland: Rowman & Littlefield.
Tait, P. (2016a), "Emotions", in M. Cheng and G. Cody (eds), *Reading Contemporary Performance*, 146–7, London: Routledge.
Tait, P. (2016b), "Introduction: Analysing Emotion and Theorising Affect", *Humanities* 5(3), 70: 1–7, DOI:10.3390/h5030070. <http://www.mdpi.com/2076-0787/5/3/70> [accessed 7 February 2017].
Tait, P. and Shim, J-S. (eds) (2006), "Theatre, Emotions and Interculturalism", *Australasian Drama Studies*, 49.
Taruskin, R. (2009a), *Music in the Early Twentieth Century: The Oxford History of Western Music* (Vol. 4), Oxford: Oxford University Press.
Taruskin, R. (2009b), *Music in the Late Twentieth Century: The Oxford History of Western Music* (Vol. 5), Oxford: Oxford University Press.
Taylor-Batty, M. and Taylor-Batty, J. (2013), *Samuel Beckett's Waiting for Godot*, London: Bloomsbury Publishing (e-book).
Taylor, B. (2009), "Discovering New Pasts: Victorian Legacies in the Postcolonial Worlds of *Jack Maggs* and *Mister Pip*", *Victorian Studies*, 52(1): 95–105.
Templeton, J. (1989), "The Doll House Blacklash: Criticism, Feminism, and Ibsen", *PMLA*, 104(1): 28–40.
Templeton, J. (1997), *Ibsen's Women*, Cambridge: Cambridge University Press.
Thien, D. (2005), "After or Beyond Feeling? A Consideration of Affect and Emotion in Geography", *Area*, 37(4): 450–6.
Thormählen, W. (2014), "Physical Distortion, Emotion and Subjectivity: Musical Virtuosity and Body Anxiety", in J. Kennway (ed.), *Music and the Nerves, 1700–1900*, Basingstoke, UK: Palgrave Macmillan: 191–215.
Thrift, N. (2004), "Intensities of Feeling: Towards a Spatial Politics of Affect", *Geogrfiska Annaler: Series B*, 86(1): 57–78.
Toye, R. (2015), "Keynes, Liberalism, and 'The Emancipation of the Mind'", *English Historical Review*, 130: 1162–91.
Tuathail, G.Ó. (2003), "'Just Out Looking For a Fight': American Affect and the Invasion of Iraq", *Antipode*, 35(5): 856–70.
Turner, G. (2004), *Understanding Celebrity*, London: Sage.
van Gogh, V. (1968) Letter to Emile Bernard, April 1888, cited in H.B. Chipp (ed.), *Theories of Modern Art*, Berkeley, CA: University of California Press: 31.
Van Hulle, D. (ed.) (2015), *The New Cambridge Companion to Samuel Beckett*, Cambridge: Cambridge University Press.
Vanderbilt, A. (1952), *Amy Vanderbilt's Complete Book of Etiquette: A Guide to Gracious Living*, New York: Doubleday.
Varnedoe, K. (1998), *Jackson Pollock*, New York: Museum of Modern Art.
Von Harbou, T. (1972), *Metropolis*, New York: Simon & Schuster.
Wallis, J.H. (1962), *The Challenge of Middle Age*, London: Routledge and Kegan Paul.
Wallis, J.H. (1964), *Someone to Turn To: A Description of the Remedial Work of the National Marriage Guidance Council*, London: Routledge and Kegan Paul.
Webster, A.D. (2014), "A flourishing future: Positive Psychology and its Lessons for Education", *Independent School*, 74, 40–6.
Wenders, W. (1987), *Wings of Desire* (film), Orion Pictures.

Wheeler D.W. and Foster, G.A. (2013), *A Short History of Film*, 2nd edn, New Brunswick: Rutgers University Press.

White, G. (2013), *Audience Participation: Aesthetics of an Invitation*, London: Palgrave.

Whitlock, G. (2007), *Soft Weapons: Autobiography in Transit*, Chicago: Chicago University Press.

Widmaier, W.W. (2010), "Emotions Before Paradigms: Elite Anxiety and Populist Resentment from the Asian to Subprime Crises", *Millennium: Journal of International Studies*, 39(1): 127–44.

Williams, P. (1994), "The Idea of *Bewegung* in the German Organ Reform Movement of the 1920s", in B. Gilliam (ed.), *Music and Performance during the Weimar Republic*, Cambridge: Cambridge University Press.

Williams, D.G. and Morris, G.H. (1996), "Crying, Weeping or Tearfulness in British and Israeli Adults", *British Journal of Psychology*, 87(3): 479–506.

Williams, R.L. and Cole, S. (1968), "Religiosity, Generalized Anxiety and Apprehension Concerning Death", *Journal of Social Psychology*, 70: 111–17.

Winter, J. (2000), "Shell-Shock and the Cultural History of the Great War", *Journal of Contemporary History*, 35: 7–11.

Wolfe, E.L., Barger, A.C., and Benison, S. (2000), *Walter B. Cannon: Science and Society*, Cambridge, MA: Harvard University Press.

Woodward, K. (1998), "Poor Hetty" in L. Berlant (ed.), *Compassion: The Culture and Politics of an Emotion*, New York and London: Routledge: 59–86.

Woodyatt, R.T. (1927), "Psychic and Emotional Factors in General Diagnosis and Treatment", *Journal of the American Medical Association*, 89: 1013–14.

Wouters, C. (1995), "The Integration of the Sexes (Etiquette Books and Emotion Management in the 20th Century, part 2)", *Journal of Social History*, 29(2): 325.

Wouters, C. (2007), *Informalization: Manners and Emotions Since 1890*, Washington, DC: SAGE Publications.

Wright, S. (2012), "Emotional Geographies of Development", *Third World Quarterly*, 33(6): 1113–27.

Wynn, M. (2005), *Emotional Experience and Religious Understanding: Integrating Perception, Conception and Feeling*, Cambridge: Cambridge University Press.

Wynn, M. (2009), *Faith and Place: An Essay in Embodied Epistemology*, Oxford: Oxford University Press.

Wynn, M. (2013), *Renewing the Senses: A Study of the Philosophy and Theology of the Religious Life*, Oxford: Oxford University Press.

Young, H. (2010), *Embodying Black Experience: Stillness, Critical Memory and the Black Body*, Ann Arbor, MI: University of Michigan.

Young, H. (2013), *Theatre and Race*, London: Palgrave.

Zehfuss, M. (2007), *Wounds of Memory: The Politics of War in Germany*, Cambridge: Cambridge University Press.

Zentner, M., Grandjean, D., and Scherer, K.R. (2008), "Emotions Evoked by the Sound of Music: Characterization, Classification, and Measurement", *Emotion*, 8(4): 494–521.

INDEX

Italic numbers are used for illustrations.

4'33 (Cage) 65
4:48 *Psychosis* (Kane) 86
9/11 terror attacks 112

Aarons, Mark 9
abstract art 95, 97–102
abstract music 58
acting techniques 76–7, 89
adaptations, literary 123–4
Adie, Major W. J. 20
Adler, Stella 77
adultery 132
advice literature 7–8, 31, 131, 132, 134–5, 136
affect and emotions 153–5
affective turn in literature 112, 114, 117, 127
Ahmed, Sara 117
Alexander, Franz 3, 27, 28, 29
All Quiet on the Western Front (film) 5
Almanac Singers (band) 12
alternative therapies 31, 44, 45–7, 49–50
Altglas, Véronique 45
analysis of music 60
anger
    in drama 77, 89
    gender differences 76
    in politics 147, 150, 154
    in private life 131, 135
anthropology and healing 40–1
apartheid era in South Africa 82
appropriation of spiritual traditions 50, 51
appropriations, literary 123–5
Arab Spring 17
asthma 27–8
Atlas Eclipticalis (Cage) 66
atonal music 59
audiences
    for drama 4, 73–5, 77–8, 81, 85–6, 89
    for music 4, 53, 56, 60, 64–6
    for television 15
Ausdruckstanz (expressionist dance) 61

Autumn Rhythm Number 30 (Pollock) 99–100, *99*

Bal, P. Matthijs 111
Balcony (Genet) 76
ballet 60, 66
Ballets Russes *54*, 60
Baraka, Amiri 81–2, *82*
Baudrillard, Jean 105
Bausch, Pina 66
Beatlemania 14, *14*
Beauvoir, Simone de 34
Beckett, Samuel 9–10, 78–9, 80–1, *80*
Bed (Rauschenberg) 101–2
Beloved (Morrison) 119
Benjamin, Walter 3
Bergman, Ingmar 88–9
Berlant, Lauren 118, 119
Bernstein, Robin 118–19
Bially Mattern, J. 156
Biess, Frank 21, 30
Big Parade (film) 5
birth control 132
birth rates 130
Black Arts Movement 81
Blain, Jenny 44
Blair, Emily 3
Blasted (Kane) 86
body and emotions 22–6, 155–6
Bono-isation of protest festivals 13
Boulez, Pierre 63
Bowie, David 12
Bracket (Mitchell) 100
Braque, George 92
Brecht, Bertolt 3–4, 75, 77–8
Brontë, Charlotte 125–6
Brooks, Geraldine 123
Brooks, Peter 114
Brown, Brené 134
bullying 17
Burke, Noel H. M. 23

Cage, John 63–5, 66
Calle, Sophie 103, *104–5*
Cannon, Walter 22, *23*, 24–7, 31, 35
Carey, Peter 123–4, *124*
Carnegie, Dale 135
Carson, Verna 39
Castano, Emanuele 111
Catholic Church 15–16
celebrities 13, 139–40
Césaire, Aimé 83
change of life 31–5
Chaplin, Charlie 5
characters migrate in literature 113, 123–6
Charles, Jack 83
cheerfulness 129, 131, 134–5, 142
Chekhov, Anton 76
child rearing advice 7–8, 131, 134–5
childhood 27–8, 131
children's literature and play 118–19
choral music 62
Choreartium (ballet) 60
choreographies 53, 60–1
Churchill, Caryl 86, *87*, 88
cinema 5–6, 9
citizenship 115
classification of emotions 149–52
Cleansed (Kane) 86
Cold War 9
collective and political emotions 152–3
commotion and emotion 19–20
communal emotion 13–14
communal music and singing 56–7, 62
communal responses to music 70
compassion and literature 115–18, 120
Compassionate Mind Therapy 50
composition of music 58–9, 63–4, 68
concentration camps, music in 57
Concerning the Spiritual in Art (Kandinsky) 92
consumerism 129, 133, 142, 143
contemporary artists 102–9
contemporary drama 88–9
contraception 132
Cooke, A. 46
courtship 130, 131, 132
Cradle Will Rock (opera/musical) 5
Crawford, Neta 150
creator gods 40–1
Crile, George Washington 23–4
Cubism 94
Cultivating Humanity (Nussbaum) 115
Cultural Politics of an Emotion (Berlant) 118
Cultural Politics of Emotion (Ahmed) 117

Cunningham, Merce 64
cyberbullying 17

Damasio, Antonio 153
dance 56, *58*, 60–1, 62, 64, 66, 70
Davidson, Larry 50
Davidson, Robert 13
de-genrefied music 58
Death of a Salesman (Miller) 38
Death of Reginald Perrin (Nobbs) 35
decision-making processes 147
definitions of emotions 153
degenerate music 58
deintensification of emotions 143–4
Der Vorleser (Schlink) 113
Desdemona (Morrison) 83–4, *84*
Dezfouli, Liza 83
Diaghilev, Serge 60
Diana, Princess of Wales 15, 137, *137*
Dickens, Charles 113, 121–2, *121*, 124
digital age 17
Ding Dong the Wicked (Churchill) 88
diseases, causes of 27–8, 29
diversity in drama 81–3
documentary drama 84–5
Doll's House (Ibsen) 76–7
domestic music 62
Dr. Strangelove (film) 9
drama 3, 9–10, 73–89
    acting and political emotion 76–8
    documentary and human rights 84–5
    emotion, diversity and rewriting the classics 81–4
    late modernism, *Waiting for Godot* 78–80
    realism 75–6
    spectator responses 80–1
    theaters of excess 85–8
    twenty-first century preoccupations 88–9
Draper, George 31
Dror, Otniel 21, 61
Dunbar, Helen Flanders 3, 27–8
Duncan, Isadora 4, 61, 62

education and drama 82
education and shame 133, *134*
Ehrenfells, Christian von 60
Eisenman, Nicole 108–9
Eliade, Mircea 42
Elias, Norbert 131
Eliot, T.S. 3
Ellis, Albert 38–9

INDEX

Ema (Nude on a Staircase) (Richter) 106–7, 106
Emancipation Approximation (Walker) 102–3
emergent models of emotions 149
emotions
    classification of 149–52
    concepts in visual arts 92–3
    definitions of 153
    intensity of 129–30, 143
    mind and 27–30
    research into 21–6, 68–71, 153
empathy
    in drama 84–5
    and literature 111, 114–23, 125, 126
    and politics 151, 158
endocrinology 23–4, 25, 26
Enduring Passion (Stopes) 31
engagement with learning 16
Enlightenment philosophy 54, 65, 130, 133, 134
Entartete Musik (exhibition, 1938) 58
envy and jealousy 137–8
Escape from Freedom (Fromm) 8
Esslin, Martin 79
ethics of reading 114–17
etiquette manuals 136
excess, in drama 85–8
expression in music and dance 60–1, 63, 67
Expressionist art 93–102
Eznack, Lucile 154

fan fiction 111
Far Away (Churchill) 88
Fascism 8
Fauvism 93–4, *94*
fear
    and the midlife crisis 31, 34
    in politics 147, 149, 158
    in private life 7–8, 131, 140–1, 143
    research into 24
feelings, concepts of 92–3, 153
Felski, Rita 111, 114
feminism 13
    See also women's movement
Fierke, Karin 155, 156
fifth wave of public health 36
Figure for Landscape (Hepworth) 97, *98*
films 5–6, 9
First World War 2–3
    See also shell shock
Fokine, Mikhail 60
folk music 56, 62

formality in relationships 129–30, 142–4
Fort, Syvilla 64
4'33 (Cage) 65
4:48 Psychosis (Kane) 86
Freud, Sigmund 2–3, 76
friendships 129, 131, 138–9
Fromm, Eric 8
Fugard, Athol 82, *83*
Furedi, Frank 111

Garber, Marjorie 117–18
Garner, Stanton 79
gender relations 132–3
Genet, Jean 76
genre fiction 120
German music, problem of 56
Gesang der Jünglinge (Stockhausen) 65
gestalt psychology and music 60
Gold Rush (film) 5
Great Depression 5
Great Expectations (Dickens) 113, 124
Great War 2–3
grief 2, 8, 15, 131, 135–7
Groen, J. 29
Gross, Daniel M. 21, 30
Groundsweller (Eisenman) 108–9
group responses to music 70
Guthrie, Woody 12

Hall, G. Stanley 31
Hall, Stuart 112
Halliday, James Lorimer 28
Halliwell, E. 49
Handke, Peter 85–6
happiness 31–2, 129, 130, 131, 134–5, 142
Harner, Michael 42, 44
Hayward, M. 46
healing, non-biomedical 41–2
health, definition of 47
hearing and perception of music 59–60
Hendrix, Jimi 12
Hepworth, Barbara 97, *98*
highbrow literature 116, 120–2
hip-hop music 13
historical research on emotions 21–2
Hochschild, Arlie 135
holistic view of the person 30, 45, 47–8
Holmes, Marcus 149
homosexuality 129, 138
hormones 23–4, 25, 26
Hour we Knew Nothing of Each Other (Handke) 86

House of Cards (television) 15
How to be Happy Though Human (Wolfe) 8
HPSCH (Cage) 66
Huebner, Bryce 157
human rights 84–5, 115
humanism 116
Hunt, Lynn 115
Huskinson, Lucy 40
Hutcheon, Linda 123
Hutton, Ronald 42

I See America Dancing (Duncan) 62
Ibsen, Henrik 76–7
Ice (2) (Richter) 107–8, *108*
immersive experiences 89
Impressionism 91–2
indigenous healing 41
individualism, impact of 50
informalization of relationships 129–30, 142–4
instruments, musical 59–60
intensity of emotions 129–30
international relations 146–9, 158–9
Internet, use of 17
Investigation (Weiss) 85
Invitation to a Beheading (Nabokov) 113
Ionisation (Varèse) 59
Island (Fugard/Kani/Ntshona) 82

Jack Maggs (Carey) 123–4
Jackson, L. 46
Jackson, Michael 14–15
Jackson, Stanley 44
Jain, Andrea 45
James, William 25, 35
Jane Eyre (Brontë) 125–6
Jaques, Elliott 34
jazz 62–3
jealousy and envy 137–8, 142
Jelinek, Elfriede 85, 86
Jones, Lloyd 113, 124
Joyce, James 3
Jung, Carl 39, 42, *43*

Kalahari San/Bushman creator god 40–1
Kandinsky, Vasily 92, 95
Kane, Sarah 86, *87*
Kani, John 82, *83*
Kardashian, Kim 140, *140*
Keen, Suzanne 118, 120, 123, 125, 126
Kidd, David Comer 111
King and I (musical) 119

King, Dana 39
King, Martin Luther 10, *11*
kissing, social 142–3
Klein, Naomi 13
Koenig, Harold 39

Laban, Rudolf von 4, 56, *57*, 58, 61
Lange, Carl Georg 25
latent models of emotions 149
Lazarus, Richard 29
Le Sacre du Printemps (Stravinsky) 53–4, *54*
Lehmann, Hans-Thies 80
leisure activities 61
Les Présages (ballet) 60
liberal humanism 116
Ling, L. H. M. 155, 159
Linklater, Andrew 150
listening to music 64–5, 71
literary criticism 112
literature 3, 111–27
  characters migrating 113, 123–6
  cueing reader response 119–23
  emotions in operation 117–19
  ethics of reading 114–17
  passionate reading 126–7
Loewenthal, Kate 40
love
  and healing 50
  medical and scientific understanding 26, 28, 31
  in private life 131, 138–9
Love and Information (Churchill) 88
Lupton, Deborah 76
Lynch, Deidre Shauna 112

macro/micro approach to emotions in politics 149–52
magazines 7–8
Malevich, Kasimir 95, *96*
Man in the Gray Flannel Suit (Wilson) 34
managed emotions 135
manners in private life 131, 142
March (Brooks) 123
March, Joseph 62
Marley, Bob 12
marriage guidance 31–3
mass media 14–15, 140, 141
Massine, Léonide 60
Matisse, Henri 164n7, 164n10, 165n13
McCarthy-Jones, Simon 50
McDermott, R. 151, 155
McLaughlin, Neil 8

Mead, George Herbert 67
Mead, Margaret 138
meaning in music 67–8
medical and scientific understanding 19–36
    body and emotions 22–6
    middle age, problems of 31–5
    psychosomatic medicine 27–30
medicalization of emotion 38
Mendl, R. W. S. 63
mental disorders 48
mental health and religion 38–40
Mercer, Jonathan 150, 155
Messiaen, Olivier 68
Metropolis (film) 5
Meyer, Leonard B. 67
micro/macro approach to emotions in politics 149–52
Middle Age Crazy (film) 35
middle age, problems of 31–5
middlebrow literature 120–1
midlife crisis 34–5
migrating characters in literature 113, 123–6
Miller, Arthur 38, 79–80
Miller, J. Hillis 111
mind and body 2–3
mind and emotions 27–30
mind-body dualism 48
Mindfulness Report (Halliwell) 49
mindfulness therapies 49, 51
Miró, Joan 96–7
misrepresentation of spiritual traditions 51
Mister Pip (Jones) 113, 124
Mitchell, Joan 100
modernism
    in art 92
    in drama 78–80, 81
    in literature 3
    in music 4, 58–60, 62, 63
Monogram (Rauschenberg) *101*
Morrison, Toni 83–4, *84*, 119
Mother Courage and her Children (Brecht) 4
mothers, influence on asthma 27–8
mourning 2, 15, 136
movies 5–6, 9
Mumford, Meg 77–8
Munch, Edvard 164n7
music and dance 4, 12–13, 53–71
    composition, analysis and expression 58–61
    engaging with music 61–3
    music and psychology 67–71
    music as narrative and the language of emotions 55–8
    1945 and after 63–6
Rite of Spring (Stravinsky) 53–4
Music of Changes (Cage) 64
musical instruments 59–60
musicals 89
Mutter Courage und ihre Kinder (Brecht) 4
Myers, Charles S. 19

Nabokov, Vladimir 113
Nafisi, Azar 113, 122–3, *122*
narrative in music and dance 54, 56, 58–9, 60–1, 64, 65–6
nation states and emotions 152–3
Nazism 8, 56–8, 146–7
negative religious coping 40
neighborhood relations 140–1
neo-shamanism 42, *43*, 44
neuro-endocrinology 23–4, 25, 26
neuroscience-based research 119, 149
9/11 terror attacks 112
Nobbs, David 35
non-biomedical healing 41–2
non-realist performance 75–6
Noonday Demon: An Anatomy of Depression (Solomon) 41–2
Not I (Beckett) 80
novels 113, 114–15, 116
Ntshona, Winston 82, *83*
Number 1 1950 (*Lavender Mist*) (Pollock) 98, 99
Nussbaum, Martha 115, 120

obedience of children 131
Offending the Audience (Handke) 85–6
Oprah's Book Club 121
O'Shaughnessy, Nicholas 8
Oxenhandler, Neal 112

painting. *See* visual arts
Palmer, Alan 112
Pargament, Kenneth 40
passionate reading 126–7
Pear, T. H. 20, 22
perception of music 59–60
performance of music 61–2
personality and disease 29
Personnage Rhythmic (Miró) 96–7
Phelan, Nancy 31
physicalist view of the person 47
Picasso, Pablo 94, 165n13
Pinker, Steven 114–15
Pirandello, Luigi 76

Pitkin, Walter B. 31
Plamper, Jan 112
Platvoet, Jan 40–1
play and children's literature 118–19
pleasures of reading 111
Poème electronique (Varèse) 65–6
political protests 10–13, 17
political self-sacrifice 156
politics and emotions 146–8
Pollock, Jackson 97–100, *99*
pop music 4–5, 12–14
Positive Psychology 16
positive religious coping 40
postcolonial literary criticism 116
postwar period 9–16
Prenez Soin de Vous (Calle) 103, *104–5*
private life 7–8, 129–44
    change and continuity 132–3
    changes 139–41
    continuities 133–5
    envy and jealousy 137–8
    grief reconsidered 135–7
    love and friendship 138–9
    twentieth century style 141–4
    Victorian model families 130–2
protest songs 4–5, 12
protests, political 10–13, 17
psychiatry and religion 38–9
psychoanalysis and emotions 25, 29, 34
psychological stress 29–30
psychology and music 67–71
psychosocial medicine 28, 30, 35–6
psychosomatic medicine 3, 27–30, 35, 47
public health 36
public life 145–59
    body and emotions 155–6
    cognitive affective and latent/emergent approaches 148–9
    collective and political emotions 152–3
    conceptions of emotions 153–5
    international relations 146–9, 158–9
    macro models and micro studies 149–52
    private life becomes more public 139–41
    representation of emotions 157–8
Punchdrunk 89
Punk music 13
Putnam, Robert 141

Quad (Beckett) 81

race, attitudes in art 102–3
railway spine 19

rap music 13
rational actors in international relations 147
rationalist music 63
Rauschenberg, Robert 100–2, *101*
Reader (Schlink) 113
reading 111, 113, 114–17, 126–7
Reading Lolita in Tehran (Nafisi) 113, 122–3
realism in art 91
realist drama 3, 74, 75–6
Reich, Steve 13
Reich, Wilhelm 8
relationships and community in therapy 50
religion and spirituality 15–16, 37–52
    emerging therapies 49–51
    ethical dilemmas of appropriation 51
    finding a place for 38–41
    medicalization of emotion 38
    non-biomedical healing 41–2
    spiritualization of emotion 42–8
representation of emotions 157–8
research into dance 70
research into emotions 21–6, 68–71, 119, 149, 153
responses to literature 119–23
Rhys, Jean 125–6
rhythm in music and dance 59, 69–70
Richter, Gerhard 105–8, *106, 108*
Rise and Fall of Reginald Perrin (television) 35
Rite of Spring (Stravinsky) 53–4, *54*
Robeson, Paul 12
Rockaby (Beckett) 80
Ross, A. A. G. 157
Roth, Martin 33
Russolo, Luigi 59
Rwanda, mental health in 41–2

Samuel, Geoffrey 45, 51
Sasley, Brent 150
Scarry, Elaine 114, 116
Scenes from a Marriage (play, Bergman) 88–9
Scenes from a Marriage (television) 34
Schenker, Heinrich 60
Schlink, Bernhard 113
Schmidt, Bettina 40
Schoenberg, Arnold 4, 59
schools and shame 133, *134*
scientific research and emotions 21–6, 68–71, 119, 149, 163
Scream (Munch) 164n7
sculptures 97, *98*
Second Viennese School music 58, 59
Second World War 9, 29, 57, 85

Seeger, Pete 12
self-control of emotions 30
self-help advice 31, 44
Seligman, Martin 16
Selye, Hans 30, 35
September 11, 2001 terror attacks 112
serialization of music 63
Sex Pistols (band) 13
sexual intercourse 31, 132
Shadow King (Dezfouli) 83
Shakespeare, William 82–4
shamanism 42, *43*, 44, 49
Shamanism: Archaic Techniques of Ecstasy (Eliade) 42
shame 130, 133–4, 139
shell shock 2, 19–21, 22, 24
sibling rivalry 138
singing 13, 56–7, 62
Six Characters in Search of An Author (Pirandello) 76
slavery, responses to 118–19
Smith, Grafton Elliot 20, 22
Snow White and the Seven Dwarfs (film) 6
social kissing 142–3
social media 17, 140
social movements, postwar 10
Solomon, Andrew 41–2
songs 4–5, 12–14
Sopranos (television) 15
sound experimentation and music 59
sound installations 66
spirit possession, belief in 40
spirituality. *See* religion and spirituality
spiritualization of emotion 42–8
Spivak, Gayatri 116, 125–6
stand-up comedy 89
Stanislavsky, Constantin 75, 76–7
states and emotions 152–3
Stockhausen, Karlheinz 65
Stopes, Marie 31, *33*
Stowe, Harriet Beecher 118–19
Strasberg, Lee 77
Stravinsky, Igor 53–4
stress, psychological 29–30
Structures I (Boulez) 63
Supermatism 95
Suprematism: Eight Red Rectangles (Malevich) 95, 96
Surrealism 95–7, 165n13
Svanberg, Jan 44
Symphony No. 4 (Brahms) 60
Symphony No. 5 (Tchaikovsky) 60

Tanztheater (dance theater) 66
television 15, 140, 141
Tempest (Shakespeare) 83
Templeton, Joan 76
terror attacks of September 2001 112
theater. *See* drama
theaters of excess 85–8
Three Dancers (Picasso) 165n13
Toneelgroep 88–9
tones, musical 59
torture, music used in 71
Trump, Donald 11, 17
trust, in politics 147

ulcerative colitis 29
Ulysses (Joyce) 3
Uncle Tom's Cabin (Stowe) 118–19
universalism of music 60, 67–8, 69, 70

value of literature 114
Varèse, Edgar 59, 65–6
Variations V (Cage) 64–5
Veltkamp, Martijn 111
Victorian emotional standards 130–1
visual arts 4, 91–109
  abstract expressionism 97–102
  concepts of emotion 92–3
  contemporary artists 102–9
  post-impressionism, expressionism and proto-cubism 93–4
  supermatism and surrealism 95–7
Volin, Michael 31
Vom Tauwind und der Neuen Freude (Laban) 58

Waiting for Godot (Beckett) 78–9, *80*
Walker, Kara 102–3
Wallis, J. H. 31–3
Waste Land (Eliot) 3
Way of the Shaman: A Guide to Power and Healing (Harner) 42, 44
Weavers (band) 12
Weiss, Peter 85
well-being 16, 47
What Happened after Nora Left her Husband . . . (Jelink) 86
Who, The (band) 12
Wide Sargasso Sea (Rhys) 125–6
Wilson, Sloan 34
Winfrey, Oprah 121–2
Wings of Desire (film) 50
Wisdom of the Body (Cannon) 26

Wolfe, W. Beran 8
Woman Destroyed (Beauvoir) 34
women
    and anger 76, 131
    and art 102–3, *104–5*, 108–9
    and dance 61, 62, 64, 66
    and drama 76, 83–4, 86, *87*, 88
    and private life 132, 133
women's magazines 7–8
women's movement 10, 11–12

Woodstock Festival 12
Woodyatt, Rollin Turner 25
Woolf, Virginia 3
World War I 2–3
    See also shell shock
World War II 9, 29, 57, 85
wounded healers 44, 47

Yalta Conference (1945) 147, *148*
yoga 31, 45–7